"Morality sometimes requires that a just war be ended before it has achieved its aims – and, occasionally, that an unjust war be prolonged. The essays in this urgently needed book greatly advance our understanding of the moral principles that determine when a belligerent must stop fighting."

Jeff McMahan, *Oxford University, UK*

"David Chan skilfully edits this outstanding collection of essays on a vital, yet under-appreciated, aspect of wartime justice. Penned by top experts, this thought-provoking volume combines searching theoretical reflections with detailed practical pieces, focusing on recent cases like Ukraine, Iraq, and Afghanistan. Highly recommended!"

Brian Orend, *University of Waterloo, Canada*

"The recognition of when and how to end wars justly (*jus ex bello*) has heretofore been neglected even in the midst of widespread discussion of other "*juses*" in contemporary moral and political discourse about war. The editor and several eminent scholars thoughtfully engage and rectify that glaring omission in this much-needed work."

George Lucas, *Professor emeritus, US Naval Academy*

Ending Wars Justly

This volume features original essays on the ethics of ending wars (*jus ex bello*). It fills a significant gap in just war theory and sets the stage for other thinkers to engage with the topic.

What makes questions about *jus ex bello* especially difficult for ethicists to answer is that the just war tradition has neglected to develop principles for ending wars justly. Until recently, debates have primarily focused on justice in going to war (*jus ad bellum*), justice in fighting a war (*jus in bello*), and justice after war (*jus post bellum*). Additionally, many contemporary conflicts are unconventional and not the kind that the traditional principles of just war theory are designed to address. The chapters in this volume address the question of how and when wars can end justly. Part 1 approaches *jus ex bello* from different theoretical angles, including just war theory, virtue ethics, pacifism, and feminism. Part 2 discusses specific aspects of recent wars: the United States' withdrawal from Afghanistan after 20 years of military involvement in the country, and the war that began with the Russian invasion of Ukraine in 2022, that is so difficult to end despite the escalating human cost.

Ending Wars Justly is an essential resource for scholars and advanced students working in just war theory, the ethics of war and peace, international relations, and military and strategic studies.

David K. Chan is Professor of Philosophy at the University of Alabama at Birmingham. He is the author of *Beyond Just War: A Virtue Ethics Approach* (2012), and *Action Reconceptualized: Human Agency and Its Sources* (2016), and the editor of *Moral Psychology Today: Essays on Values, Rational Choice, and the Will* (2008).

Routledge Research in Applied Ethics

The Ethics of Drone Design
How Value-Sensitive Design Can Create Better Technologies
Dylan Cawthorne

New Omnivorism and Strict Veganism
Critical Perspectives
Edited by Cheryl Abbate and Christopher Bobier

Human Freedom in the Age of AI
Filippo Santoni de Sio

Procreative Responsibility and Assisted Reproductive Technologies
Davide Battisti

Ethics and Situational Crime Prevention
Thomas Søbirk Petersen

Rethinking Informed Consent in the Big Data Age
Adam J. Andreotta

A Philosophical Case for Ecological Pessimism
Toby Svoboda

Ending Wars Justly
Theory and Applications
Edited by David K. Chan

For more information about this series, please visit: https://www.routledge.com/Routledge-Research-in-Applied-Ethics/book-series/RRAES

Ending Wars Justly

Theory and Applications

Edited by David K. Chan

Routledge
Taylor & Francis Group
NEW YORK AND LONDON

First published 2025
by Routledge
605 Third Avenue, New York, NY 10158

and by Routledge
4 Park Square, Milton Park, Abingdon, Oxon, OX14 4RN

Routledge is an imprint of the Taylor & Francis Group, an informa business

Library of Congress Cataloging-in-Publication Data
Names: Chan, David K., editor.
Title: Ending wars justly : theory and applications / edited by David K. Chan.
Description: New York, NY : Routledge, 2025. | Includes bibliographical references and index.
Identifiers: LCCN 2024057074 (print) | LCCN 2024057075 (ebook) | ISBN 9781032593074 (hbk) | ISBN 9781032593166 (pbk) | ISBN 9781003454144 (ebk)
Subjects: LCSH: Just war doctrine. | War--Moral and ethical aspects.
Classification: LCC KZ6396 .E53 2025 (print) | LCC KZ6396 (ebook) | DDC 172/.42--dc23/eng/20241220
LC record available at https://lccn.loc.gov/2024057074
LC ebook record available at https://lccn.loc.gov/2024057075

ISBN: 978-1-032-59307-4 (hbk)
ISBN: 978-1-032-59316-6 (pbk)
ISBN: 978-1-003-45414-4 (ebk)

DOI: 10.4324/9781003454144

Typeset in Sabon
by SPi Technologies India Pvt Ltd (Straive)

Contents

Contributors

Michael Blake is Professor of Philosophy, Public Policy, and Governance at the University of Washington, USA.

David K. Chan is Professor of Philosophy at The University of Alabama at Birmingham, USA.

Yvonne Chiu is Associate Professor of Strategy & War at the U.S. Naval War College, and Jeane Kirkpatrick Fellow at the American Enterprise Institute, Washington, DC, USA.

Andrew Fiala is Professor of Philosophy and Director of the Ethics Center at California State University, Fresno, USA.

Jennifer Kling is Associate Professor of Philosophy and Director of the Center for Legal Studies at the University of Colorado, Colorado Springs, USA.

Eric Patterson is President and CEO of the Victims of Communism Memorial Foundation, and Scholar-at-Large at Regent University in Virginia Beach, USA.

Jordy Rocheleau is Professor of Philosophy at Austin Peay State University, Tennessee, USA.

Cheyney Ryan is Senior Research Fellow at the Institute for Ethics, Law, and Armed Conflict, Blavatnik School of Government, at the University of Oxford, UK.

Elad Uzan is Junior Research Fellow in Philosophy at Corpus Christi College, and a Marie Curie Fellow at the Faculty of Philosophy, at the University of Oxford, UK.

Preface

After I finished a book on the ethics of war in 2012, I started thinking about addressing new topics. I soon realized that the ending of wars is an interesting and important topic. Not only have there been inconclusive and morally unsavory endings in many recent wars, but it seems that it could be wrong to immediately end a war that was unjustly begun, as exemplified by the American invasion of Iraq in 2003. A war that arguably violated principles of *jus ad bellum* should not have been started, but once Americans invaded and overthrew the Saddam Hussein regime, an immediate withdrawal would have been morally objectionable. It would have left Iraq without a government to maintain basic security and services and to stop sectarian violence that was unleashed by the invasion. While it may be argued that the duties that the United States had after it defeated the Iraqi military were matters of *jus post bellum*, American troops were still deployed in large numbers and involved in fighting insurgents. Clearly, post-invasion Iraq was not in a state of peace after a war that had supposedly concluded, so the ethical questions remained as to how and when American forces should end their participation in the fighting that began with the invasion. Thus, the question that provoked my interest was a paradoxical one: whether a war entered into unjustly should nevertheless be continued because ending the war would be unjust. In other words, how could it be unjust to stop fighting an unjust war? Even for wars that were started and fought justly, such as a humanitarian intervention, might they be difficult to end justly, as it could be wrong simply to declare "mission accomplished" and leave?

In 2021, US forces were finally withdrawn from Afghanistan on President Biden's orders under an agreement signed by the previous Trump administration, and the Taliban immediately returned to power. Not only did the war end with a failure to achieve the stated goals of 20 years of American military engagement in that country, but the United States was faulted for a haphazard withdrawal that led to the collapse of the Afghan government and betrayal of those Afghan allies left behind to face retribution from the Taliban. Soon after, in February 2022, I organized a session on behalf of the North American Society for Social Philosophy at the American Philosophical Association meeting in Chicago on "The End of the U.S. War in Afghanistan." Three papers were presented, two of which are in this anthology. As the session had a small attendance, I decided to get the papers published together with invited contributions in a volume on the topic of ending wars justly. Hence, this project was begun.

There is a small set of literature on the topic, and many of these were papers presented at the 2012 Ethics, Law, and Armed Conflict (ELAC) workshop at Oxford University and subsequently published in the journal *Ethics*. The authors were among those I approached for contributions. I also approached others I knew from my own work in the ethics of war. In the end, the contributors here come from the latter group as those whom I invited from the first group had moved on to new projects. This has turned out to be a blessing in disguise, as the quality and breadth of approaches presented in the papers here make this book highly original, with many fresh ideas that complement rather than replicate previous work.

I am grateful to have the support of the Routledge editors to get reviews and approvals quickly and efficiently, and also to have contributors who accepted tight deadlines to get their papers to me. Getting this book out in the shortest time possible, as hard as it is to do in academic publishing, was important to me. How to end wars properly is a topic on which there is a lot of disagreement and is much discussed in military and political circles in connection with current and past wars. Since this book project started, a new war in Ukraine has added to the urgent need to find ways to end wars in the most ethical way. As Ukraine's civilians keep paying a high price in a war with no end in sight, the choice between giving up on just self-defense and continuing to pay that high price in human lives and suffering could not be more of a dilemma for the country's leaders and its allies. And while papers were being written, Israel, after experiencing a shocking and brutal terrorist attack on October 7, 2023, had launched a military campaign to eliminate Hamas terrorists in densely populated Gaza, inevitably causing immense death and suffering among Palestinian civilians without any prospect of escaping the fighting. While the American and Israeli governments have disagreed about how and when to end hostilities, this new war is being savagely fought and has broadened to involve other parties in the Middle East.

To conclude my acknowledgements here, I should mention that four of the papers in this book were workshopped in draft form at an invited session during the American Philosophical Association meeting in New Orleans in 2024. This session was arranged with the assistance of Elyse Purcell, Secretary-Treasurer of the Central Division of the APA at the time. Finally, but not least, I thank my wife, Agnes, for her forbearance on the weekends and summers that I devoted to furthering this project at a time when I was also serving as department chair.

Introduction

David K. Chan

1 The Problems with How Wars End

Unfortunately, war is a repeated occurrence throughout human history in every part of the inhabited world. The devastating effect of war on human existence is undeniable. What takes place during war are actions that are considered morally wrong outside of war in civilized societies. Ethicists working across the two millennia of the just war tradition have approached the subject of war by distinguishing between what is morally justified and unjustified in starting a war and in how soldiers fight during a war. These requirements for just war take the form of principles of *jus ad bellum* and *jus in bello*. The aftermath of war is now also a subject for ethical discussion in the form of *jus post bellum*. The papers in this volume are concerned with a question that does not seem to fit within the three parts of modern just war thinking: What is the difference between a just and unjust ending of war? If *jus ad bellum* is concerned with decisions made before going to war and *jus in bello* with decisions and actions during the war, what ethical principles can help decide whether the war should continue? Ideas about *jus post bellum* tell us what should be done by all parties after the fighting stops. Thus, there needs to be a fourth area for just war thinkers to consider, namely *jus ex bello*. The questions that need to be addressed in this area are particularly pertinent to war today, where words such as "quagmires" and "endless wars" have been used to describe post-Second World War military conflicts that involve the United States and other nations that purportedly seek to fight wars ethically.

Why then is there insufficient attention given to the ethics of ending wars? The answer lies in assumptions that are made about how principles of *jus ad bellum* apply not only to the beginning of wars but throughout a war after it begins.[1] Consider that the conditions under which a state goes to war are likely to change after the fighting begins. In the simplest case, a war should end once the just cause is achieved and there is no longer a cause that justifies continued fighting. In other instances, the human and moral cost of

DOI: 10.4324/9781003454144-1

the war reaches the point where that which was considered proportionate before the war is exceeded. If after a war begins, *jus ad bellum* principles are reconsidered, there are wars that would no longer be justified if continued. Alternatively it may be held that, once the fighting starts, it is not *jus ad bellum* but *jus in bello* that provides the principles for making decisions about the war. But again, if the fighting is morally unjustified due to violations of *jus in bello* that happen in the heat of battle or from decisions made out of desperation, the war cannot continue as a just war. Considering the matter in either way with *jus ad bellum* or *jus in bello*, there does not seem to be a need for further principles of *jus ex bello* to be developed and applied.

Given all of the above, the essays in this volume implicitly and explicitly pose the obvious question: Should *jus ex bello* be separated from *jus ad bellum*, *jus in bello*, and *jus post bellum*? And is the division of war into stages governed by different moral requirements based on reality? Wars do not break down neatly into stages. Fighting may pause and restart and change in intensity. Is a prolonged ceasefire the ending of a war, and is the breakdown of the ceasefire the beginning of a new war, or the continuation of the earlier war? Should *jus post bellum* apply when the fighting pauses or only when the fighting ends permanently? If *jus ad bellum* principles continue to apply after the war starts, should they apply in the same way or take a weaker or adjusted form?[2] If a war that is justly begun could become unjust, could a war that is unjustly started become a just war to be continued based on the application of *jus ad bellum* principles in the middle of the war?[3] Or is the only just option to end any unjustly begun war immediately? If *jus ex bello* is decided by principles of *jus ad bellum* applied later in the war, then should having an exit strategy be a requirement of *jus ad bellum*? In addition, should *jus ex bello* also include considerations of *jus post bellum*, as the time to end a war may not be right when conditions for a lasting peace are not met? Clearly, *jus in bello* has to take some account of *jus post bellum*, as some ways of fighting a war make it harder to secure permanent peace with a defeated enemy. Should it also be a consideration of *jus ex bello* what kind of peace will result from ending the war at that point? For example, would ending a war in a way that leaves a repressive regime in power be unjust even if continued fighting violates the principles of *jus ad bellum* or *jus in bello*? Does this then mean that it is *jus post bellum* that should be used to determine if it is just to end a war at that point? And if so, should steps needed to meet the requirements of *jus post bellum* be taken before the fighting ends rather than after the war is over?

Connecting *jus ex bello* with other requirements for just war found in *jus ad bellum*, *jus in bello*, and *jus post bellum* provokes questions about whether ending wars should be about justice at all. One reason to be skeptical about the connection between the ethics of ending war and the goal of justice in terms of just cause is that there are internal contradictions within just war requirements.[4] Although just wars are fought to correct injustices, they are also supposed to have the goal of peace. Is peace (or ending wars) always compatible with justice (or is it even a matter of justice)? Would prolonging a war to achieve a just cause lead to more suffering and resentment after the war? On the other hand, is justice satisfied to end a war through compromise without achieving some or all of the just cause? How should pragmatic (or proportionality) considerations be weighted in moral decision-making regarding the ending of wars? Are there moral benefits that can make up for acceding to a compromise without full justice? One obvious benefit is the avoidance of further unjust harm to civilians that results from continuing a war. And the avoidance of such harm may be required by just war principles of proportionality and discrimination. What this shows is that whether the just cause is achieved (or achievable) is only one of many considerations when deciding on the ending of a war. Not only are there other requirements of justice, but there are also prudential considerations to take into account. Added to all that is how there are many cases in which both sides in a war have competing claims to justice, even if one side is mistaken or disingenuous about it. So should the decision about ending wars be morally evaluated from one side or both sides? What say should the unjust side have, or should the losing side have? How could the ending of a war be just if only one side accepts the ending as just? Can a demand for the losing side to surrender unconditionally be just, even if the winning side has just cause? If not, is a real peace, that is, a permanent and lasting end to conflict and not the mere cessation of current hostilities, one that is better achieved by giving up some of the winning side's claims regarding justice in the outcome that follows the end of fighting?

If justice has to be a requirement for ending wars, there arises a worry that war is a moral trap.[5] For justice in ending wars may not be possible at all. The costs of achieving the just cause for which the war is fought include numerous injustices that accumulate during the war, and the longer that the fighting continues, the greater these costs are. At any point in the war, ending the war would be unjust, as would be the continuation of the war. The only way to avoid such a moral trap is not to fight wars at all. But even this pacifist position is unsatisfactory as it leaves unjust and evil actors in place to engage in acts of aggression and repression. As long as there are such actors in the world, many of whom are in positions of power and have the capability of committing large-scale and grave injustices against individuals and neighboring countries, it is inconceivable that leaders of liberal states, as well as some of their citizens, do not act on a moral obligation to defend the basic rights of human beings to live in peace and security. Is war too heavy-handed an approach to take against evil regimes? Is there always a non-violent alternative? If not, the choice of war may be morally legitimate, and leaders have to make a tragic choice of doing evil to stop evil. But it is the nature of tragedy that there are no good endings. Every war in history, even the ones fought for the noblest of reasons, has been immensely evil for those who experience it, be they soldiers or civilians.

As mentioned earlier, it is not a simple matter to consider a war ended. What does it mean for a war to end? One view is that wars do not really end at all. All we do is to tell stories of the ending of wars in order to find meaning in war and perhaps to serve the ideological framework that undergirds war. Suppose that wars do end. How do we know it has ended? It cannot be merely a break in fighting, as in a truce or a ceasefire. Although stopping actual combat may be required for humanitarian reasons or to provide opportunities for negotiating the end of a war, ending a war justly seems to require more than a cessation of fighting. Would justice allow for troops to be deployed after fighting stops, or should they be withdrawn from the frontlines? For instance, if a country was invaded, justice ought to require not only that the invaders stop their advance, but that they also withdraw from the territories that they had illicitly seized. So how demanding should conditions of *jus ex bello* be? If the mere cessation of fighting is not sufficient, is political reconciliation between opposing sides necessary? Is regime change necessary, and what if that cannot be achieved without further fighting? Is punishment for war crimes necessary for wars to end justly, or will it be perceived as victor's justice and an obstacle to reconciliation? Would it be more just not to punish those who are defeated for the sake of fostering or realizing a more lasting peace? Or is it morally better if punishment is meted out to those on every side deemed to have committed war crimes since it cannot be compatible with justice to allow criminals, some of whom have acted heinously, to get away scot-free?

If the victors in war, even those who have just cause for fighting, have to be generous with the losers to end a war without recrimination and resentment, this does not mean that justice does not have a place in the ethics of ending wars. Perhaps justice in ending wars involves a change from violent to non-violent means of seeking just political ends, rather than giving up on previously held ends. Then, contrary to Clausewitz, war should not be regarded as merely an extension of politics, and the ending of war should be a resumption of politics that war has disrupted. Thus, war and politics are fundamentally different, and politics cannot be carried out through war.

Given the difficulties described above in achieving peace with full justice in terms of vindicating international law and securing the rights of individual human beings, perhaps answers in the ethics of ending wars need to be found outside of the just war framework. Ending a war right may not be the same as ending a war justly. One issue with just war theory and laws of armed conflict that developed from it is their focus on what states may or may not do in war. It is important to consider what part individual citizens (soldiers or civilians) play in ending wars justly. Is it necessary that they do their part, or is it only what the state decides that matters? Intuitively, it does not seem that an agreement to end hostilities worked out between leaders without the input and buy-in from citizens would be a good way to end a war. A disconnect between leaders and citizens may be reflected both in unpopular wars and unpopular peace. In the latter case, it may be a peace in name only. Historically, wars have flared up again and again between the same adversaries. This makes a strong case for the importance of reconciliation after a war, which may require that demands for justice, reparation, and punishment be tempered. In relation to this, how should the moral impact of a war's end on individual soldiers (those who died, those who survived, and those to whom promises were made) be taken into account in deciding about the ending of a war? Would a failure to achieve just ends be a moral harm to those who died and suffered in the course of fighting for a cause that had been declared as worth killing and dying for?

Going beyond states and individuals, how and what may international organizations contribute to *jus ex bello*? States do not negotiate an end to war in a vacuum, as other non-belligerents may have an interest in what takes place after the war ends. The latter may also have a part to play in underwriting or securing a peace agreement and supporting reconstruction and reconciliation between adversaries. Admission to the international community and membership in international bodies help to incentivize nations to keep the peace after a war is over, making a war's ending more than a mere ceasefire or armistice. In mentioning the role of other states that are not part of the war, we move beyond just war theory's focus on the rights and duties of those directly or indirectly involved in war. What should other states and international organizations do to bring about the end of wars that they are not involved in? In what ways does international law need to be reformed in order to give these parties such a role and to perform the role effectively?

A final question, concerning the adequacy of any account of *jus ex bello*, is that of whether there is more than one kind of ending of wars that could be just. Should different kinds of wars have different just endings? Already, traditional just war theory has been challenged by kinds of war and ways of fighting that were not envisaged when the principles of the theory were formulated. Wars are taking place involving non-state groups, vastly asymmetric in capabilities, with no clear distinction between combatants and non-combatants. There is no battlefield to which fighting is limited, and modern weapons eliminate safe sanctuaries for civilians as they are capable of massive destruction and deployed in populated areas. Thus, there should be no "one size fits all" approach to evaluating the justice of war-making and war-fighting. There is unlikely also to be such an approach to war-ending. The ethics of ending wars may have to be applied flexibly and take into account what is particular and unique in each war. This is evident from the examples that are discussed in this book, whether in the theoretical section or the papers specifically concerned with two of the major conflicts of the 21st century.

What are the lessons that should be drawn from Afghanistan and other war endings? The United States invaded Afghanistan in 2001 after the September 11 terrorist attacks perpetuated by Al-Qaeda, who were sequestered in Afghanistan as they planned the attacks. Twenty years later, the final withdrawal of US military forces took place in a chaotic manner that led quickly to the restoration of the Taliban, who had been driven out of power when the United States invaded. Arguments continue among military strategists, international scholars, and political thinkers about when and how the United States should have ended the war and departed from Afghanistan. Should the Americans have left after they had eliminated the Al-Qaeda bases in Afghanistan quite early after the invasion began? Was the United States justified or obligated to remain in Afghanistan to rebuild the country and to set up a government that respected human rights in a way that the Taliban did not? Should the United States have left once it became clear that the war with the Taliban was unwinnable and that continuing to support the unpopular Afghan government would require a massively larger and indefinite deployment of American fighting forces? And if US withdrawal was ethically (and legally) required, should it have been done in a different way from the precipitous and haphazard way that it ended up doing? Was it moral harm to its fallen soldiers and abandoned allies that none of the central war aims that were proclaimed to justify the American presence, apart from the elimination of Al-Qaeda, had been achieved in the end?

President Putin of Russia launched a large-scale invasion of the independent state of Ukraine on February 24, 2022, and the brutal war that began has continued unabated at this point in time. Entire cities in Ukraine have been decimated, and millions of Ukrainians have been killed or displaced. The Russians have not succeeded in overthrowing the government of Ukraine, and the United States and European allies have provided large amounts of military assistance to shore up Ukraine's ability to fight the larger and better-equipped Russian forces. There is nevertheless no Ukrainian victory in sight at the time of writing, and Russia has kept its hold on Ukrainian territories that it captured earlier in the war. Meanwhile, missile and drone attacks have been repeatedly launched against civilian areas in Ukraine beyond the battle-lines, including attacks on shopping centers, hospitals, and schools. It would be greatly beneficial to ordinary Ukrainians for these attacks to end so that their lives can resume with normality and safety, and millions of displaced Ukrainians could return to (and rebuild) their homes, but a peace deal that allows Russia to keep all or some of the territories that it seized by force would be unjust for the nation of Ukraine. Thus, the ongoing war illustrates the difficulty of answering the question of how this and other wars should end, and how they could end justly. Pertinent questions include whether pursuing a peace deal with an aggressor constitutes appeasement that does greater harm in the long run, as illustrated by the 1938 Munich Agreement that ceded Czech territory to the Nazis. Is Ukraine obligated to seek a compromise rather than continuing to fight if it is in no position to drive the Russians out of its territory, given Russia's greater strength in numbers and equipment, and Putin's willingness to order the Russian military to carry out brutal violations of international law? Is it worth insisting on the prosecution of Russian war criminals, including President Putin? Should anything be done to address Russia's expressed fear of Western expansion to its borders, which it used as one of its justifications for its invasion of Ukraine? Above all, is it ethical for Ukraine and its Western Allies to expect Ukrainian citizens to continue to suffer and die with no endgame in sight?

2 Editor's Guide to Papers

The essays in this volume are original contributions to the ethics of ending wars. Until now, the essays presented at the 2012 Ethics, Law, and Armed Conflict (ELAC) workshop at Oxford University, and subsequently published in the journal *Ethics* in 2015, have set the table for examining this subject. Many of the papers in this volume written by a different team of scholars discuss or cite some of the views expressed in those earlier essays, but none of them replicate those views. Instead, they critique these views or offer alternative views. Some approach the topic within the framework of the just war tradition, similar to the 2015 *Ethics* papers, but others base their views on a rejection of the just war approach. The essays here raise new questions and provide new insights, proposing new answers on a very complex subject. They will provoke scholars to do further research and readers to rethink how wars should end.

The first paper that begins the **Theory** part of this anthology is by Yvonne Chiu, "Beginning the End: Unilateral vs. Collaborative Conceptions of War Termination Ethics." Chiu points out the conceptual shortcoming in a *jus ex bello* that approaches war termination from a unilateral perspective, as there is an *ethic* of cooperation in warfare, manifested in a belief that it can be right to cooperate in war on matters such as prisoner exchanges, regulations for POW treatment, wearing uniforms or other identifying symbols, and weapons bans (Chiu 2019). On a practical level, wars are interactive and could only end when opposing sides have agreed to stop fighting and settled on the terms of peace. To wit, "each side's respective conceptions of victory, loss, or draw must be minimally compatible with the other side's conceptions." A unilateral *jus ex bello* neglects to account for the reality that victory is more than a statement of superior military coercive power, as it makes a statement (about justice) that the other side acquiesces to. In her paper, Chiu discusses how a cooperative, procedural justice approach such as that found in classical Greek hoplite warfare would not generate sufficient justice to yield sustainable war termination in wars today. Instead, "cooperation between belligerents to work from mutual or compatible theories of victory can make it possible to determine a victor and therefore yield an ending to a war," based on a shared understanding of what is decided in war. A case of incompatible conceptions of what military outcomes signify is found in the "asymmetry trap" that involves unilateral just war limits on the militarily stronger party's permission to fight back against an injustice where it must violate *jus in bello* in order to fight at all. This leads Chiu to suggest that justice is ill served by judgments of *jus ex bello* that systematically prioritize *jus in bello* over *jus ad bellum*.

In his paper, "Wars to Stop Aggression and to End Genocide: Beyond Just Endings," David K. Chan presents an alternative to the just war framework for making ethical decisions about ending wars. Chan uses a virtue ethics approach[6] that considers war to be a great evil that could never be morally justified but may be correctly chosen as tragic choices against regimes that are greater evils than war itself, prime examples being regimes that carry out unrestrained aggression and genocide. On this approach, wars should end at the point when continued fighting makes war the greater evil. But wars often create evils that are so great that nations that go to war leave behind a state of affairs that is more evil than existed before the war, even if they reduce the prior evils. This leads Chan to consider a version of Rodin's "war trap" that could be used as an argument against going to war at all. Would this leave us unable to fight against evil regimes in the world? In response, he proposes two considerations that affect whether a war, begun to stop aggression or end genocide, could bring less evil after the war is over. One is that continuing a war to pursue regime change could be the right choice against regimes that are evil in nature. The other is that the evils of a war to achieve regime change could be reduced by how the war is fought, so these evils should be given less weight in comparison with the evil of the regime. Chan suggests, using a discussion of examples from Kuwait and Libya, that his approach to ending wars is more useful than applying *jus ad bellum* considerations in *jus ex bello*.

Andrew Fiala's contribution, "Victor's Justice and the Myth of Ending Wars Justly," brings up the problem of Victor's Justice, or superpower impunity, when war crimes are punished after the war. For wars to end justly, according to just war theory and international law, punishment of war crimes (broadly defined using the Rome Statute of 2002 to include crimes against peace, genocide, and other crimes against humanity, and crimes in the course of war) is necessary as a condition of *jus post bellum*. This is a view that has been espoused by many in the just war tradition. But the punishment of the defeated without punishing similar crimes by the victorious side (or by the side that did not win but is powerful enough to defy calls to punish their war criminals) violates this requirement of justice. Numerous examples in the history of war, even in the Second World War (the Good War), show that war crimes committed by the victors are routinely ignored or pardoned by the victorious powers. Extending his critique of just war theory in his book *The Just War Myth*, Fiala argues that "the problem of victor's justice gives us further reason to see the popular application of just war concepts in mythological terms." Almost all wars fail to end justly (2008). Fiala suggests that with a just war not being a realistic possibility under present circumstances, we should follow Larry May in accepting a kind of contingent pacifism.[7]

Jennifer Kling's paper, "Bodies that are 'Ready-to-Politics': a Feminist Approach to *Jus Ex Bello*," approaches the subject of this book from a different angle. Kling defines *jus ex bello* not as just war theorists would, but rather as "when the conditions of possibility for the space of politics to arise are met." She challenges Clausewitz's view of war as a continuation of politics, replacing it with a relational understanding of politics derived from feminist critiques. In arguing for this, she points out that war is about domination while politics is about friendship, reason, and persuasion, so the ends of war and politics are not the same. Drawing on the feminist analyses of Bat-Ami Bar On, Hannah Arendt, and Susan Brison, among others, she argues that war and politics exclude each other conceptually, psychologically, and materially. The space of politics can arise but only in a fragile and embodied way, and the conditions for its possibility provide "a robust tracking concept for the occurrence of *jus ex bello*," that is, the transition from war to politics. A war is ending well "when social, material, and embodied mini-spaces of politics start to emerge." Thus, on Kling's account of *jus ex bello*, "peace treaties or the restoration of order – in the sense of negative peace – do not signify by themselves that war has ended, in the sense of switching ends." The switching of ends from domination to political freedom "involves shifting the material, social, and embodied conditions of possibility that either enable or prevent the emergence of the space of politics."

Cheyney Ryan writes about the ideology of modern warfare, reflecting on what it means for wars not to end in his paper "Endless War and the Ideologies of War." In his account, Western modernity has produced a "Peace Narrative" whereby civilized nations in the West fight "civilized wars" that end in the triumph of "civilization" and a peaceful world. But the Peace Narrative has paradoxically led Western nations into endless wars, as exemplified by the United States' "War on Terror." Ryan argues that the reality of endless war throughout Western modernity reveals "the extent to which war is *baked in* to our very institutions and ideologies." He believes that the problem of endless war undermines the idea that peace can be achieved through war, showing instead that "war cannot end war [just as] crime cannot end crime." Instead of denying away the uncivilized and endless wars as aberrations or the intrusion of premodern "tribalism" into modern civilization, there is a need to challenge what he terms "the war system." Drawing on a framework from his recent work (Ryan 2024), Ryan understands war not as a series of discrete events but as a system with an ideological configuration. The ideology serves a legitimizing function in justifying war and "*motivating* it, so that people will engage in it." The problem of endless war has resulted in a legitimation crisis. Justification and motivation have become unhinged, with fewer and fewer people willing to fight in the wars that the West engages in today, as "the motivation to fight comes from the meaning that a person finds in doing so, but the endless nature of modern war has rendered war increasingly devoid of meaning."

Elad Uzan's contribution, "Ending Wars and the Problem of Moral Hazard," begins the **Applications** part of this anthology by asking the question of whether Ukraine is obligated to seek a compromise ending to the war with Russia by making territorial and other concessions. Just war theory presumes that invaded countries have a right to fight in self-defense and continue to do so until their just aim is achieved. But at what cost to human life and well-being? On the one hand, it is unjust to reward an aggressor that violated territorial sovereignty and international norms. Doing so poses a moral hazard as it encourages further aggression in the future by this and other aggressors. On the other hand, leaders have a duty to prevent harm to their soldiers and civilians. Uzan points out that those who think that Ukraine should seek a compromise by making concessions to Russia do not base their view on an understanding of how the reasons for and against compromise should be weighed. Uzan sets out such a model here. He argues that "any compromise – whether understood as obligatory or optional – must be carefully structured to avoid rewarding aggression and should ensure that the benefits of peace outweigh the moral costs, thus maintaining justice." He uses his proposed framework as a way to determine the circumstances under which a state, such as Ukraine, might seek compromise peace and how it can do so without undermining moral principles. Part of his proposal includes the need for outside support from allies and international organizations to enforce a compromise and to partly ameliorate the costs of the compromise to Ukraine, in terms of concessions of territorial control and reparations needed to rebuild after the war, that are not borne by Russia. In his view, such international support would mitigate the moral hazard of concessions to Russia and reduce the cost to

Ukraine of those concessions. In this way, and only in this way, a compromise end to the Ukraine War negotiated with Russia may become an option and even an obligation for the Ukrainian government.

Jordy Rocheleau, in his paper "Just War Continuation and Just War Exit in Afghanistan," takes on a view about continuing and exiting wars that is held by, among others, Darrel Moellendorf, who was one of the contributors to the 2012 ELAC workshop at Oxford. This is the view that *jus ad bellum* requirements only apply in full to the decision to initiate war and are not conditions that must continue to be met in order to keep fighting the war. In other words, the decision whether to continue or end a war is not determined by whether *jus ad bellum* conditions hold at the point that the decision is made. Rocheleau makes the case that war cannot be ethically continued if just cause and last resort are no longer satisfied. He rejects the presumption in favor of continuation without needing to meet the full slate of *jus ad bellum* conditions. While Moellendorf suggests a reduced threshold for just cause in continuing war and proposes further principles of *jus ex bello*, namely "all due haste" and "costs minimization" (2015), Rocheleau argues that obligations to prevent harm and relational duties to dependent parties cannot justify the massive infringement of the rights to life and self-determination involved in war. Instead, the pursuit of humanitarian measures may be carried out by less violent means after the fighting is stopped. Rocheleau applies his analysis to the US withdrawal from Afghanistan, and he concludes that "the U.S. was obligated to withdraw from Afghanistan when it did, and probably many years before."

Eric Patterson's paper, "The Afghanistan War and *Jus Post Bellum*: A Look at Three Milestones for Peace and Security," is an updated and expanded version of a paper that previously appeared in the *Washington University Review of Philosophy* (Patterson 2022). Patterson rejects just war scholarship that treats war as linear and that takes considerations for initiating war, fighting in war, and peace after the war as separate categories with little interaction or overlap. Instead, he focuses on *jus post bellum* across all phases of warfare, linking *ad bellum* and *in bello* criteria in a way that is both broader and deeper than narrower conceptions of *jus ex bello*. The conditions required for *jus post bellum* are: "*order* (governance, rule of law), that develops into *justice*, and takes steps toward long-term *conciliation*." Order is the fundamental condition for justice and conciliation: "one cannot establish enduring *justice* and *conciliation* without basic *order* – the first step." Patterson discusses how these requirements apply to three *jus post bellum* milestones in Afghanistan. In looking at each of the three periods, he finds that order was not achieved in any of them. In the first *post bellum* phase (2002–2005), "secularist cookie-cutter models" were employed that "lack culturally relevant mechanisms for peace." In the second *post bellum* phase (2009-2012), attempts were made to engage with tribal leaders and bring lower-tiered Taliban leaders in from the cold. However, corruption, political instability, and an ineffective Afghan military meant the security dimension of order was not in place. In the third *post bellum* phase (2012–2022 and beyond), the Taliban's quest for order post-US withdrawal is being stymied by internal and external rivals. Patterson concludes that the 20 years of America's war in Afghanistan left "not *order*, much less *justice* or *conciliation*," and thus a failure in terms of *jus post bellum*.

In his paper, "Meaningful Lives and Meaningful Deaths: Narrative Values and the Retreat from Afghanistan," Michael Blake is concerned with understanding the force of John Kerry's famous question during testimony at the US Senate about ending US involvement in the Vietnam War: How do you ask a man to be the last man to die for a mistake? The assumption behind the question is that while the United States can sometimes rightly ask American soldiers to risk their lives, it cannot justly ask the same of them for a mistaken war. Blake, noting that "the soldier in question, after all, loses as much in either case," asks what moral distinction is being made here. He suggests the mistake referred to in Kerry's question does not concern the overall justice of the war, as just war theorists have it. Instead, it has to do with "how it is that those who participated in that war might understand their lives and the meanings they assigned to their lives." Blake shares Susan Wolf's (2010) view that "meaning can be grounded in how the world is remade by those projects in which our labor is mixed." If so, there might be a link between the meaning in the life of a soldier and the success of that war in which the soldier participates. Kerry's question then rests on there not being any possibility of success in Vietnam, not on the injustice of the war. But a corollary of the account is that ending a war without success renders the lives of those who have already died meaningless. Thus, as illustrated in Afghanistan, there is a moral tragedy involved in ending a war without making the world better in terms of achieving what the soldiers fought for. Continuation with little hope of success would mean more lives that are lost without meaning, but ending the war would guarantee that the lives already lost are meaningless.

Notes

1 Dill (2015) distinguishes between "repeated" and "adjusted" applications of *jus ad bellum* principles to the continuation or ending of wars.
2 If war should only be started as a last resort, must it end as soon as another non-war option opens for achieving the just cause? Should proportionality be applied differently after the war begins by discounting "sunk costs"?
3 We may call this a "paradox of bootstrapping." Suppose a country invades another country and the invaded country mounts self-defensive actions that

involve incursions and occupation of the aggressor's territory and take actions that harm civilians of the aggressor nation.

4 Another reason for skepticism is that there is no guarantee that the just side would be victorious, as many wars have ended without justice, for example, with an aggressor holding onto seized territory. And in some wars, neither of the opposing sides has just cause for going to war.

5 See Rodin (2015).

6 See Chan (2012) for details of this approach.

7 See May (2015).

References

Chan, David K. 2012. *Beyond Just War: A Virtue Ethics Approach*. Basingstoke: Palgrave Macmillan.

Chiu, Yvonne. 2019. *Conspiring with the Enemy: The Ethic of Cooperation in Warfare*. New York: Columbia University Press.

Dill, Janina. 2015. "Ending Wars: The *Jus ad Bellum* Principles Suspended, Repeated, or Adjusted?" *Ethics* 125 (April): 627–30.

Fiala, Andrew. 2008. *The Just War Myth: The Moral Illusions of War*. Lanham, MD: Rowman and Littlefield.

May, Larry. 2015. *Contingent Pacifism*. Cambridge: Cambridge University Press.

Moellendorf, Darrel. 2015. "Two Doctrines of *Jus ex Bello*." *Ethics* 125 (April): 653–73.

Patterson, Eric. 2022. "The Afghanistan War and *Jus Post Bellum*: A Look at 3 Milestones for Peace and Security." *Washington University Review of Philosophy* 2: 62–77.

Rodin, David. 2015. "The War Trap: Dilemmas of *jus terminatio*." *Ethics* 125 (April): 674–95.

Ryan, Cheyney. 2024. *Pacifism as War Abolitionism*. New York: Routledge.

Wolf, Susan. 2010. *Meaning in Life and Why It Matters*. New York: Princeton University Press.

Part I

Theories of War Endings

1 Beginning the End: Unilateral vs. Collaborative Conceptions of War Termination Ethics

*Yvonne Chiu**

Ending a war is as much, if not even more, of an ethical ordeal as starting one, and practitioners and philosophers alike devote insufficient attention to its challenges. Large-scale conventional wars call attention to every aspect of warfare, including the importance of war termination, that low-intensity conflicts—such as the "forever wars" of recent memory, especially Afghanistan and Vietnam—do not. Ending these different types of wars, however, is equally—though differently—complicated, but in all cases, the need for the defeated party to acquiesce to its loss is too often overlooked.

The ethic of cooperation in warfare helps belligerents end wars with a greater likelihood of sustainable peace, but there are trade-offs and lingering questions. On the surface, cooperation between enemies is essential to end the war—after all, both sides have to agree to lay down arms, whatever the terms are—but the role of cooperation in war termination runs more deeply still and presents its own challenges and dilemmas. The importance of cooperation in war points to a conceptual shortcoming of the *jus ex bello* literature, which approaches war termination from a unilateral perspective, making it impossible to sustain even if it can be initially implemented. More so than ethical evaluations of other stages of war (e.g., *jus ad bellum* and *jus in bello*), the ethics of ending war (*jus ex bello*) requires taking into account the interactive nature of warfare, which has not only practical but ethical implications.

1 The Role of Cooperation in the Ethics of War

The most antagonistic of human activities—warfare—is also surprisingly saturated with cooperation between enemies. Not temporary alliances of

* Views are the author's own and do not represent those of US Naval War College, Department of Navy, Department of Defense, or the US government.

DOI: 10.4324/9781003454144-3

convenience against a mutual foe that mean "the enemy of my enemy is my friend" for now, but rather cooperation between antagonists even as they are trying to kill each other. This cooperation manifests in different ways—for example, prisoner exchanges, regulations for Prisoners of War (POW) treatment, wearing uniforms or other identifying symbols to distinguish oneself from and to protect civilians, and weapons bans—and it spans the spectrum of formality from random, isolated instances to institutionalization in international law.

Cooperation between enemies is so commonplace in some areas of warfare that it goes unnoticed, and its structures and corresponding behaviors are often taken for granted, especially once they are institutionalized in the law, and practitioners of such cooperation themselves often miss the cooperative aspects of their interactions or would not describe them in cooperative terms.

The peculiar thing about cooperation in warfare is not only that there is cooperation at all—already significant in itself—but that there is beyond that an *ethic* of cooperation in warfare, a belief that it is right to cooperate in war. This ethic is more than mere pursuit of self-interest, for, in individual cases, it often cuts against the self-interest of those engaging in cooperation in ways that make it harder for them to win the war. It is in these cases that the ethic of cooperation takes its most counterintuitive and interesting forms.

Even when cooperation clearly promotes everyone's self-interest, other motivations will creep in as well, for example, belief in human rights, a sense of warrior honor, or attention to efficiency. Cooperation between enemies as they try to kill each other requires some modicum of honesty, sincerity, trust, and predictability. As a result, cooperation between enemies generates a political and moral legitimating effect on the activity because it creates a veneer of respect, trust, and mutual recognition of humanity—whether or not that actually exists in the particular case—over the relationship between the opponents (Chiu 2019, 23–26).

The ethic of cooperation in warfare is still relevant when it comes to ending wars because, until they can come to an agreement, the belligerents will continue threatening and trying to kill each other. When and how to end a war is as important an ethical question as when and how to start and fight the war. This integral phase of war is too often overlooked, which is often a reason war breaks out—because of how an earlier war was concluded.

2 Ending Wars Quickly

War is destructive to everyone, even the winner, and the benefits of not fighting usually outweigh whatever gains there might be from winning a war. To that end, it often behooves everyone to cooperate to end a war quickly.

The most prominent example of this comes from classical Greek hoplite warfare, circa 700–500 BCE. Although the conditions of classical Greek hoplite warfare may seem irrelevant for considering the ethics of war termination today, it can be instructive for discerning what might be required for getting to the necessary agreement, the limits of that agreement, and what might be missing now under contemporary circumstances.

During this time period, Greeks fought each other in a variety of ways, mostly in reflection of their geography; for example, mountainous city-states favored skirmishes and missile attacks, while plains and coastal city-states developed cavalry-centric militaries. Most of the major city-states (e.g., Athens, Sparta, Thebes, Corinth, Argos, and Mantineia) were situated on small, rolling plains in valleys, engaged in small farming, and were surrounded by mountains. The lack of natural protection or shelter meant that there was no advantage to flanking horsemen, so the heavily armed and armored hoplite infantry marched to flat battlefields a short distance away to fight in phalanx formation.

Classical Greek hoplites' characteristic form of decisive shock battle arose from both the strategic constraints of the terrain and the harvesting demands of Greek agriculture (primarily grains, olives, and grapes). Hoplites were drawn from independent small farmers, most of whom owned enough land—usually 10–15 acres—to sustain their families. Agricultural production was labor intensive, margins were slim, and timing was critical, so they had little free time for drilling or fighting. It afforded the small landowners only one or two months a year during which they had time to fight, so they cooperated to keep wars so short that they lasted only a day or even just an hour. Geographic and agricultural constraints made limited war necessary, so winners and losers alike needed to curb both casualties[1] and time spent in conflict. Thus, they opted for brutal yet bounded engagement and quick resolution.

While hoplite wars were frequent—all Greek city-states expected to fight every summer—they were also short and decisive. There is a certain artificiality to ending the encounter within a prescribed time limit (including overtime) and accepting whatever outcome results at the end of the designated process. While there was no hard-and-fast time limit to Greek hoplite warfare, it concluded within the day, once it became clear which side had prevailed on that day, and they did not revisit the result the next day in hopes of a different outcome or total annihilation of the other side. The end of the war was considered decisive enough that survivors could return to the pressing matters of their daily lives (farming, harvesting, etc.).

Warfare as Procedural Justice

One way to think about the classical Greek hoplite model is as pure procedural justice, à la Rawls (1999, §14), such that whatever outcome results from correctly followed procedures is considered just—or at least acceptable. This does not mean that independent designations of justice were of no concern to classical Greeks, but they were willing for a time to accept a procedural justice approach in exchange for other benefits.

Misunderstandings of the Procedural Justice Model of War

This model has been frequently misunderstood: there are many flawed variations of this "short and sharp" model—such as "shock and awe"—although some of them have been well-intentioned in their own ways. For example, some 19th-century European and American jurists saw "short, sharp, and decisive" as the only solution given the inefficacy of humanitarian laws governing warfare, because they thought the humanitarian laws prolonged the war and the suffering, and they reasoned that unconstrained wars would at least be shorter, thus reducing harm overall, and, as Francis Lieber said, be "better for humanity, for peace and civilization" (Witt 2012, 184).[2]

However, these unconstrained "short and sharp" models of warfare miss one essential aspect of the brief and brutal classical Greek hoplite wars, namely, the limited cost of defeat: for example, victory did not necessarily confer the right to occupy the loser's territory. Such restraint made it possible for losers to accept the trade-off of a somewhat arbitrary procedure for the benefits of brevity. Like other features of classical Greek hoplite warfare, this requires extensive cooperation between belligerents. Brevity and brutality, but with limited losses, were not unilaterally imposed: the norms and rules are essential and agreed upon. Without that buy-in, war—no matter how sharp—cannot function as an instrument of procedural justice, and as a result, would lose the ability to limit destruction. Once the cooperative element slips away and it becomes a one-sided effort to pummel the opponent into submission, the humanitarian potential evaporates as well (Chiu 2019, 147–150).

What Makes a Cooperative, Procedural Justice Approach Possible?

The structural constraints of geography and agricultural production are possibly unnecessary but unfortunately definitely insufficient for sustainable cooperation between enemies for war termination. The classical Greek hoplite model of brief and definitive war also seemed to require an extraordinary coincidence of shared language, religion, culture, and values, as well as close quarters, expectations of repeated interactions, and the ability to credibly punish defection. Moreover, all sides must *perceive* one another as sharing these characteristics (Chiu 2019, 157).

Although the classical Greek hoplite model does not and likely could not be replicated today, it is instructive for what might be required to reach an agreement for war termination. Such shared features are conducive—even if strictly unnecessary—to ending all wars, not just short ones. Common understanding, made possible by shared language and culture, could help parties to communicate during negotiations over war termination terms as well as to trust one another to adhere to the procedure and to maintain peace terms as agreed.

Clearly, these are necessary but insufficient conditions, as many people with shared characteristics have fought—perhaps all the more viciously for their commonalities—and continue to fight one another without ever developing a shared ethic to end war quickly or at all and have no desire to do so.

While in theory shared characteristics would make this easier, it is still required that all parties at least tacitly acknowledge and accept the trade-offs offered by this particular process of war. Therein lies the challenge: what about substantive justice? When for any reason (whether the pursuit of substantive justice or merely a high-stakes gamble) one party or another is unwilling to make this trade-off on offer—eschewing the pursuit of substantive justice in favor of mere procedural justice but with limited losses and more time spent in peaceful *modus vivendi*—this arrangement falls apart.

3 The Contemporary Place of Justice in War Termination

Regarding the pursuit of substantive justice through warfare, the pendulum has swung to the other side in contemporary law. In stark contrast to the classical Greek hoplite model that treats war as a tool for conflict resolution, contemporary Law of Armed Conflict (LOAC)—which includes both customary international law and treaty laws such as the Geneva Conventions and Hague Conventions—is an extensive and ever-growing body of regulations governing what constitutes *jus in bello* or what is morally permissible in fighting. This body of law explicitly rejects the procedural justice approach embodied by the classical Greek hoplite model, whose procedure permits any actions while *in bello*.

Nonetheless, contemporary international law's almost-exclusive focus on *jus bello* means that it unwittingly ends up in a similar place as the classical Greek hoplite model. Contemporary international law has little to say about *jus ad bellum* beyond restricting legitimate wars to those of self-defense (United Nations 1945, Art. 51). This narrow treatment of *jus ad bellum* says that all aggressive wars are unjust and that only defensive wars are just. By starting at an arbitrary time with whatever territorial boundaries happen to exist now—whenever "now" is, and regardless of how those borders came to be—the law deems "just peace" to be merely the absence of violent conflict. As such, considerations of *jus ad bellum* effectively drop out of the international laws of war, and concern with *jus in bello* fills the entire moral space (Chiu 2019, 205).

Fighting justly is essential, but requiring this cannot substitute for just cause. Some would go so far as to subsume *jus in bello* under *jus ad bellum* (e.g., just war revisionists), but even if one holds them separate (e.g., traditional just war theorists), *jus in bello* cannot rectify the grievances that are raised by just cause.

Especially given past injustices, a time-slice principle of self-defense cannot now be the only legitimate cause for war. However, with contemporary LOAC, so long as proper procedures were followed (*jus in bello* was achieved), international law has little of substance to say about the substantive justice of the outcome. As a result, it unwittingly operates within a procedural justice framework. By focusing so heavily on *jus in bello*, international law implicitly assumes that following proper procedures while fighting would generate sufficient justice to yield sustainable war termination. Certainly, fighting justly could help to yield stable post-war peace. For example, cooperation for a "fairer" fight would not directly address the questions of justice that fundamentally animate the war, but it would help to mitigate one additional reason people might have for reopening the war, while the opposite—fighting in ways that are perceived as manifestly "unfair"—can generate new resentments and future conflicts (Chiu 2019).

4 The Future of Cooperation to End Wars

But, however "fairly" or justly a war is fought, *jus in bello* alone is insufficient for stable war termination. *Jus ad bellum* is significant, not just philosophically, but for people's political judgments about whether or not to accept a particular conclusion to the war. Agreement on just cause is difficult to come by, so absent agreement on just cause, what might promote sustainable peace?

Although not strictly necessary, given how helpful shared characteristics between enemies (e.g., language, culture, and religion) can be for cooperating in and ending warfare, there is a certain irony if some form of Kant's perpetual peace theory comes to pass. Due to trade, other economic ties, political commonalities, and greater trust and communications between societies, societies could come to share more relevant characteristics and have more information about how others think; this could eventually lead to less antagonism between enemies. As the circumstances for war and the number of wars decline, however, peace will get harder to establish, because the wars that do occur will be *more likely* to be between those without shared underlying understandings. Perhaps then, intractable conflicts would mostly take place between enemies with different cultures, languages, and religions. Ironically, however, cooperation between enemies could become relatively more difficult to establish and sustain (Chiu 2019, 158).

5 Generosity vs. Duty

Given the difficulty of cooperation in war and war termination, could something other than cooperation on procedure yield sustainable war termination? If one had to take a unilateral approach to ending war justly and sustainably, what might that require? Could generosity, for example, help to end wars with some reasonable expectation for sustainable peace? During the long, convoluted Second Peloponnesian War, Sparta attempted to settle enmities with Athens in the middle of the Pylos and Sphacteria battles (425 BCE) by arguing for magnanimity on the part of Athens:

> [2] Indeed if great enmities are ever to be really settled, we think it will be, not by the system of revenge and military success, and by forcing an opponent to swear to a treaty to his disadvantage; but when the more fortunate combatant waives his privileges and, guided by gentler feelings, conquers his rival in **generosity** and accords peace on more moderate conditions than expected. [3] From that moment, instead of the debt of revenge which violence must entail, his adversary owes a debt of **generosity** to be paid in kind, and is inclined by honor to stand by his agreement.[3]
>
> (Thucydides 1996, IV.19.2–3, emphasis added)

Both translations of "generosity" are from the Greek *arete* [ἀρετή or a variation thereof].

Setting aside whether the Spartans were talking in good faith here if these words are taken at face value, what is the role of the virtue of "generosity" in ending wars? Is some amount of generosity needed for successful war termination, including the *maintenance* of the peace, after all the harm and devastation of war that could engender new resentments?[4]

If so, what kind of generosity? This is partly what rebuilding the defeated country is about; for example, post-WWII reconstruction in Europe, such as the Marshall Plan, spent over $13bn (equivalent to over $170bn today), in addition to other aid packages and loans. This was a huge sum of money, but it was also an attempt to stave off future resentments that could inflame back into war,[5] as money is essential for rebuilding infrastructure, establishing and maintaining social order, and other essential post-war recovery.

Generosity requires more than mere financial outlay, however. Philosophers and political theorists usually translate *arete* [ἀρετή] as virtue, but there is a connotation of specifically "manly" virtue, although that too is difficult to translate. Words do not have to be translated the same way every time, especially when they are multifaceted concepts whose meaning and emphasis shift slightly with their contextual usage. Thucydides used *arete* [ἀρετή] at other points in his history, and another aspect of *arete* [ἀρετή] is "forthrightness," as in "being a stand-up guy." What does that mean? It could mean honesty, integrity, or straightforwardness, which would be consistent with Thucydides' accounts of Spartan general Brasidas's emphasis on men matching their words with their deeds.

Taking forthrightness specifically: What does it mean as a virtue? It requires honesty, sincerity, and integrity—the ability to do in the future what one said today one would do. This helps to make justice possible because people can then respond accurately and accordingly to one's statements. It makes genuine agreement (whether explicit or tacit) possible. An important part of war termination is coming to that agreement, which requires forthrightness—with all its components—of both the victor and the defeated.

If *arete* is conceived as forthrightness, however, this moves the concept away from generosity, strictly speaking, and toward something closer to duty.

Is it generosity or duty when a victor rebuilds the country it defeated after the war? Maybe it is duty since the victor is the one who destroyed that country. This is, perhaps, what Colin Powell called the "Pottery Barn rule": "you break it, you buy it." This implies, however, that one was wrong to have broken the object, but what if the victor is the one who had just cause? Perhaps it was attacked first and was merely defending itself or defending an innocent third party. Is it generosity or duty when the victor rebuilds a country that it defeated—justifiably—after the war? Considering that to be a form of generosity generates a weaker conception of *jus post bellum*.

Perhaps it is indeed generosity and therefore not ethically required as a duty. Yet generosity might be required for lasting peace, which may be required for justice. For example, Germany was in the wrong in both WWI and WWII. It was justly defeated both times. Rebuilding it the way the US and Western allies did—not just the infrastructure but also its form of government and, crucially, integrating it into an entangled Europe in a variety of ways—helped to make long-term peace possible.

If post-war subsidies and reconstruction are more likely to yield stable long-term peace, then it is at least prudent to attend to *post bellum* justice. But might post-war aid then be a duty? (This is the implication of the "you break it, you buy it" principle.)

Some understandings of acceptable *jus ad bellum* might point in the direction of obligatory post-war aid. For example, one reconstruction of classical Chinese just war theory as found in *The Seven Military Classics* (which includes Sun Tzu's *The Art of War*) draws out a theory of good governance as a justifiable cause for war. In this reconstruction, installing good governance in a badly governed state is a justifiable reason to go to war—that is, to install justice. Furthermore, the ruler's good governance of his own state is what will enable him to win wars (Chiu 2024). In this philosophical reconstruction of classical Chinese just war theory, physical reconstruction and political reform (if not outright absorption of a territory) after a war is arguably not generosity, but rather a duty.

That it would be a duty, as opposed to merely being generous, to rebuild and otherwise attend to *jus post bellum* seems to be morally and practically preferable, especially when considering the well-being of civilians harmed by the war. Generosity is supererogatory, which means it is not required, and it can have the whiff of paternalism or *noblesse oblige*—although in some cases, accepting that may be preferable to the alternative.

However, magnanimity can carry connotations of inequality, so that the resulting terms or conditions for ending the war might always be more tenuous in comparison with terms reached through cooperation, which implies relevant equal standing or peer-ship along relevant lines (such equality is implicit in the modern LOAC).

An illustrative example of the difference this might make comes from Adam Smith, who said the pursuit of self-interest has value. Smith has received both praise and criticism for this idea, but understanding the context is important. When *The Wealth of Nations* (1776) was written, Great Britain was still a monarchical (albeit constitutional) and recently feudal society. Being able to rely on a person's pursuit of self-interest might actually have been more predictable and consistent—and therefore better—than having to rely on someone to feel generosity, beneficence, or *noblesse oblige*, which is usually more *noblesse* and less *oblige*. People's whims are far more mercurial, inconsistent, and unpredictable, and that hinders trust and the ability to make agreements. Negotiations between peers, based on duty, might also be more sustainable because it implies that there is some moral recourse possible, some appeal that one could make for fairness, justice, and even rights.

6 How Permanent Must War Termination Be?

How permanent must an end to war be? How long must peace last for the next war to be considered a new war—even if it is influenced by the previous war—and not merely a continuation of the old one? Some of that depends on historians looking back at conflicts, taking longer views, and finding a narrative arc after the fact that influences the characterization of the fighting. For example, the Second Peloponnesian War is actually comprised of two different wars: the Archidamian War (432–421 BCE), which concluded with the Peace of Nicias (421 BCE), and was followed by the Decelean or Ionian War (413–404 BCE). Although wars were frequent among the Greeks, the Peace of Nicias's terms were meant to bind for 50 years, although it only lasted eight years, which still seems long enough to constitute a definitive end of a war.

Is there a trade-off between cooperation and definitiveness? Wars that are fought and ended cooperatively between enemies might, ironically, tend to generate less-than-definitive outcomes. If warring parties can reach agreements about how to fight, they could theoretically also trust each other enough to establish truces, pauses, or even ends of wars, with the understanding that they might revisit the issues at hand later. This is the dynamic of the classical Greek hoplite model, which traded permanence for duration and opted for shorter wars with the understanding that they would fight repeatedly. The circumstances of classical Greek hoplite warfare are unusual, however; as pitched battle only yields a definitive outcome when both sides agree that it will determine the outcome, and usually only one party—the one with superior firepower—is interested in that (Chiu 2019, 151, 155).

It is not, however, clear that endings to non-cooperative wars are generally any more definitive. The "short and massive" model seeks absolute conclusiveness—the price for which is enormous destruction for the opponent—but even then, neither quick resolution nor final settlement is guaranteed or even particularly likely, as results can always be contested with future wars. Unless the enemy is annihilated *en masse*, hope for a definitive outcome in non-cooperative wars hinges on the aftermath of the war rather than the war itself, for example, by fundamentally transforming the political, social, and cultural systems of the defeated (e.g., Germany and Japan after World War II); this would require a massive endeavor, with no guarantee of success. Open-ended and non-cooperative warfare has the *potential* for more definitiveness, but that lies in paving the way for post-war transformation and not in the outcome of the war itself. In doing so, it also destroys more, which may seed long-run resentments and eventually renewed conflict. Kant's concerns with the importance of building trust between nations even during conflict in order to make future peace possible are relevant here; the brutality of a "short and massive" war can destroy trust and engender long-term resentments that reignite future conflict. Overall, this model generates much higher variance in its results—and not even necessarily definitive ones (Chiu 2019, 153). Perhaps limited definitiveness *à la* classical Greek hoplite warfare—which is offered in exchange for limited damage—is the best that can be achieved, whether through cooperative or non-cooperative means.

Given the degree of definitiveness sought from the end of a war, it is all the more important to be clear about what battlefield victory means to the participants, because they will have to agree on its meaning. Does it mean the victor gains claims over the opponents' bodies? Property? Territory? Form of governance? And what is the extent of those claims?

Understanding the limitations of military force to yield decisive, accepted political outcomes means that both political leaders and military strategists should take greater account of whether the way the war is fought and won might set the stage for future conflict, as the origins of war can often be found in a previous war. Considerations of post-war scenarios should not be limited to post-war peace (e.g., *jus post bellum*) but should also address future *jus ad bellum*.

7 Implications for *jus ex bello*

Questions about post-war duties should lead us to consider the relationship between *jus ex bello* and *jus post bellum*; perhaps a fuller conception of *jus ex bello* is needed, one that is enveloped within a broader theory of *jus post bellum*. How does an ethic of cooperation between enemies to end wars connect with the extensive existing literature on *jus ex bello*, the ethics of ending wars? The *jus ex bello* literature looks at the conditions required for just war. Justifications for *continuing* war are informed by but separable from justifications for starting a war (e.g., Moellendorf 2015).

As soon as the war begins, circumstances can change immediately, and conditions for justified fighting may no longer hold (the opposite can also be true: once war begins, even if it was unjustified, there may now be reason for continuing it under new circumstances[6]). The idea of *jus ex bello* is that one must continuously reevaluate the justice of the war, and once conditions for justice are no longer met, the parties should stop fighting.

Interactive Nature of Warfare

One of the many challenges of developing an effective theory of just warfare is that it cannot be done in a vacuum. This is true for any specific ethical issue in war, but especially so for war termination. Whether there is a winner and a loser, or there is a stalemate such that both sides can lay claim to victory, each side's respective conceptions of victory, loss, or draw must be minimally compatible with the other side's conceptions. There must be a shared understanding of how the war could sustainably end.

A conception of victory means knowing what political end state constitutes "winning" for you: Does victory require the military defeat of the enemy such that it brings them to the bargaining table? Occupation of enemy territory? Annihilation of the enemy's population? Change in the enemy's government? Change in the enemy's policy? Making the enemy feel continually insecure through ongoing harassment or terrorism? Preservation of one's dignity despite military defeats? Something else? Whatever one's conception of victory, there must be an idea of what *political achievement* one is aiming for by means of military achievement.

The victor's conception of victory must be compatible with the loser's conception of defeat, which also requires having some conception of what defeat would look like for both parties—for the opponent and for oneself—as soon as the fighting begins, if not earlier. For obvious and understandable reasons, people do not like to think about what would entail defeat for themselves, which is only the first problem with reaching sustainable war termination. The second major problem is that it is common for one side to view the other's conception of defeat as a mirror image of one's own conception of victory when, in fact, the opponent's conception of defeat may be entirely different.

One famous example comes from the US war in Vietnam. When US Colonel Harry G. Summers, Jr., who fought in both the Korean War and the Vietnam War, said to his counterpart in Hanoi a week before Saigon fell to the North Vietnamese Army (NVA), "You know, you never beat us on the battlefield—for the United States did indeed win most of the major battles in the Vietnam War—NVA Colonel Tu replied, "That may be so, but it is also irrelevant" (Summers Jr. 1995 [1982], Chapter 1). There are many other historical and contemporary examples of similarly incongruous conceptions of victory and defeat, usually to the detriment of the militarily stronger.

It may be easier to reach a shared understanding between enemies about what constitutes victory and defeat and what victory and defeat signify when both sides are fighting in a more conventional fashion. Warfare is rife with misunderstanding, and the more proscribed range of actions in conventional warfare means there are fewer things to misinterpret, and thus slightly more possibility of reaching common understanding. In asymmetric war, where there is a mismatch of fighting capabilities and therefore strategies, it is more difficult to come to a common understanding, especially if political victory for one side does not require conventional military victory on the battlefield.[7]

So, how could compatibility be generated between antagonists' conceptions of victory and of defeat? This requires some kind of shared understanding, however grudging, between the opponents on what victory and defeat look like and what they require.

Unfortunately, that shared understanding is not achieved peacefully—it can be and usually is coerced. One can think of shared understanding as acquiescence or acceptance, ultimately, but that cannot be planned in advance, and with few exceptions, it certainly is not agreed upon in advance.

There are some major exceptions, such as the 18th-century norms of "pitched battle" in Europe (Whitman 2012) or institutionalized norms of the ethic of cooperation in warfare, such as civilian immunity, specific POW treatment, or chemical weapons bans (Chiu 2019). These exceptions mostly have to do with questions of *jus in bello*, however, and place restrictions on what can be done in the course of fighting. With the major exception of classical Greek hoplite warfare (c. 700 to 500 BCE), these do not address pressing questions of *jus ex bello*.

However, cooperation and shared understanding are no less important for ending a war and equally problematic to achieve. By and large, at the beginning of a conflict, the enemies not only disagree on the political end state, but also none of them knows in advance what their opponents will ultimately agree to or how to settle that agreement. Hence, they fight over it.

This is what the fighting is about, ultimately; it is an attempt to coerce the other side into accepting one's conception of victory and defeat. Admittedly, the ensuing agreement may only be a Hobbesian one. But ultimately, for there to even be a possibility of stable peace for some reasonable period of time, the conception of victory and defeat has to be shared—even if only in a Hobbesian sense—by the losing side.

This highlights one serious shortcoming of *jus ex bello*: *jus ex bello* imposes unilateral responsibilities—for example, I should stop fighting because I no longer have just cause—but *jus ex bello* cannot be unilaterally determined, because the other side must agree that it is no longer going to fight. Otherwise, it continues fighting after I have stopped, and I have just cause again (now self-defense) because I have been unduly attacked.

So taking into account the interactive nature of warfare is not just a practitioner's problem but also an ethicist's/philosopher's problem, because it has implications for the *ethical* judgments about war.

Jus ex bello neglects to account for the reality that military victory is more than a statement of superior military coercive power: military victory carries a political meaning that people (rightly or wrongly) acquiesce to, and the termination of military operations is more than merely a declaration of the injustice of continued military action. It makes a statement (about justice) that the other side acquiesces to, again in a Hobbesian sense. Most importantly, when one side deems that *jus ex bello* conditions are reached, it is also saying that the other side *should*, for the same ethical reasons, also cease military operations.

Thus *jus ex bello*—and just war theory more generally—is interactive. Or should be, if it wants to be anything more than an analytic exercise.

Can War Termination Be Unilateral?

It seems that there can be no end to war unless all sides hold mutual or compatible conceptions of what it means to be victorious: how victory is decided and who decides. These, in turn, rest on particular conceptions of the scope, nature, and function of warfare. If there is no *mutual* understanding of a theory of victory, then there must be at least *compatible* understandings between antagonists. What does victory in war decide: a narrow geopolitical claim, a degree of international influence, a designation of honor or prestige, or questions of right? All operating theories of victory have developed gradually over time, changed significantly across human eras, and co-exist with other held theories; this presents a challenge in aligning belligerents' understanding of victory. Cooperation between belligerents to work from mutual or compatible theories of victory can make it possible to determine a victor and therefore yield an ending to a war.

Are there ways to install lasting peace without parties coming to a shared understanding, however reluctantly? Annihilation is always a possibility when no agreement is possible. If there is no other party to speak with, even acquiescence is unnecessary, and enmities could be permanently settled. This is one implication of the Melian Dialogue, in Thucydides's history of the Second Peloponnesian War: the disparity between the strong and the weak is so large that they are of different species, and the weak do not need to be reasoned with or accorded any dignity. In these circumstances, justice has no relevance, and one party can simply annihilate the other. One might also see that as an implication of the way the Second Peloponnesian War finally ended. The 50-year Peace of Nicias (421 BCE) was broken after less than 8 years, in part because it reinforced the pre-war status quo ante and the military asymmetry between Sparta and Athens, but the peace between Sparta and Athens after 404 BCE lasted a little longer because Sparta had destroyed Athens's military capabilities on sea and land by defeating its fleet and tearing down its Long Walls. So perhaps annihilation is the only way to achieve lasting peace.

However, the ending of the Second Peloponnesian War could also teach the opposite lesson, that annihilation, too, only works temporarily. The aftermath of the Second Peloponnesian War did not lack for conflict, including not only extended Persian civil conflicts of succession but also continuous intra-Greek wars between shifting alliances, often with Persian involvement on one side or another. (This also points to the importance of third parties, who are often themselves involved, acquiescing to the outcome.) Less than 100 years after the end of the second Peloponnesian War, Athens and its Grecian golden age had collapsed and were replaced by various empires (Macedonian, then Roman). So it seems that annihilation in order to terminate war is not necessarily a better prospect for post-war peace than nominal acquiescence.

Having a conception of the circumstances necessary for favorable *jus ex bello* before the war begins will increase the parties' chances of getting there, and they should continuously update their respective conceptions as the war itself continually changes. Identifying the conditions for *jus ex bello* is insufficient, however. One needs conceptions of victory and defeat in order to make possible the identification of *jus ex bello* conditions, and conceptions of victory and defeat are useless unless they are compatible with the opponent's. This is difficult enough when there are only two parties in question, exponentially more so as additional parties get involved, as is inevitably the case.

This is one reason why, for example, contemporary calls for Ukraine and Israel to unilaterally end their wars as quickly as possible are problematic both ethically and pragmatically. In the former case, some prominent policy figures have called for Ukraine to cede significant parts of its territory (e.g., Donbas and Crimea) and make other unilateral concessions in order to end the Russian invasion, such as giving Russia a guarantee of Ukrainian neutrality (Barnes 2024) or ceding land to Russia in exchange for NATO membership (Sabbagh 2023).[8] Similarly, there have been calls for Israel to unilaterally cease fire or withdraw from Gaza in order to end the conflict (United Nations 2024).[9] (These have been driven by a mix of concerns, including geopolitical stability, financial and human costs of these wars, and ethical judgments.).

Interestingly, calls for Russia and Hamas to end the wars that they began are much less vehement. One reason could simply be who is a more receptive audience. One could certainly call for Russia and Hamas to end the wars that they began, but they will not listen, so why bother? Better to focus one's efforts on the party that might listen, especially if one provides major military aid to Ukraine and Israel that might influence their decision-making. Prudential concerns with limiting conflict escalation and maintaining geopolitical stability also push one toward focusing pressure on the more receptive party; even if the status quo ante was unjust, some aversion to the risk that a revised geopolitical order would be even more unjust is warranted.

However, this same asymmetry in attention points to the underlying problem with unilateral war termination: short of annihilating the opponent, a belligerent cannot unilaterally end a war because war is interactive, and the only cessation possible without the opponent's acquiescence is surrender. Unlike other categories of just war theory, *jus ex bello* cannot be determined unilaterally.

Tension between Sovereignty Norms and Unilateral jus ex bello

Counterintuitively, unilateral conceptions of *jus ex bello* are also problematic given contemporary international law's foundation in state sovereignty. The roots of contemporary international law lie in the 19th century when international law was conceived as law between states; it was grounded in the concept of state sovereignty, "and the defining attribute of state sovereignty was precisely the right to go to war" (Holquist 2004). Thus, the UN Charter (United Nations 1945) upholds a principle of state territorial integrity by forbidding the aggressive "threat of use of force against the territorial integrity or political independence of any state" (Art. 2.4) and outlines procedures for defensive responses against "threats to the peace, breaches of the peace, and acts of aggression" (Chap. VII).

Other considerations have entered international law over the years, however, including the protection of individuals, especially via the conception and enforcement of civilian immunity. Most notably, the first rule of customary international law is civilian distinction:

> Rule 1. The Principle of Distinction between Civilians and Combatants. The parties to the conflict must at all times distinguish between civilians and combatants. Attacks may only be directed against combatants. Attacks must not be directed against civilians.
>
> (ICRC, Customary IHL Database)

Rights of state sovereignty are thus circumscribed in various ways but not taken away—neither legally nor normatively. The UN Charter acknowledges this tension when it declares that "nothing in the present Charter shall impair the inherent right of individual or collective self-defense if an armed attack occurs against a Member of the United Nations, until the Security Council has taken measure necessary to maintain international peace and security" (United Nations 1945, Art. 51). By this, the UN Charter means that it does not intend for the sake of civilian protection to hinder the ability of a state to fight in its own self-defense. However, it does not provide any meaningful approaches for resolving the tension with individual civilian protections.

This normative question is at the crux of the debate between liberal cosmopolitans (e.g., Beitz) or individualists (e.g., McMahan) and liberal nationalists of various kinds (e.g., Walzer, and D. Miller). How should foundational state sovereignty operate alongside civilian protection and its grounding in assumptions of the individual as the primary unit of normative analysis?

Both moral philosophy and international law must somehow adjudicate the tension between individual rights and the right of states (which are comprised of individuals) to self-defense, and both still leave much for individual judgment. The requirements proposed in the body of literature on *jus ex bello* often present normative challenges to the law, but they need more development in order to navigate the tension between state privileges and individual rights.

8 The Roles of *jus ad bellum* and *jus in bello* in *jus ex bello*

The "Asymmetry Trap"

The expectation that contemporary war would be fought within the bounds of certain cooperative norms can be exploited in order to try to pressure the other party into unilateral war termination. Michael Walzer (2023) recently wrote about an "asymmetry trap" for Israel: Hamas's strategy is to put Israel in a situation such that Israel must kill large numbers of civilians if Israel wants to fight at all, for example, by building a sophisticated tunnel system and hiding Hamas forces in those tunnels while Gazan civilians are left aboveground. Whether Israel bombards Gaza with missiles or puts its troops on the ground to get close enough for more targeted missions, it will kill a lot of Gazan civilians—which is Hamas's intent—and this leads to calls for Israel to end the war on proportionality grounds, among other reasons.[10]

Although the traditional just war theory principle of *in bello* proportionality does permit the killing of civilians—within bounds of proportionality—let us assume that in this "asymmetry trap," the superior military power must indeed violate proportionality guidelines in order to fight at all. This "asymmetry trap" can be an effective strategy to compensate for one's comparative military weakness and, as such, also raises critical questions about justice, especially about the relationship between *jus ad bellum* and *jus ex bello*. If it is impossible to fight for a just cause without violating *jus in bello* requirements, does it mean that one cannot fight at all? For example, given the number of civilians who would also be killed in order to kill Hamas leaders and fighters, does it mean that Israel should not have responded in self-defense after Hamas's October 2023 attack?[11] Do proportionality considerations take precedence over self-defense? Do *jus in bello* requirements take lexical priority over *jus ad bellum*?

Probability of Success Principle

The constraints posed by the "asymmetry trap" resemble the limitations presented by the "probability of success" principle in just war theory. One interpretation of the probability of success requirement is that it limits a weaker party's justification for fighting against an injustice if it has no chance of winning; with respect to *jus ex bello*, it would also mean that once fighting had begun, a party must cease fighting if circumstances became such that it no longer had a chance of winning.

For example, no probability of success is one reason frequently given for advocating that Ukraine, despite having been unjustifiably invaded in 2022, seek accommodation with Russia: Because Ukraine cannot hope to seize back all of its territory that Russia had taken since 2014, Ukraine is merely wasting resources (including lives) by continuing to contest this effective stalemate so it is unethical to do so, the argument would say. If this is right for countries of relative capacity, such as Russia and Ukraine, then it is even more so for wars between entities with even greater military and geopolitical disparity.

However, this claim relies on a mistaken empirical assumption. In the contemporary Russia-Ukraine case, and generally when people say "no chance of winning" in the just war theory context, they (perhaps unwittingly) envision conventional military conflict. Materially speaking, however, that there is no chance of conventional military victory does not mean that there is no chance of winning. One need only look to the American war in Vietnam and to both Soviet and American wars in Afghanistan to see that the militarily weaker party can win, not by winning pitched battles but rather by winning the insurgency. This is because military engagements are not purely physical—they are also political. As Clausewitz noted, there is no such thing as a purely military action (Clausewitz 1989 [1832], 607). Therefore, outlasting the enemy can be an effective military strategy. This is why agreement, or at least acquiescence, on war termination is critical, because both sides must have compatible conceptions of what the military outcomes signify. The necessity of agreement or acquiescence is neglected in conventional conflicts because conventional military engagements are already grounded in various norm agreements that include some nominal acquiescence on the political significance of the military outcome. Because agreement on war termination is bundled with other assumptions, its role is frequently overlooked.

This mistaken empirical assumption only reinforces the problematic ethical judgment: from the perspective of promoting substantive justice, it is troubling to say that those without adequate military power cannot ethically fight a war, even as a last resort.

Pursuit of Substantive Justice

What if justice lies with the stronger? While stronger parties do not warrant much sympathy, and there is a natural and often well-founded suspicion of the stronger, justice matters no less when it lies with the stronger—and sometimes it does lie with the stronger. It is similarly problematic when stronger parties are unduly constrained in the pursuit of justice, for example, if the stronger party faces a weaker opponent's intentional strategy to sacrifice its own civilians so that the stronger party cannot ethically fight a war to rectify a serious injustice (the aforementioned asymmetry trap).

More importantly for our purposes today, this argument is problematic if we are interested in questions of justice, which are, after all, the object of just war theory. Just as it is problematic for the probability of success principle to limit a weak party's ability to fight a just war, it is likewise problematic for the asymmetry trap to limit a strong party's justification for fighting back against an injustice.

From the perspective of promoting justice, it is no less problematic to say that the stronger party cannot fight despite its just cause. Both the probability of success principle and the asymmetry strategy (which exploits the proportionality principle) make moral claims about prudence: that if one cannot win at all or without killing disproportionately large numbers, then one should not fight, perhaps not even in self-defense.[12] In making these claims, the probability of success principle and the asymmetry strategy limit the pursuit of substantive justice, which is problematic, especially when it hinders one's claims of legitimate self-defense.

So how should one weigh separate, simultaneous claims of justice from across different phases of war? What is the proper relationship between *jus ad bellum* and *jus ex bello*? How should just cause be weighted in deciding when one cannot fight or when one must stop fighting? Whether a hindered party is weaker or stronger, justice is ill-served by judgments that pursue *jus ex bello* by systematically prioritizing *jus in bello* over *jus ad bellum*.

9 Conclusion

In addition to concerns about how they might limit the pursuit of substantive justice, both the "asymmetry trap" and strong interpretations of the probability of success principle take unilateral approaches to *jus ex bello*. Generally, unilateral approaches to *jus ex bello* overlook two essential elements of warfare:

1 The outcome of war is unpredictable: with few exceptions, no one knows for certain who will win, and this is one reason why parties will roll the dice by going to war. For the same reason that games/matches are actually played in sports competitions to determine the outcome instead of simply crowning the stronger player as the winner, drilling/training/practice are not the same as playing or fighting the real thing. As with any activity of contestation, chance and circumstance on the day play large roles in military outcomes.[13]
2 Both sides have to agree that the war is over, and the two sides may hold incompatible conceptions of victory and loss, neither of which requires a conventional pitched battle. Certainly, the belligerents disagree on what "justice" requires, which is why they fight, so disagreements about what "winning" and "losing" often follow.

Philosophical approaches to *jus ex bello* by and large take insufficient account of the interactive nature of warfare, with implications for the ethics of war, since unilateral approaches to *jus ex bello* are ineffective for just, stable, and lasting war termination.

While ethical analyses of each stage of war consider the effects of interaction between opponents, *jus ex bello* requires that taking account of interaction and compatibility between enemies be essential in a way that it is not at the other stages. One could decide upon *jus ad bellum* and *jus in bello* unilaterally and act upon those judgments unilaterally; however, one could decide but could not act upon *jus ex bello* unilaterally.

When it comes to the ethics of war termination, we should think about the complex web of relationships between the different principles of just war theory. Traditionally, all conditions have to be met for *jus ad bellum*, and traditionally, there are two tiers of principles within *jus ad bellum* (just cause + legitimate authority + right intent, then last resort + proportionality + probability of success). Should they all be weighted equally? If not, how should they be weighted relative to each other?

Just war theory should not be principles in a vacuum. One can engage with just war theory in that way, but then it is simply a logical exercise. Just war theory needs theories and principles developed for *war*. This requires a process of Rawlsian reflective equilibrium between abstract principles of war and considered convictions in practice. The reality is that just war principles are fought over. They have purchase not entirely because they are championed by the victorious, but at least *in part* because they are championed by the victorious.

Notes

1 While combat casualties were high (about 15 percent fatalities, with total casualties under 20 percent) and could not have been sustained repeatedly and over time in an extended conflict, it was an acceptable trade-off in exchange for brevity and decisiveness for the small hoplite armies of these small city-states (Hanson 2000).

2 For example, Francis Lieber wrote in US General Orders No. 100, which helped lay the foundation for contemporary international laws of war, "The more vigorously wars are pursued, the better it is for humanity. Sharp wars are brief" (Art. 29). Requiring warfighters to use the less destructive methods would increase overall harm done and it is "best and most humane [to fight] as intensely as possible so as to be through with it as soon as possible" (Witt 2012, 235).

3 Also translated "generosity" in Norton Critical Edition and Loeb Collection. The original Greek is as follows:

2 νομίζομέν τε τὰς μεγάλας ἔχθρας μάλιστ᾽ ἂν διαλύεσθαι βεβαίως, οὐκ ἢν ἀνταμυνόμενός τις καὶ ἐπικρατήσας τὰ πλείω τοῦ πολέμου κατ᾽ ἀνάγκην ὅρκοις ἐγκαταλαμβάνων μὴ ἀπὸ τοῦ ἴσου ξυμβῇ, ἀλλ ἤν, παρὸν τὸ αὐτὸ δρᾶσαι πρὸς τὸ ἐπιεικές, καὶ ἀρετῇ αὐτὸν νικήσας παρὰ ἃ 3 προσεδέχετο μετρίως ξυναλλαγῇ. ὀφείλων γὰρ ἤδη ὁ ἐναντίος μὴ ἀνταμύνεσθαι ὡς βιασθείς, ἀλλ ἀνταποδοῦναι ἀρετήν, ἑτοιμότερός ἐστιν 4 αἰσχύνῃ ἐμμένειν οἷς ξυνέθετο.

4 On the role of generosity in ending wars, one might compare the Augustinian Christian tradition that requires that, like the disciplining father or the wise magistrate, any wars waged be motivated solely by love for and aim only at the well-being of the opponent; thus, it means not merely that peace becomes possible but also the required just governance (*Letter* 138.14). These strict conditions for intent reflect Augustine's limited concern for worldly peace, as even the maximal earthly peace that could be achieved by a City of Man inherently lacks the justice that can only be achieved by the City of God. However, not all earthly societies are morally equal and they can be better or worse morally, depending on the nature and terms of their achieved peace (Augustine 1887, 19.21, 19.24; Weithman 2001, 243–244).

5 Mixed motives are, of course, a concern. For example, although the United States also spent heavily to rebuild Iraq (over $35bn between the years 2003 and 2007, which was more than the equivalent spent in Germany and Japan), there are frequent accusations about ulterior motives for its 2003 invasion of Iraq. The more decentralized and federal a governmental system, the more difficult it is to both discern and pursue unified intent; the question then is how to evaluate disaggregated, complex, or multifaceted intentions, across individuals acting as a collective entity.

6 See, for example, Cécile Fabre (2015), on a belligerent lacking justification at t_1 but perhaps having acquired justification for continuing to fight at t_2; or Moellendorf (2015) who, with some exceptions, rejects a conception of proportionality that only looks forward and allows for some accumulation.

7 Most large-scale wars are mixtures of conventional and guerrilla.

8 This would have significant geopolitical ramifications, for example, access to major SLOCs (sea lines of communication).

9 Calls for unilateral cease-fire in the service of broader, long-term strategic goals such as regional coalition-building (e.g., Ross and Makovsky 2024) fall into a different category, although this still raises the question of whether unilateral cease-fire could hold if the opponent has no interest in it.

10 Walzer advocates instead a "responsibility principle".
11 This raises additional questions about what "self-defense" permits.
12 They might differ in the party they constrain: the asymmetry strategy allows an actor with "no hope of success" to use the proportionality principle to constrain the stronger party in the conflict, while the probability of success principle constrains the weaker party in the conflict. Because these principles evaluate relative capacity between particular belligerents, one might find an argument that a strong party (e.g., Ukraine) that is deemed to have no probability of success against a stronger party (e.g., Russia) is questioned about whether it is morally permitted to fight, even though a weak party (e.g., Hamas, objectively weaker than Ukraine) can use the asymmetry strategy to fight a stronger party (e.g., Israel).
13 Cf. Clausewitz on chance as an essential element of warfare.

Bibliography

Augustine. 1887 [c. 413–426 ce]. *De civitate Dei contra paganos* (*Concerning the City of God Against the Pagans*). Translated by Marcus Dods. In *Nicene and Post-Nicene Fathers, First Series*, Vol. 2, edited by Philip Schaff. Buffalo, NY: Christian Literature Publishing Co.. Revised and edited for New Advent by Kevin Knight. http://www.newadvent.org/fathers/120119.htm

Barnes, Julian E. 2024. "Vance Describes Plan to End Ukraine War That Sounds a Lot Like Putin's." *The New York Times*, September 13, 2024. https://www.nytimes.com/2024/09/13/us/politics/vance-trump-ukraine-russia-war.html

Chiu, Yvonne. 2019. *Conspiring with the Enemy: The Ethic of Cooperation in Warfare*. New York: Columbia University Press.

Chiu, Yvonne. 2024. "Seven Military Classics: Martial Victory through Good Governance." In *Warfare Ethics in Comparative Perspective: China and the West*, edited by Sumner B. Twiss, Bingxiang Luo, and Benedict S. B. Chan. Chapter 6: 91–112. London: Routledge, Taylor & Francis Group.

Clausewitz, Carl von. 1989 [1832]. *On War*. Edited and translated by Michael Howard and Peter Paret. Princeton, NJ: Princeton University Press.

Fabre, Cécile. 2015. "War Exit." *Ethics* 125(3): 631–652.

Hanson, Victor Davis. 2000. *The Western Way of War: Infantry Battle in Classical Greece*. Berkeley, CA: University of California Press.

Holquist, Peter. 2004. "The Russian Empire as a 'Civilized State': International Law as Principle and Practice in Imperial Russia, 1874–1878." Grant Proposal to the National Council for Eurasian and East European Research, July 14, 2004.

International Committee of the Red Cross (ICRC). n.d. Customary IHL (International Humanitarian Law) Database.

Lieber, Francis. 1898. Instructions for the Government of Armies of the United States in the Field. Originally Issued as General Orders No. 100, Adjutant General's Office, April 24, 1863. Washington, DC: Government Printing Office. A.k.a. the Lieber Code.

Moellendorf, Darrel. 2015. "Two Doctrines of *Jus Ex Bello*." *Ethics* 125(3): 653–673.

Rawls, John. 1999 [1971]. *A Theory of Justice*. Revised edition. Cambridge, MA: Harvard University Press.

Ross, Dennis and David Makovsky. 2024. "Why Israel Should Declare a Unilateral Cease-fire in Gaza." *Foreign Affairs*, May 1, 2024. https://www.foreignaffairs.com/middle-east/why-israel-should-declare-unilateral-cease-fire-gaza

Sabbagh, Dan. 2023. "Nato Official Apologises Over Suggestion Ukraine Could Give Up Land for Membership." *The Guardian*, August 16, 2023. https://www.theguardian.com/world/2023/aug/16/nato-official-suggests-ukraine-could-give-up-territory-in-exchange-for-membership

Sawyer, Ralph D. 1993. *The Seven Military Classics of Ancient China* (武經七書). Translated by Ralph D. Sawyer. New York: Basic Books.

Smith, Adam. 1981 [1776]. *An Inquiry into the Nature and Causes of the Wealth of Nations*, edited by R. H. Campbell and A. S. Skinner. Indianapolis, IN: Liberty Fund.

Summers, Harry G., Jr. 1995 [1982]. *On Strategy: A Critical Analysis of the Vietnam War*. Novato, CA: Presidio.

Thucydides. 1996. *The Landmark Thucydides: A Comprehensive Guide to the Peloponnesian War*, edited by Robert B. Strassler. Translated by Richard Crawley. New York: The Free Press.

Thucydides. 1998. *The Peloponnesian War: A New Translation, Backgrounds, Interpretations*, edited by Walter Blanco and Jennifer Tolbert Roberts. Translated by Walter Blanco. Norton Critical Edition. New York: W.W. Norton & Co.

Thucydides. 2014 [1919]. *History of the Peloponnesian War, Volumes I–IV*. Translated by C. F. Smith. Loeb Classical Library 108. Cambridge, MA: Harvard University Press.

United Nations. 1945. Charter. San Francisco, June 26, 1945, entered into force October 24, 1945.

United Nations. 2024. "General Assembly Overwhelmingly Adopts Historic Text Demanding Israel End Its Unlawful Presence, Policies in Occupied Palestinian Territory within One Year." Meetings Coverage GA/12626, September 18, 2024. https://press.un.org/en/2024/ga12626.doc.htm

Walzer, Michael. 2023. "Gaza and the Asymmetry Trap." *Quillette*, December 1, 2023. https://quillette.com/2023/12/01/gaza-and-the-asymmetry-trap/

Weithman, Paul. 2001. "Augustine's Political Philosophy." In *The Cambridge Companion to Augustine*, 1st edition, edited by Eleonore Stump and Norman Kretzmann. Chapter 16: 234–252. Cambridge: Cambridge University Press.

Whitman, James Q. 2012. *The Verdict of Battle: The Law of Victory and the Making of Modern War*. Cambridge, MA: Harvard University Press.

Witt, John Fabian. 2012. *Lincoln's Code: The Laws of War in American History*. New York: Free Press.

2 Wars to Stop Aggression and to End Genocide: Beyond Just Endings

David K. Chan

1 Just War Endings

Traditionally, just war theory was concerned with justice in initiating war (*jus ad bellum*) and justice in the conduct of war (*jus in bello*). More recently, the importance of justice after wars (*jus post bellum*) has been recognized as a third component of just war theory. One reason why there has not been a developed *jus ex bello* is the assumption by ethicists that wars should be terminated once any of the conditions for justice in going to war no longer applies. For instance, if there is no longer a just cause, the war cannot continue as a just war and should be ended. If an invasion has been reversed, or if a humanitarian crisis has been averted, then it cannot be just to continue fighting unless there is a new just cause to fight for. Similarly, a war has to be assessed beforehand as proportionate in terms of the harms that it involves in relation to the benefit of attaining the just cause. It is often the case that wars have turned out to be much more destructive and deadly after hostilities have commenced, and such wars would thereby violate the proportionality requirement of *jus ad bellum*. At that point, what was once considered a just war turns into one that is unjust and fighting should stop.[1]

Attempts by just war theorists to formulate a *jus ex bello* doctrine have brought to light new problems that cannot be settled by the assumption that wars should end when they no longer satisfy one or more of the conditions of *jus ad bellum*.[2] Consider the principle of proportionality. Political leaders have often underestimated the costs of achieving the goal that they set out to achieve in war. There is a paradox involved in making new assessments of proportionality. If x is the degree of harm that it is considered justified in order to achieve the just cause, and the amount of harm that has already occurred up to that point is x without the just cause being attained, is it appropriate to continue fighting if it is now thought that a further amount of harm y, which is less than x, is what has to take place to attain the just cause? On the one hand, x plus y is more than x, the greatest

DOI: 10.4324/9781003454144-4

amount of harm that was considered proportionate before the war commenced. So it cannot be just to continue the war, and it should be terminated. On the other hand, y is less than x, and if further fighting will achieve the just cause with its attendant benefits, then the overall cost-benefit accounting of the war would be better with more fighting than with a war that is ended without attaining the just cause. On this view, a fresh evaluation of proportionality should be made that discounts x as "sunk costs" that are not relevant for deciding whether the war should continue.[3] The main criticism of this view is that fresh evaluations of proportionality may be repeated if the just cause is not attained after y has occurred, leading to a war with an amount of harm (x plus y plus z plus ...) that could not possibly be offset by the benefits of attaining the just cause. The defense of this view is that the harm (deaths and destruction) done if a war is terminated without the just cause being attained could be redeemed by attaining it with further harms y, and if y is proportionate for attaining the just cause, giving up means that the harms x were incurred for no benefit at all.

Clearly, nothing about proportionality as a principle of *jus ad bellum* will resolve this question of how sunk costs should count in assessments of proportionality when deciding whether it is just to continue a war that was just when it started. However, I would suggest that the problem goes beyond that of whether and how the principle of proportionality should be used in *jus ex bello*. While it may be a just cause to end the evils of aggression, occupation, and human rights violation, it is an unfortunate fact that the use of war as the means to eliminate those evils often compounds rather than eliminates existing evils. A sunk-cost approach to the *ad bellum* proportionality calculus in *jus ex bello*, in which it is suggested that "only the harm foreseeable in the future, not the harm inflicted in the past, determines whether exiting the war is morally required" (Dill 2015, 629), is not only wrong-headed but illustrates clearly the deficiency in the modern just war approach[4] to the ethics of war. The very idea of proportionality enables the harms of death and destruction to be discounted by the benefits that success in war brings in a utilitarian fashion. Rodin says it is "arguably worse" for a war to "cost 500 lives but make no contribution to the morally good war objectives at all" than to achieve those objectives disproportionately by adding 200 lives to the maximum of 1,000 fatalities that were initially judged proportionate (Rodin 2011, 363). Thus, if a state cannot achieve the war's objective with 1,000 fatalities, it should achieve it with 1,200 fatalities even though it could have stopped the fighting with 500 fatalities at the point that the disproportionality of the entire war is recognized. But it is surely morally worse for 1,200 people to die than for 500 people to die for what in the end is an unjust war.[5] This is a moral judgment that can be made without reference to what the war is fought for. In evaluating war, it is the massive evil of killings and other harms in war that provides the basis for the moral presumption against the use of war as a legitimate means to achieve any purpose.[6] It seems to me that in the discussion of *jus ex bello*, assessments of proportionality exemplify how just war thinking has abstracted away from the evils of war and how problematic it is when war is legitimized by just war principles as an acceptable means to be considered for achieving good ends.[7]

2 Evils of War, Aggression, and Genocide

In my view, the way in which just war theory justifies war on the basis of satisfying a checklist of conditions is insufficiently attentive to the massive evil of war itself. While the evil of war does not make pacifism morally obligatory, it sets a very high bar for war to be used as a means to achieve any purpose. War is such a great evil that it should only be unleashed in the face of genocidal and expansionist regimes that are comparable in evil to the Third Reich under Hitler and not in every case where *jus ad bellum* requirements are met.[8] Even then, bringing about the evil of war as the lesser evil is not a justified act, though war may be rightly chosen by a virtuous leader facing a tragic choice between war and the existence of a greater evil.[9] The evil of mass killing and destruction in war should not be balanced in a utilitarian ledger against beneficial effects, even that of preventing greater evils.[10] In contrast, proportionality and other requirements of *jus ad bellum* would make war something that state leaders could have a **right** to choose, and thereby do no wrong in so choosing. In a tragic dilemma, war may be the correct choice, but what is chosen involves evil acts that it is wrong (and damaging to the character of moral agents) to do. Thus, we need to move beyond the idea of justifying war to that of making war as rare as possible, which is resorted to only in exceptional cases such as the situation that the Allies faced with Hitler's Germany. Even so, the evil of Nazism does not make any of the lesser harms of war justified, as the way that a war is fought against evil regimes should be as limited as possible. A principle of *jus ad bellum*, such as proportionality, whether at the point of the war's beginning or at a later time when sunk costs can be set aside, does nothing to remove what is evil about starting and continuing a war.[11]

My view is more restrictive than just war theory without going as far as absolute pacifism. I will here consider two examples of the kind of wars that could be rightly chosen as the lesser evil.[12] In the case of a ruthlessly expansionist evil such as Nazism, a war to stop brutal and unrestrained aggression rather than to let such evil stand may indeed be the lesser evil and be rightly chosen as such. However, when Nazi Germany had been rendered unable to pursue its aggression and forced to retreat to its borders, continued fighting may be the greater evil, and it is arguably morally better to leave Germany contained but under Nazi rule (this assessment does not require that the Nazis could not continue to do some evil within Germany's borders). Based on a choice between evils, the war could have ended at the point where Nazi aggression had been halted, without taking the fight into Germany in pursuit of regime change. In doing otherwise, the Allies had chosen to carry out greater evils than those they had been fighting to eliminate.[13]

The second case of a war that may be rightly chosen as the lesser evil is that of humanitarian intervention to prevent large scale genocides. If the Nazis had continued to carry out the mass extermination of Jews within Germany after withdrawal from the rest of Europe, that evil alone could be greater than the evils of waging a humanitarian war to stop them. This applies also to other genocides that have occurred in more recent history, such as the Rwandan genocide. In considering war as legitimate only if it is the lesser evil, we need to recognize that once the genocidal activities are ended and the capability of the regime to resume such activities on a massive scale is degraded, a continued occupation that is being resisted often produces a state of war that is more evil compared to whatever remaining human rights violations that the regime may undertake after the intervening forces withdrew (Chan 2012, 137–138). It would then be morally better for the humanitarian intervention to be done in a way that stops the evil of genocide quickly (not incrementally),[14] followed by withdrawal, despite leaving the perpetrators in power.

Obviously, there is something highly unsatisfactory about this account of ending wars to stop aggression and end genocides. It will be objected that leaving the Nazis and other genocidal regimes in place would set the stage for them to resume their evil activities. It would eventually necessitate another war when their evil activities return to the previous level. Moreover, my stance may result in a failure to prevent the smaller scale human rights violations that are evil but not evil enough to make war a legitimate way to stop them. It seems that my account makes the virtuous leader into a moral egoist who keeps her hands clean in avoiding war but allows what is evil, but not massively so, to continue at the hands of others in order to avoid responsibility for the evils that wars to stop aggression and genocide would necessarily involve.

Now, it should be noted that while the objection above may be appropriate to level against pacifists, my view is not a pacifist one. It is not entirely correct to say that a leader who acts in the way that I described is too concerned to keep her hands clean of war. She would already have undertaken a war against a brutal aggressor or a genocidal regime, but she would choose to end the war earlier than a just war thinker would recommend, as she would not accept that the decision to continue a war is derived from states having the right to carry out wars of self-defense and humanitarian intervention. The idea that the threat posed by the evil regime that she fights must be eliminated completely by war, based on the right of national self-defense or of defense of individual rights, goes far beyond the point at which war would become the greater evil. Moreover, in saying that the virtuous leader should not continue using war as the means to stop what has become a lesser evil, I am not saying that she should stop doing anything about the threats to peace and human rights that may continue after a war to stop aggression or genocide. It is rather that as war is itself evil, the means that are chosen, at the point that the evil of the regime that perpetuated aggression or genocide has been greatly reduced, should not include war. Instead, non-violent means to resist evil, of the kind proposed by some anti-war pacifists, could be chosen after fighting stops (though the leader I imagine is no pacifist, as she would wage war until the point at which war is more evil than the regime's evil actions).

Nevertheless, I need to develop my account of ending wars to stop aggression and end genocide by considering the aftermath of an early end to such wars. War is evil not just in what happens during war, but in its consequences, which include evils created by war (Chan 2012, 76–83). This is the basis for the so-called "Pottery Barn rule" that is used to make the case that those who initiate war need to rebuild the state that has suffered the damage of war. In stopping aggression or genocide, the nation that goes to war for such ends, unless it is also engaged in nation-building, will often be unable to leave behind a state of affairs where everything is what it was before, minus only the aggression or the genocide. There will likely be many new evils that began as the result of the war itself, and these, added to the lesser human rights violations that may continue with the non-removal of the genocidal regime, may make continued military activities the lesser evil.[15] And if engaging in a war in which new evils are created does moral damage to its participants (leaders and soldiers), then walking away at the stage that I suggested above may also result in moral damage, albeit of a different kind from that of mass killing in war.

Consider a case of humanitarian intervention to prevent genocide, in which military force is required to push the regime's soldiers who are committing atrocities away from their victims. The weaponry used in the fighting will kill the regime's soldiers who are resisting, as well as some civilians from the population who are being rescued. Homes and infrastructure will be damaged or destroyed. If the regime remains in power and is not deterred, it may become even more repressive after the withdrawal of the intervening forces. It may be entirely predictable that once the foreign forces leave, the conditions in the country for the population that is the target of atrocities may be worse than before the intervention. If the evil of genocide was sufficient to make war the right choice to protect the victims, then the conditions created during the intervention could also make it right for the outside force to remain. However, if the intervention continues, there will be more evils created by the very fact of the intervention itself. As these evils add up, the intervention cannot be terminated on the basis of its being the greater evil. In other words, as long as the intervention provokes a worsening state of affairs even as it reduces the human rights violations of a genocidal regime, it will have to be continued as the lesser evil.

It would now seem nearly impossible for interveners to ever exit the kind of war described above at a point that leaves behind a situation with less evil than before the intervention. My account of ending wars when war has become the greater evil compared to aggression and genocide cannot succeed because I had not taken into account how war changes the situation by creating new evils. David Rodin suggests that war may involve moral entrapment in which "there can be compelling moral reasons to continue fighting wars that are, in their totality, unjust," so the only way to escape the war trap may be not to get into a war (Rodin 2015, 675). Rodin was writing about how the sunk-cost dilemma may make it obligatory to continue with a war that is overall not proportionate and therefore unjust. While I reject the use of a principle such as proportionality (among other principles in *jus ad bellum*) to justify war, I have now described how going to war as a humanitarian intervention, even when that is rightly judged the lesser evil, may lead to greater evils that can only be avoided by not carrying out such intervention at all. Thus, war could also be a moral trap when carried out against the greater evil of genocide.

As stated earlier, the other kind of war that may be a lesser evil in my view is a war against a Hitler-like regime engaged in massive and brutal military aggression. It is not difficult to imagine how stopping the aggression by going to war could reach a point where, due to war's consequences, continuing the war would be a greater evil compared to the threat of aggression, but not continuing the war would leave a state of affairs that is a greater evil than before the war began. Such a dilemma would again constitute a moral trap that can only be avoided by not going to war at all.

3 The War Trap Argument for Pacifism

Do wars that are legitimate to begin as the lesser evil often have as their outcome a state of affairs that is more evil than the greater evil of aggression and genocide that the war was begun to alleviate? If so, then there is an interesting reason to endorse pacifism. Conditional pacifists argue that there is no such thing in reality as a just war in which all requirements of *jus ad bellum* are met. The argument made here in terms of the war trap is that while at the start, there may be greater evils than war, such as Nazi military expansionism and regimes that carry out genocides, and such wars may seem legitimate at the start as the lesser evil, wars once begun lead to great evils that have to be added to the reduced evil that the evil regimes may still do after being defeated. Not only is war not a neutral means, as it is itself evil, but war does not involve a fixed amount of evil. Instead, war is a temporal sequence of events with unavoidable consequences that add up cumulatively to greater evils once war begins. While war may no longer be the lesser evil in comparison to the evil acts that the weakened regime is capable of doing, it is indeed the lesser evil compared to the evils created in the war added to what the regime may still do. This means that the war should be continued. However, doing so only makes things worse, as there would be more created evils. The pacifist can make the case that regardless of how evil an aggressor or a genocidal regime is to start with, since there cannot be a good moral ending to war after it begins, even wars against Hitler-like regimes should never be fought.

This sort of pacifist argument seems to leave us resigned to the existence of evil in the world once non-violent means are exhausted because to stop evil regimes by going to war only leaves us with more evil at any point at which the fighting is ended, and yet the evil perpetuated by such regimes cannot be reduced without war being used as the means of last resort. A just war theorist may see this as a reason not to treat war as evil in the same way that injustice is evil. If this is accepted, then war may be considered an evil but the evil acts of aggressively expansionist and genocidal regimes are always evils of a far worse kind. However, I think the premise is untenable. The killings in defensive war and humanitarian interventions are evils in the same way that the killings carried out in aggression and genocide are evils. And I would also argue that the just war theorist who considers war as a neutral means, that may be either good or evil depending on what its purpose is, ends up failing to take seriously the evil of mass killing and destruction taking place in fighting even the "good" wars.

The most obvious answer to the pacifist who makes the war trap argument is that if the evil regime is removed from power by continuing the war all the way to achieve that outcome, the consequences can be better than stopping the war earlier. And this can be true even if the continuation of the war created greater evils that could have been avoided by stopping the war earlier. In other words, complete victory accomplishes immense good that could not have been achieved earlier, and the good of totally defeating evil regimes may outweigh even the accumulated evils taking place in extending the war. The Western Allies' victory over Nazi Germany illustrates this well. While it may be true that taking the war into Germany to depose the Nazi regime involved much greater evil than the Nazis could have carried out at that point in the war, the total victory achieved enabled the Western Allies to reform and restructure German society and the rest of Western Europe into a democratic and peaceful community of nations.

It can be argued that this result is ultimately worth the price of even the most terrible and destructive war seen on European soil.

The following are two problems for this response: first, the example may be the exception that proves the rule. So many contributing factors have to turn out right that it can hardly be assumed that total victory is always worth the cost. For instance, the Marshall Plan to fund the rebuilding of a devastated Europe after the war is unlikely to be repeated in other wars. In fact, the political will to pay for the recovery of one's former enemy is difficult to muster in most cases. Moreover, the decisions made during the Second World War were based on many non-moral considerations. For instance, the Western Allies feared that the Soviet Union would occupy the whole of Germany, and this provided a strong incentive to continue advancing into Germany. The second problem with the case being made using this one example is that we may be drawing the wrong lesson from it. If the lesson is thought to be that war should continue until war aims are fully achieved regardless of the evil of war, as the good of achieving those aims would ensure that the evils of war are not the greater evils in the final reckoning, then it should be recognized that achievement of war aims is something that can never be assured while the evils involved in war are inevitable. If the majority of wars do not succeed in achieving their declared aims, even if they are prolonged, then the decision to continue wars when the evils of war are greater than the evils of the partially defeated regime is a choice of greater evils for little or no good. In fact, this line of reasoning has been used repeatedly in past wars as a reason to continue wars which are more costly than assumed at the beginning of the war. This is basically another version of the redemption argument to continue wars in the face of higher costs when success has not been achieved. In most cases, the continuation of wars simply results in further evils created without the redemptive good of achieving a just cause.

So we need to take the war trap argument seriously. To counter the argument, I will have to explain how, in my view of war as legitimate only when it is the lesser evil, pacifism is not obligatory despite the problem of how to end wars. If a moral case can be made for continuing a war against evil regimes, then it is not necessarily a problem that such a war is not ended when the point is reached where the evil regime is unable to commit a level of evil that is greater than the evil of continued war. What would such a case look like?

4 The Moral Case for Continuing a War

I presented an argument that war, when it ends, always leaves a state of affairs that is a greater evil than the evil of those expansionist and genocidal regimes that war may legitimately be used to fight. This argument is premised on the accumulation of created evils as war continues, and on further evils that stretch beyond the ending of the war. My initial proposal was that war should be ended when the ability of a regime to pursue brutal aggression or genocide is greatly reduced. However, this is often not a permanent result, and the regime is likely again to engage in great evils in the future. And when the intervening forces stop fighting and withdraw, they also leave behind the death and destruction of war that they contributed to, including new violence and repression unleashed by the intervention. This leaves us in the paradoxical position where it is both the case that there is greater evil in stopping after military action has begun and also greater evil in not beginning a war in the face of brutal aggression and genocide. I will now propose two ways to reject the pacifist alternative of avoiding the war trap by not going to war at all. As the kind of evils that I think are worse than war, namely Nazi-like and genocidal regimes, are intolerable evils, the pacifist response to the paradox is a highly unsatisfactory one.

My first proposal is to choose war as the lesser evil not only when war is compared with the evil *actions* of others[16] but also compared with the evil of *actors* that stay in power by carrying out such atrocities. The Nazi regime in Germany in the 1930s and 1940s was evil in nature, as its very existence was predicated on carrying out terribly evil actions on a large scale. Genocide against the Jews and others considered to be inferior races, and the quest to create an expanded living space as the Aryan homeland through brutal domination over Europe and North Africa, were not incidental policies but reflect what Nazism was essentially about. Thus, even if such a regime had been defeated in the lands that it seized, and even if its infrastructure for carrying out genocide had been dismantled, its potential to repeat previous atrocities would eventually be actualized once again if it was allowed to remain in power. Such potential for evil built into the nature of the regime should be included in evaluating whether a war to remove the regime and replace it with a decent one is a lesser evil. Thus, I need to revise my previous claim that war must end when the actual evil that one is fighting has been reduced to a level below that of the evil of continued fighting. I should say instead that despite war being a great evil, fighting for regime change and not just stopping ongoing atrocities may be the right choice when dealing with a Nazi-like regime. And if regime change is to be achieved, the war should not be terminated at a point where the regime, while unable to carry out its evil activities because it has been weakened by an intervening force, is able to stay in power.

There is a second way to avoid the war trap implication of not being able to end wars with less evil than before the war, which is to discount or give less weight to the evils that are expected to follow if the fighting stops at the point where an evil regime is defanged, as the created evils of war need not occur or could be ameliorated. It is possible that the regime left in power when the fighting stops may be weakened or be deterred from repeating its evil actions by other means. The potential of a regime to carry out future atrocities may be disrupted through non-military means after the fighting ends. To some extent, the magnitude of evils created in war is within the control of those fighting to stop aggression and atrocities. The war might have consequences that are less evil if it were fought with greater care to reduce harm to civilians so that a return to a decent existence would be possible after the war. If this makes it possible for war to end with a state of affairs that is less evil than the state of affairs before the war, then war may rightly be chosen as the lesser evil given the state of affairs at the start of the war, without having to fear falling into a war trap in which things get progressively worse the more fighting that is done. This way of judging whether war is the lesser evil takes account of actual evils of the regime when war begins as well as potential evils created by war but puts greater weight on actual evils that are less of a matter of speculation.

Now, the two ways to avoid pacifism presented here may seem to point in different directions regarding when a war should end. However, they in fact represent two different possibilities. Depending on how the war turns out, the right decision about ending a war may be one or the other of the two scenarios. In the first case, the state fighting an expansionist or genocidal regime may carry on fighting, even after the ability of the enemy to carry out evil actions on a large scale has been degraded, because of the evil nature of the regime. In the second case, the fighting should stop at the point where the enemy is so weakened that it could be prevented by non-military means from resuming aggression or atrocities at the previous level. At the point where the immediate evil acts are stopped altogether or largely reduced in scale, the right decision to make about ending the war is one that depends on a judgment about the nature of the evil-doers in the opposing regime and about the possibility of preventing future atrocities through non-violent means with the threat of force as a deterrence, and perhaps with the hope of reforming a regime that had committed evil acts but is not itself essentially evil.

This way of making the right decision about whether to end a war is undoubtedly a matter of judgment, but no more so than the decision to start a war in the first place, which, in my virtue ethics approach to war, is a tragic choice that requires a judgment about whether a state is faced with an evil worse than the evil of war.[17] If the just war approach is deemed by some to be preferable because there are principles that set out what is required for a war to be just, the criticism I have made against this is that to judge with a checklist of conditions is not the way that the evil of fighting a war can be properly taken into account, for war needs to be evaluated as a great evil and not as a neutral means that is good or bad depending on its purpose. I also think that the ease and simplicity of applying just war theory is illusory and dangerously so.[18] Each principle in just war theory requires interpretation for its application, and there is much subjectivity involved in doing so. The principles are subject to bad faith as they can be used in opposing ways depending on what facts are selectively brought to the table. As I have already mentioned, the problem of how to evaluate proportionality in a war that is not going well provides a good illustration of how there is usually no intuitive answer as to whether it is just to continue a war.

The problem of an ethical ending to war may seem to depict the problem of exiting a war as a trap, which cannot be avoided unless a state does not go to war even when there is a just cause. Either it can be just to violate proportionality after a war has started, or it is not enough to justify a war using *jus ad bellum* conditions since wars often do not go as planned and earlier assessments need to be revised. Pacifists may see this as lending support to never going to war. However, I have proposed a way to make a decision about whether to continue fighting a war or to end a war, and this way of deciding is consistent with my view that war is rightly chosen only when it is the lesser evil. Thus, pacifism is not the only answer to the challenge of how to end wars justly. Some wars may be rightly chosen as the lesser evil, and such wars may end by choosing the lesser evil once the evil actions of an aggressive or genocidal regime are reduced or stopped. And other wars should continue because the evil nature of a regime makes it more evil to allow that regime to stay in power.

5 Kuwait and Libya

To illustrate the application of my proposal in the last section, I will discuss two real-world examples of responding to aggression and to genocidal intent. On August 2, 1990, the Saddam Hussein regime of Iraq launched an invasion of the neighboring state of Kuwait and succeeded in occupying the entire country in just two days. The Emir and government of Kuwait were overthrown, and a puppet government under Iraqi control was set up. The invasion was motivated by economic reasons and historical grievances, which did not provide just cause. Indeed, there was unanimous international condemnation, with the United Nations passing resolutions that imposed economic sanctions on Iraq and that set a deadline for Iraqi compliance with demands to withdraw from Kuwait or face the use of force to liberate Kuwait. The Iraqi regime did not comply, and an international coalition of 42 nations led by the United States was formed to take military action against the Iraqi occupiers. Aerial and naval bombardment of military targets began on January 17, 1991. This escalated when Iraq retaliated with missile attacks on Israel and coalition targets in Saudi

Arabia. Ground forces were sent into Kuwait on February 24, 1991, with the coalition quickly overwhelming the mismatched Iraqi occupation army and achieving a decisive victory in less than 100 hours, with Iraqi troops fleeing back into Iraq. A ceasefire was declared, ending the war on February 28, 1991.

It would not be difficult to show that the coalition war to liberate Kuwait satisfied the requirements of *jus ad bellum*. My approach would require a judgment as to how evil the Iraqi regime's actions in invading and occupying Kuwait were compared to the evils of the war that was carried out by the coalition to liberate Kuwait. What I would answer here concerns the ending of the war. There was some controversy when American President George H.W. Bush declared an end to fighting without sending troops into Iraq to depose Saddam Hussein. Based on the idea that the just cause of liberating Kuwait had been achieved and the mandate of the United Nations had been fulfilled, this was the right decision. Critics of the decision argued that Saddam Hussein continued to be a threat to its neighbors, including Israel, and continued to violate the human rights of the Kurds in the north and Shiites in the south of Iraq and that the only way to end such potential and actual crimes was to extend the war until Hussein was deposed.

The question for me is how the evils of carrying on with the war against the Iraqi regime compare with the evils that the regime could perpetuate after the war ended without its removal from power. Although deciding at the time on the answer would have required a judgment ahead of later events, we now have factual answers about both sides of the comparison. The United States did eventually invade Iraq in 2003. And in the intervening years, we have evidence about how much evil Saddam Hussein could do when left in power. It seems quite clear that if the consequences of a United States invasion of Iraq in 1991 would have been similar to what happened with the invasion in 2003, the evils of continuing the 1991 war were clearly greater than the evils of having Saddam Hussein constrained by non-military means such as sanctions during the years between the two Persian Gulf Wars. This is not to minimize the latter evils, but they certainly were not close to Hitler-like evils.[19] The 2003 invasion, on the other hand, unleashed violent forces in Iraq and led to a drawn-out insurgency, sectarian violence, and the creation of the terrorist group Al-Qaeda in Iraq and the terrorist state of ISIS that exported terrorism to the West and harshly repressed people in its territories. It also led to war crimes, including torture of prisoners and killing of civilians, committed by United States forces and private contractors as they faced insurgent and terrorist attacks. It seems then that my answer to the question of whether it was morally right to end the war in 1991 at the point that it did should be that it was indeed right.

In 2011, on March 19, a NATO-led coalition began military action against the forces of Libyan leader Muammar Gaddafi to enforce United Nations Security Council Resolution 1973, which was adopted on March 17 in the first-ever application of the Responsibility to Protect (R2P) doctrine. The R2P doctrine was formulated and accepted by the international community in 2005 in order to provide a legal basis for humanitarian interventions in states that carry out genocide, ethnic cleansing, and other grave human rights violations within their borders. At the time that Resolution 1973 was passed, Libya was in the midst of a civil war as opponents of Gaddafi's dictatorship began an uprising inspired by the Arab Spring protests in nearby countries. Armed rebels had taken control of large cities, including Benghazi. Gaddafi had announced that he planned to obliterate the city and its population,[20] and this was viewed as a genocidal aim by Western leaders. As Gaddafi's forces prepared to attack Benghazi, Western leaders pushed for an intervention to prevent an impending genocide from taking place. By going to the United Nations under the R2P framework, there was a legal basis for a coalition of Western powers to take military action within the borders of a sovereign state for humanitarian reasons. Using my approach to the ethics of war, we would need to ask whether the genocide of the population of Benghazi, if carried out, would be a greater evil than the evils of a military intervention by outside forces. Conceivably, it would have been, though the genocide would not be on the scale of that perpetuated by the Nazis against the Jews, or the Hutus against the Tutsis in Rwanda.

My interest here once again is what the morally appropriate ending of the intervention should have been. The NATO alliance intervened by imposing a blockade and launching cruise missiles and air strikes on Gaddafi's troops to drive them away from Benghazi. Thus, a brutal and indiscriminate attack that could have exterminated the city's inhabitants was averted. However, NATO forces continued their attacks on Libyan territory, including the capital Tripoli, in an obvious effort to help rebels overthrow the Gaddafi regime. Eventually, NATO's military actions weakened Gaddafi's forces to such an extent that it brought about Gaddafi's overthrow, capture, and killing by the rebels as he fled the city of Sirte. Only at that point was NATO's intervention in Libya declared finished in October of that year.

There has been much criticism of how NATO countries had exceeded the UN mandate in turning a humanitarian intervention into a war to remove a regime that had been repressive at home and had sponsored terrorist attacks on Western targets. These critics believe that the intervention should have ended after preventing genocide in Benghazi and destroying enough of Gaddafi's military capability so that he could no longer threaten to commit genocide even though he would continue to be a repressive ruler who violated human rights. Defenders of the NATO actions argued that it was better to remove Gaddafi from power once and for all, even if there were evils created by the bombing campaign carried out after Benghazi had been saved from genocide. As in my answer to the question concerning ending the war to liberate Kuwait, a judgment needs to be made about which alternative constitutes the greater evil.

Those who think that it was right to continue attacks until Gaddafi was removed from power would say that the limited nature of NATO's intervention reduced the evils that the humanitarian war created, while there was clear evidence of Gaddafi's willingness to treat his people brutally in order to hold onto power. Even if he could not carry out genocide after NATO stopped him at Benghazi, he had no qualms about committing crimes against humanity and had a record of doing so. To bolster this case, we could look at what had been happening in Syria, where President Bashar al-Assad, another Middle Eastern dictator with a history of brutal repression, had been engaged in fighting a civil war against rebels seeking to overthrow him since 2012. The Assad regime had been credibly accused of attacking rebel-held cities indiscriminately using chemical weapons, barrel bombs, and cluster munitions, and of carrying out massacres.[21] At the time of writing, there are thought to be 12 million refugees displaced by the Syrian civil war, either internally or fleeing to neighboring countries and the West.

However, the evils created by NATO's taking sides in the Libyan civil war by helping rebels overthrow Gaddafi go beyond the death and destruction during the period of the bombing campaign. After Gaddafi's overthrow, rival militias and armed groups engulfed the country in lawlessness, violence, and human rights violations, causing immense suffering for the Libyan people.[22] The subsequent years were characterized by chaos and disorder without a central government capable of taking control and restraining warring militia groups. While it is possible that the aftermath was the result of historical and social factors, NATO's intervention on the side of the rebels before Gaddafi's fall played an important part in the evils of the post-Gaddafi era.[23] NATO leaders had chosen to side with the rebels in the civil war to engineer Gaddafi's removal without using their own troops on the ground. Thus, they were in no position to disarm militia and rebel groups and to keep order while a new government was formed. The strategy of aerial bombardment was chosen to avoid casualties among the intervening forces but shifted the risks to civilians in more ways than just that of being killed by the bombs. The intervention was not done with a commitment to rebuilding Libya, as there was no political will to do so. In fact, expecting Gaddafi to be deposed by rebels echoed American strategy when the first Gulf War ended. At that time, President Bush encouraged the Kurds and the Shiites in Basra to rise up against Saddam Hussein.

What Bush did not do was bombarding Iraqi forces while the uprising took place, and the rebellion was brutally quashed by Saddam Hussein's forces. The lesson here is that interveners should not engage in pursuing regime change unless they do what they can to reduce the evils of violence during and after the process of overthrowing the regime, which necessitates interveners to act in ways that unavoidably expose their soldiers to harm.[24] Pursuing regime change in the way it was done by NATO in Libya was not the lesser evil compared to leaving Gaddafi in power at the time of the intervention.

As I said earlier, humanitarian interventions have to be ended quickly once the evil of genocide is ended or averted because continued intervention brings evils of its own. However, if it is judged that a regime is evil in nature and it is the lesser evil to continue fighting to achieve regime change, then the intervention should be done in a way that reduces the created evils of the intervention and achieves real benefits when regime change happens. Since continued fighting brings great evils, the success of the war must be a great enough good for it to be the lesser evil to extend the war. Given how NATO chose to carry out the humanitarian mission from the air, it could not be the lesser evil to continue with the intervention to achieve regime change, even if it was true that Western leaders feared Gaddafi was still capable of genocide. It was thus morally wrong for NATO to pursue regime change as an extension of the humanitarian intervention that was authorized by the United Nations.

6 Further Applications

As this chapter is being prepared for publication, there is a new military crisis in the headlines that is relevant to the issues discussed here. On October 7, 2023, the anti-Israel terrorist organization Hamas launched a devastating attack from Gaza into southern Israel, indiscriminately massacring over a thousand people, including elderly people and children, and committing horrible atrocities including rape. The terrorists also took a number of hostages into Gaza, some of whom were subjected to torture and public humiliation. Israel exercised its right to defend itself and protect its citizens by starting a war in Gaza to eliminate Hamas and free the hostages, which, at the time of writing, has continued for several months and is estimated to have caused the deaths of 40,000 people in Gaza, a large proportion of whom were children. These casualty numbers increase with each day that the war does not pause or end. Israel ordered and forced the evacuation of Palestinians from their homes, leading to a sudden refugee crisis, severe shortages of basic necessities, and the destruction of buildings, infrastructure, and hospitals. There has been strong and repeated pressure from the international community for a permanent end to the fighting with the release of hostages and the return of refugees to their homes. At the very least, there have been calls for a humanitarian pause or ceasefire. However, the Netanyahu government in Israel has maintained that it has the right to continue the war until Hamas is completely wiped out and all hostages freed, regardless of the cost to civilians in Gaza. Critics have been horrified at the evils created by the continued attacks carried out by Israeli forces in heavily populated areas, with a lack of safe spaces and access to food for civilians. Some have described the crisis and the death toll in Gaza as genocide, and a case has been brought in the International Court of Justice against the Israeli government.

Events on the ground are too fast moving, and there are facts that will only be understood with some distance and perspective, so it is not wise to draw immediate conclusions about all the ethical and political issues involved in this latest chapter in the complex struggle between the state of Israel and Palestinians in territories occupied by Israel since the Six Day Arab-Israeli War in 1967. Nevertheless, there is a need for ethical decision-making, and my proposals in this chapter provide a useful framework to answer the question of when Israel should end the fighting in Gaza. Gaza is not a state, and Hamas does not represent the Palestinian people (even though it had been elected in the past as the government in Gaza when Israel previously withdrew). However, as violent terrorists committed to destroying the state of Israel, Hamas is indeed an evil that may have to be defeated by military means. Yet the urgent question that needs to be answered as the war drags on is whether the point had been reached where continuing to wage war in Gaza was a greater evil than the evil of Hamas. This is the framework that I think should be used in discussing the ending of any war, and I would suggest it provides a more useful way of addressing the issue than going back to *jus ad bellum* considerations.[25]

Notes

1 Fabre (2015, 645–652) shows that we also need to consider the possibility that an initially unjust war could acquire justification to continue.

2 A number of articles on justice in ending wars, all of which note the lack of attention to the ethics of war termination, were presented at a 2012 Ethics, Law, and Armed Conflict workshop at Oxford University. These articles, some of which are cited in this paper, have been published together in a special issue of *Ethics* in 2015.

3 David Rodin discusses this "sunk-cost dilemma" in Rodin 2015, 686–692. It is also discussed in earlier articles by Rodin, as well as by Moellendorf (2015, 662–665).

4 Proportionality and likelihood of success were added to the requirements of *jus ad bellum* more recently, and traditionalists such as James Turner Johnson, who take the classical Augustinian approach, reject these additions as utilitarian principles that do not fit into the framework of rights and duties found in the just war tradition.

5 While Rodin (2011, 361–362) thinks that the right thing to do is to carry on fighting, he grants that the war is overall unjust on the basis of its not being proportionate.

6 Throughout the history of just war theory, there have been thinkers who view war as good or evil depending on what it is used for. Pacifists, on the other hand, view war as inherently evil that cannot be used for any purpose.

7 I note again that my discussion about proportionality in *jus ex bello* assumes that proportionality should be included in *jus ad bellum*. This is mostly true of modern just war theorists and is part of how they discuss *jus ex bello*, but as previously noted, traditionalists such as James Turner Johnson would reject the more recent inclusion of proportionality, likelihood of success, and last resort as incompatible with the nature of just war theory as a non-consequentialist account of rights and duties. Nevertheless, the principles of just cause, legitimate authority, and right intention also raise issues about how they apply when deciding to end the fighting. Moreover, these principles would support fighting even when doing so creates greater evils, reinforcing my objection that just war theory fails to take proper account of the evil nature of war. Thanks to Andy Fiala for prompting me to clarify.

8 This is the position that I argue for in Chan 2012. Clearly, most who describe war as evil do so in terms of the consequences which follow from actions that are necessary in war-making. As these evils are intentional and foreseen harms produced in a culpable way, war involves not just evil actions but also evil-doers, but I make a distinction between evil-doers and evil persons whose evil acts reflect their character. Thus, the evil of war does not depend on there being evil persons, though often there are (see Chan (2012, 70)).

9 A distinction in moral dilemmas between morally right decision and morally right act is one that has been made by Rosalind Hursthouse (1999, 44–51).

10 That evil can be greater or lesser does not mean they can be measured and compared to decide which evil is greater or lesser, such that the disvalue of a lesser evil can be discounted if there is more value in preventing a greater evil. I reject such a utilitarian way of choosing between evils in Chan (2012, 72–74).

11 Moellendorf (2015, 661) introduces the term "proportionality budget" to label "the *ante bellum* judged total of morally permissible costs that a belligerent party may bring about or contribute to in its pursuit of a just cause." The idea that killings in war may be "budgeted" for similarly to material costs reflects a failure to recognize the moral evil of such killings. Moellendorf's phrase encapsulates what I think is problematic about proportionality as a *jus ad bellum* requirement for just war, apart from other problems with it, such as there being no consensus on what proportionality means and the amount of speculation involved in applying it.

12 The first example clearly involves a just cause for war, while the second is considered to involve a just cause only if humanitarian intervention is accepted as a just cause. In my view, they are both wars that may be legitimately chosen as lesser evils without appealing to a principle of just cause. The reason my account is more restrictive than just war theory is that, although it is hard to draw a clear line of how evil an enemy is for war to be the lesser evil, many wars that satisfy the just cause principle obviously do not involve evil threats on the scale of Nazi aggression.

13 This is discussed in Chan (2012, 101–102). Many of the military actions by the Allies after that point during the Second World War, such as the Dresden firebombing, illustrate the greater evil of continued fighting.

14 Humanitarian interventions often last too long when the countries that engage in such interventions use a small intervening force, partly because they do not want to be seen as invaders and partly due to lack of support at home for a war that does not serve national interests.

15 Following Lee (2012, 86), I will henceforth use the term "created evil" to refer to evils that arise out of war itself as opposed to the "resisted evil" that war is aimed at reducing or ending. One difference from Lee's usage is that I am considering the created evil at the point of continuing or ending war, whereas Lee is using it for assessing *jus ad bellum* proportionality. Another difference is that the resisted evil for Lee is "the *wrong* that provides a just cause," whereas I take the actions of brutal aggression and genocide as themselves the evils to be resisted.

16 By evil actions, I mean actions that foreseeably cause intolerable harm in a culpably wrongful way. This definition of evil is one that I take from the philosophical account in Card 2002.

17 It is a feature of my virtue ethics approach that there is no set of rules or a calculus available for making the right choice. Instead, a political leader of good character will possess practical wisdom, which is an ability derived from experience to make correct practical choices in a reliable manner (see Chan (2012, 103, 110)).

18 According to Andrew Fiala (2008), the concept of a just war allows those who wage war to provide rationalizations of what they do for realist reasons, making war a morally possible choice, and therefore it is more frequently resorted to.

19 Andy Fiala has suggested to me that the sanctions on Iraq caused such great harm to Iraqi civilians that arguably, an invasion of Iraq after the liberation of Kuwait would have been the lesser evil. Thus, it is necessary to not only take account of what evils the Iraqi regime could do but also the evils created by measures short of war, such as the sanctions imposed on Iraq. While I still think an invasion of Iraq in 1991 would have been the greater evil, even taking the harms of sanctions into account, I will add that the sanctions and embargoes were more harmful than they needed to be and based on the false premise that pressure that included limiting the flow of food and medicine into Iraq was needed to force the regime to give up its WMD programs. Instead, similar to why war should not be used to depose the regime, sanctions should have been lifted or eased once they became a greater evil than the evil perpetuated or threatened by the regime against its people and its neighbors.

20 In a speech on Libyan State TV, Gaddafi declared he would "cleanse Libya house by house," calling those opposed to his rule "rats" and "cockroaches," who he said were "serving the devil" (see BBC News 2011).

21 Regarding barrel bombs dropped on Syrian cities, see al-Saleh 2015.

22 See Amnesty International 2021 for a report on conditions in Libya ten years after the uprising began, and also BBC News 2020.

23 Claudia Gazzini, a Libya specialist quoted in Beaumont 2021, says, "If you start with the NATO-led intervention, the big lesson learned was that this planted the seeds for the disarray that followed. A very idealistic invocation of responsibility to protect led to full and violent regime change."

24 Michael Blake (2014, 145) argues for an interpretation of the so-called Pottery Barn rule as "Do not enter into an invasion intended to transform another society, unless you are able to commit to doing all the work required to transform that society – and doing it all yourself."

25 An earlier and much shorter version of this paper was presented with the title "Ending War Justly" on the Main Program of the American Philosophical Association Pacific Division Meeting in Vancouver, Canada, on April 14, 2022. Thanks to Michael Blake, who served as commentator, and to audience members for their questions. Thanks also to Andy Fiala for reading a full length draft and suggesting improvements.

References

al-Saleh, Raed. 2015. "Stop the 'barrel bombs' in Syria." *The Washington Post*, March 27, 2015. https://www.washingtonpost.com/opinions/stop-the-barrel-bombs-the-deadliest-weapons-in-syrias-civil-war/2015/03/27/c983d024-cf4e-11e4-8a46-b1dc9be5a8ff_story.html

Amnesty International. 2021. "Libya: Ten Years After Uprising Abusive Militias Evade Justice and Instead Reap Rewards." February 17, 2021. https://www.amnesty.org/en/latest/press-release/2021/02/libya-ten-years-after-uprising-abusive-militias-evade-justice-and-instead-reap-rewards/

BBC News. 2011. "Libya Protests: Defiant Gaddafi Refuses to Quit." February, 22, 2011. https://www.bbc.com/news/world-middle-east-12544624

BBC News. 2020. "Why Is Libya So Lawless?" January 23, 2020. https://www.bbc.com/news/world-africa-24472322

Beaumont, Peter. 2021. "'War weary' Libya Reflects 10 Years on from Gaddafi and Arab Spring." *The Guardian*, April 26, 2021. https://www.theguardian.com/world/2021/apr/26/war-weary-libya-reflects-10-years-on-from-gaddafi-and-arab-spring

Blake, Michael. 2014. "The Costs of War: Justice, Liability, and the Pottery Barn Rule." In *The Ethics of Armed Humanitarian Intervention*, edited by Don E. Scheid, 133–147. Cambridge: Cambridge University Press.

Card, Claudia. 2002. *The Atrocity Paradigm: A Theory of Evil*. New York: Oxford University Press.

Chan, David K. 2012. *Beyond Just War: A Virtue Ethics Approach*. Basingstoke: Palgrave Macmillan.

Dill, Janina. 2015. "Ending Wars: The *Jus ad Bellum* Principles Suspended, Repeated, or Adjusted?" *Ethics* 125 (April): 627–630.

Fabre, Cécile. 2015. "War Exit." *Ethics* 125 (April): 631–652.

Fiala, Andrew. 2008. *The Just War Myth*. Lanham, MD: Rowman & Littlefield.

Hursthouse, Rosalind. 1999. *On Virtue Ethics*. New York: Oxford University Press.

Lee Steven P. 2012. *Ethics and War: An Introduction*. New York: Cambridge University Press.

Moellendorf, Darrel. 2015. "Two Doctrines of *Jus ex Bello*." *Ethics* 125 (April): 653–673.

Rodin, David. 2011. "Ending War." *Ethics and International Affairs* 25, no. 3: 359–367.

Rodin, David. 2015. "The War Trap: Dilemmas of *jus terminatio*." *Ethics* 125 (April): 674–695.

3 Victor's Justice and the Myth of Ending Wars Justly

Andrew Fiala

In the 2003 film, *The Fog of War*, former US Secretary of Defense Robert S. McNamara posed a significant worry about war crimes and the aftermath of war (Morris 2003). Referring to war crimes committed by the US in the Second World War, including intentional firebomb and atomic bomb attacks against civilians, McNamara said, "If we had lost the war, we'd all have been prosecuted as war criminals… But what makes it immoral if you lose and not immoral if you win?"

This remark points toward the problem of "victor's justice." The most obvious version of this problem occurs when the victors put the losers on trial while also ignoring crimes that those victors themselves have committed. This results in McNamara's worry that if you win, you get away with your "crimes" but if you lose, you get prosecuted for them. The problem of victor's justice provides a significant reason to be skeptical that wars can be ended justly. It also reminds us that in the real world, few (if any) actual wars live up to the ideal standards of just war theory. The Second World War is often viewed as the paradigm of a just war. However, if this war did not end justly—if its ending involved a one-sided application of victor's justice—then we ought to remain skeptical. We can take steps to improve the way that wars end—such as creating and supporting international war crimes tribunals. However, the empirical and historical reality of the non-ideal world reminds us that there will be challenges to actualizing the just war ideal. We ought also to be aware of the tendency to mythologize warfare. It is a myth to think that victor's justice can be easily eliminated. It is thus also a myth to think that wars typically (or ever) end justly.

The argument in favor of skepticism can be articulated briefly as follows:

1 For a war to end justly, war crimes must be fairly and fully prosecuted, and victor's justice must be avoided.

DOI: 10.4324/9781003454144-5

2 Victor's justice is common. War crimes committed by the victors are routinely ignored or pardoned by the victorious powers.
3 Therefore, most wars do not end justly.

I do not intend this as a deductive syllogism but as a "for the most part" generalization: most wars will fail to end justly because of the problem of victor's justice. My approach here is similar to the kind of argument I have made elsewhere regarding what I call "the just war myth" (Fiala 2008). The just war myth occurs when we believe that it is easy to fight wars justly, that our side fights justly, and that we win the wars we fight because we fight justly. The problem of victor's justice gives us further reason to see the popular application of just war concepts in mythological terms. Wars typically do not end justly because the perpetrators of war crimes often escape justice. However, in the popular and patriotic imagination, it is often thought that the good guys win, that we are the good guys, and that war crimes do not go unpunished. One thrust of my argument is to disabuse the popular imagination of that kind of mythic faith in the application of just war theory. Moreover, a further point holds with regard to conversations among scholars who advocate in favor of just war principles as a theory of the justification of war (for a review of the scholarship, see Fiala 2023). The ideal theory of a just war ought to include stipulations about fair prosecution of war crimes (in an account of *jus post bellum*), and proponents of that ideal theory ought to also bear in mind the fact of victor's justice as found in the non-ideal world.

This chapter has three main parts. The first two are focused on elucidating each of the premises in the above syllogism. The last part of the paper extends the discussion to point toward a conclusion that can be broadly understood as a kind of contingent pacifism.

1 For a War to End Justly, War Crimes Must be Fairly and Fully Prosecuted, and Victor's Justice Must be Avoided

I begin by explaining and justifying the first premise of the argument, which is the primary normative claim that drives this chapter. I will turn to the second empirical/historical premise in the next section of the paper, where I consider some cases of victor's justice. I derive this basic principle from consideration of the primary rationale behind a just war, which is supposed to be to pursue a just cause. Just causes of war are typically understood as responding to the crime of aggression, preventing atrocities, and pursuing justice for the victims of war crimes. Brian Orend explains this as follows, in his summary of the just war tradition: "The just causes most frequently mentioned include: self-defence from external attack; the protection of innocents; and punishment for wrongdoing" (Orend 2001, 87). Orend explains this with reference to Michael Walzer's contemporary theory of just war in *Just and Unjust Wars* (Walzer 2006, originally published in 1977) and that of the deeper just war tradition. Indeed, Orend notes that Francisco de Vitoria subsumed all of this under the general category of responding to "a wrong received" (Vitoria cited in May 2006). Vitoria, writing in the 16th century, emphasized that wars are not fought justly when they seek to expand an empire or aggrandize a prince. Rather, Vitoria explains, just wars are supposed to be responsive to a preceding wrong. In the tradition that develops from this basic claim, the primary wrong identified as a just cause for war was initially understood as international aggression. However, during the post-Second World War era, prevention of atrocity has come to be understood as providing a just cause for war under the general rubric of humanitarian intervention.

To achieve the aim of responding to a wrong received, I maintain that war crimes must be fairly and fully prosecuted and punished. In the scholarly literature on war crimes (see May 2007) and in the emerging realm of international law, as seen in the International Criminal Court (ICC) founded on the Rome Statute of 2002, there has been an attempt to distinguish among various "wrongs." The Rome Statute identifies four categories as falling under its jurisdiction: the crime of genocide, crimes against humanity, war crimes, and crimes against the peace (Rome Statute 2021). I discuss these distinctions briefly in what follows. However, in general, I will use the concept of "war crimes" in a broad and inclusive sense intended to encompass each of these areas of concern and connected to the general notion of a just war as responding to a "received wrong" of the sort identified by these categories. I contend that a just war is supposed to respond to all of these crimes (or wrongs) in a way that is linked to a basic conception of justice. There are also consequentialist and pragmatic considerations at play in discussions of the ethics of war. However, I contend that the primary rationale for a "just" war is a war fought in pursuit of justice in response to these sorts of wrongs.

The basic conception of justice here is grounded in a kind of natural law theory, which includes a focus on retributive justice. Of course, the just war tradition has a more complicated focus that is not only interested in retribution. There are consequentialist considerations in the modern just war theory, as well as natural law and retributive elements. As James Turner Johnson has explained in discussing war crimes tribunals:

> The aim of a just war is not simply to end the fighting, for peace without justice is no real peace at all. Rather, just war tradition requires a peace with justice, a peace in which the rule of law is established or restored, one in which civil society does not need to cope with the ongoing fear of powerful figures who perpetrated evil acts during the conflict and remain free to engage in similar acts again.
>
> (Johnson 2006, 194)

Expanding on Johnson's idea of "peace with justice," we can fill this in with both deontological and consequentialist considerations. Among the deontological concerns is the idea that perpetrators of injustice ought to be punished. We might expand this somewhat and suggest that there is a *duty to bring war criminals to justice*. This means that war criminals are viewed as responsible for their crimes. And that one of the goals of a just war is to hold them accountable. This, in turn, means that claims of necessity, duress, ignorance, or institutional inertia cannot excuse those war criminals or justify failing to prosecute them for their crimes. Michael Walzer explains:

> If there are recognizable war crimes, there must be recognizable criminals. If there is such a thing as aggression, there must be aggressors. It is not the case that for every violation of human rights in wartime we can name a guilty person or group of persons. The conditions of war supply a plethora of excuses: fear, coercion, ignorance, even madness. But the theory of justice should point us to the men and women from whom we can rightly demand an accounting.
>
> (Walzer 2006, 287)

Nonetheless, Walzer notes that it is difficult to actualize the process of assigning blame and establishing accountability. This is especially complicated given the fog of war, the diffusion of responsibility in large social phenomena such as war, and the way that structures of command and obedience tend to change the way that accountability works. Walzer says that "moral accounting is difficult and imprecise" (Walzer 2006, 303). Nonetheless, I contend that even with all these caveats in place, the idea that there is a duty to bring war criminals to justice still holds as a basic normative commitment in the idea of justice in war.

There are also consequentialist concerns, including the problem of fear and the threat of recurrence of wrongdoing. Consequentialist concerns include both the need to prevent wrong-doers from continuing to do wrong and the need to deter other wrong-doers from perpetrating similar misdeeds. Moreover, the idea of peace with justice can be used to support the idea that for a war to end justly, victor's justice must be avoided, since "victor's justice" is, by definition, not really justice. When victor's justice occurs, the stronger party gets away with its crimes (violating the deontological duty to punish wrongdoing). With victor's justice, the weaker party is also often punished in a manner that is not equitable, fair, or just. And if the victorious party fails to punish crimes committed or supported by its military personnel and political leaders, there will be no preventive or deterrent effect.

The problem identified here as "victor's justice" also occurs when the stronger party "loses" in a war (or does not "win" in any recognizable way)—but, due to its strength, is able to prevent those who are responsible for war crimes from being extradited or punished. Something like this occurs when dominant global or regional superpowers meddle or intervene in less powerful countries. We might call this "superpower impunity."[1] Superpower impunity is a form of "victor's justice," broadly construed, which ironically does not depend on victory. Regional and global superpower interventions can include full-fledged invasions, border wars, missile and bombing campaigns, targeted assassinations, cyber-attacks, and so on. Yet even when the superpower intervention fails to achieve victory, the superpower is insulated from accountability. These superpowers are rarely prosecuted for their aggression or for other war crimes committed as they intervene. This makes one wonder whether the concept of "victor's justice" is really only about *victory* in the strict sense. However, I maintain that the concept remains useful and of interest because it is familiar from the literature.

Of course, all of this is made more complicated depending on our understanding of the basic idea of *justice*. My supposition here is that the basic idea of justice found in the just war tradition, including in the newly developing idea of *jus post bellum*, is *retributive*. However, there are obvious complexities. In its development as a "Christian" theory of the justification of war, the tradition includes an element of *caritas* or love (Elshtain 2004; Steffen 2012, Chapter 1). With this in mind, there may be a place for *restorative justice* in the just war theory and in discussions of *jus post bellum*. I will not discuss this possibility here (but see Scheid 2016). Nor will I discuss the notion of *reparations* for victims of war crimes or related notions of *transitional* or *transformative* justice (but see articles in Ferstman and Goetz 2020). Rather, my primary focus is on an account of *retributive justice* that includes the need to vindicate the victims of war crimes and punish those who have committed war crimes. As noted above, there may be reasons not to prosecute, including Walzer's notion of the difficulty and imprecision of delivering justice. These excuses and other pragmatic or consequentialist concerns may explain the difficulty of delivering justice. However, they do not lessen the demand for justice.

This conception of justice is found within much of the contemporary discussion of war crimes and *jus post bellum*. To cite an important example, it is the spirit of retributive justice that guides the ICC. The Rome Statute that founds the ICC affirms that "most serious crimes" "must not go unpunished." It states a fundamental resolve "to put an end to impunity for the perpetrators of these crimes and thus to contribute to the prevention of such crimes" (Rome Statute 2021). The notion of impunity is, I maintain, a retributive one. However, we should also note that the Rome

Statute speaks here of prevention (or what can be more broadly understood as deterrence), which points toward consequentialist considerations that go beyond strict retributivism.

The focus on retributive justice has been articulated by just war theorists in a number of ways. One important focus is the idea that the punishment should fit (or be *proportional*) to the crime. Williams and Caldwell put it this way in a consideration of *proportionality* as a value in thinking about *jus post bellum*:

> In assessing postwar efforts to promote justice—particularly retributive justice—a sense of proportionality seems essential. If punishment for crimes against peace or war crimes is appropriate at all, the punishment must fit the crime.
>
> (Williams and Caldwell 2006, 316)

In general, according to the logic of the just war tradition, for a war to end justly, war crimes must be punished fairly and fully—that is, in ways that are proportional to the severity of the crime.

Now, let me cite a couple of other scholars who share the basic intuition of my first premise. The idea was described by Kellogg (2002), as follows:

> If Just War is undertaken to right wrongs done by a group or groups of people to another—if in fact the only acceptable reason for going to war is, as Michael Walzer and other Just War theorists contend, to do justice—then stopping short of trying and punishing those most responsible for war crimes and crimes against humanity which either led to war or were committed in its prosecution may be likened to declaring "checkmate" and then declining to take your opponent's king. It makes no strategic sense, since the purpose for which war was undertaken is never achieved. It makes no legal sense, since the criminal activities the war was undertaken to rectify or curtail are allowed to continue unchecked. What is worse, it makes no moral sense, since justice is not done for the victims of atrocities in such an outcome to war.
>
> (Kellogg 2002, 88)

Building on Kellogg's account, I suggest that there are *moral*, *legal*, and *strategic* reasons to avoid victor's justice. However, there are subtleties that must be considered. An account provided by Alex Bellamy (2008) indicates a difference between a *minimal* and a *maximal* conception of *jus post bellum*. A minimalist conception holds that just wars are fought to defend the rights of those who are attacked and that, beyond that, there is nothing further required for a war to be justified. We might suppose that once those rights are defended—say, if a border is secured and the enemy is driven out—then nothing further is required. A maximalist conception holds that just warriors have other obligations, including the obligation to prosecute those who commit war crimes. This distinction is useful and might be used to argue against my first premise. A minimalist might say that the prosecution of war criminals is not a requirement of justice, assuming that the rights of those who are defended have been secured. Of course, Kellogg and Johnson seem to make a stronger, more maximal sort of argument: that justice requires a just prosecution of war criminals. Furthermore, the problem of victor's justice is not merely that war crimes are not punished—as when the border is secured and the criminal enemy is left alone behind that stabilized border. Rather, the problem is that the victors often do punish the losers. Moreover, the crimes committed by the winners are typically not in fact punished (or rarely punished). It seems that even a minimal account of *jus post bellum* would at least require war crimes prosecutions for the misdeeds of those who purportedly have justice on their side.

Another useful account of the need to prosecute war crimes was articulated by Gary Bass in 2004. In explaining the importance of war crimes prosecutions in relation to the idea of *jus post bellum*, Bass explains:

> A central element of an account of *jus post bellum* will be the question of war crimes trials. After all, *jus post bellum* must take seriously the demands of *jus ad bellum* and *jus in bello*; when they have been violated, the violators should be punished.
>
> (Bass and Bass. 2004, 404)

Bass's analysis is helpful since he articulates the complexity of the task, along with the fact that there are other values at stake in thinking about the ethics of war. Bass notes that there may be a conflict between the duty to end a war and establish peace (what he calls the "duty of peace") and the duty to pursue punishment for war crimes (the "duty of justice"). As Bass explains, justice is one good among many. Peace, stability, and reconciliation are other important goods. Of course, as we saw, Johnson suggests that justice and peace must be more closely linked in his idea of peace with justice. However, Bass suggests that there may be reasons to prefer peace without justice.

With this on the table, let me clarify what I mean in my first premise by the phrase, "for a war to end justly." There may be other ways for a war to end. A war could end in atrocity and exhaustion. A war could end in a stalemate across an armed frontier. A war could end when one party simply surrenders. Or a war could end with mutual reconciliation and forgiveness. However, if we expect a war to end *justly* (in the sense of retributive justice and natural law that I've been employing here), then war crimes ought to be punished—and they ought to be punished fairly and comprehensively.

This means that victor's justice should be avoided: war crimes perpetrated by the stronger party should be punished, and there should not be an unfair prosecution of the losing party. If victor's justice occurs, that is, if war crimes are not punished fairly, then we would not say that the war ended justly.

2 Victor's Justice Is Common

Now let me support the second premise, which is that victor's justice is common. Of course, it is not so obvious what exactly we might mean by victor's justice. In fact, I suggest that there are two versions of the problem. I will first examine these two versions (in part 2a). Then I'll describe some real-world cases (in part 2b) that show us that this problem is common.

2a Victor's Justice: Strong and Weak Versions of the Problem

A simple definition of victor's justice is that this is what occurs when the winners punish the losers. Presumptively, this is an unjust kind of punishment: the notion of victor's justice is ironic—the term "justice" should be put in scare quotes, signifying that it is not really justice. Now it may be that the vanquished do in fact *deserve* to be punished because of the crimes they have committed—and so are punished "justly." This would occur when a putative war criminal is captured or arrested and is put on trial at some tribunal in which evidence is presented, in which the accused is able to respond to and rebut that evidence, when the actions that they are accused of are indeed considered "criminal," and when conviction and appropriate punishment follow from such a proceeding. For the sake of the present paper, I will not discuss in any detail how all of this might work or any of the technical details of how such a tribunal might be constituted, what might count as evidence or rebuttal, and related questions of what counts as a criminal action in war and what counts as an appropriate punishment. There is a large literature that discusses these details, which I will assume supports the basic idea that some actions are in fact criminal when done in war and that some kinds of tribunals can legitimately prosecute and punish war criminals. The literature on war crimes often considers war crimes tribunals at the end of the Second World War as good examples of how this might occur (see May 2007; Walzer 2006). However, it is important to note that these paradigmatic examples are problematic since they were, in fact, one-sided tribunals in which the victors punished the vanquished while failing to punish their own crimes. A more recent and less problematic example is found in the ICC, which intends to be a neutral adjudicator of war crimes. However, as we will see, the ICC is fundamentally flawed since strong war-fighting nations, including the United States, Russia, Israel, and China, do not recognize its jurisdiction.

At any rate, the problem of victor's justice occurs when culpability, liability, and justice are not equally or neutrally administered. This occurs, most obviously, when the victors are not also punished or held liable for their crimes. This problem makes most sense when we understand crime and punishment on a retributivist scheme, assuming that some actions are criminally wrong and that punishment for those crimes is deserved. The problem will be different when understood from a consequentialist point of view, where "justice" is reconceived as a matter of prevention, deterrence, reparation, or some other non-retributive value.

According to Wringe, one of the ways of conceiving the problem of victor's justice is that it simply has nothing to do with justice. Wringe says, "what the Victor's Justice objection suggests is that when war criminals receive harsh treatment, they are not receiving this harsh treatment because of the crimes they have committed but for some other reason" (Wringe 2006, 168). The "other reason" may be a matter of exploitation (perhaps if the victor wants to extract war bounty under the rubric of reparations—such as occurs when pirates demand ransom or payoff from those they have defeated). Or it may be a way of vaunting and glory-seeking—such as happened in the ancient world when vanquished enemies were marched through the streets and publicly executed. Perhaps it is tied to a political agenda that aims to take further advantage (such as might occur when the victor demands a revision of borders or the dismantling of a political system, religion, or party, as part of "punishment"). However, at its root, this "other reason" is most generally understood as a matter of power and domination. We might call this the "strong form of victor's justice." It is "strong" because it is simply a matter of strength: the strong do what they can and the weak take what they get. This is also "strong" in the sense that it creates a strong or significant objection to the claim that this is justice. The strong form of the problem of victor's justice is a fairly typical phenomenon in war that can be traced back to Thucydides' account of the impunity of the victorious Athenian army in the Melian Dialogue. Thucydides tells us that the Athenians claimed: "Justice is only in question between equals in power, while the strong do what they can and the weak suffer what they must." The Athenians, of course, committed war crimes as they killed and enslaved the Melians they had defeated. However, they got away with those crimes (at least in the moment), due to their strength and power. The weaker Melians were not able to complain or respond or put the Athenians on trial. Of course, Thucydides seems to recount this episode as a warning against hubris: the apparent impunity of the Athenians can be seen as part of a tragic scene that eventually leads to their downfall (Lucas 2013). Nonetheless, the doctrine that we now call "realism" can be traced back to the Melian episode, from which realists take the following lesson: it is better to be strong than weak, and it is better to administer "justice"—understood here as power—than to receive it from a stronger enemy.

A weaker version of the victor's justice objection holds that the problem is not that the powerful victor acts with absolute impunity but, rather, that victor's justice leaves the crimes of the victorious party unpunished. Notice that this weaker victor's justice objection does not require that the victorious party be cruel and rapacious in forcing a kind of "punishment" upon the vanquished. The victor, in this case, need not commit injustices in the administration of justice or unjustly use a phony legal proceeding (a so-called kangaroo court) to exact revenge or extract booty. Rather, in the weaker version of victor's justice, the primary problem is that the crimes committed by the victors are left unpunished. They are left unpunished because the victorious party has no desire to prosecute the crimes that were committed by its own forces; there is no neutral third party that has the power to put those war criminals on trial, and the party that lost the war is not able to do so. Furthermore, the victorious power often has no interest in or incentive to investigate and acknowledge its own crimes—because in doing so, it would undermine its own claims about having justice on its side. There are also domestic political incentives that may lead the victorious party simply to ignore or even pardon its own war criminals. And so, on the weaker version of the problem of victor's justice, the difficulty is that crimes remain unacknowledged and unpunished.

2b Two Examples of the Common Problem of Victor's Justice

It should be obvious that this paper depends upon an account of what counts as a war crime. As I've been discussing it here, I intend the concept to be broadly construed to include, as the ICC does, genocide, crimes against humanity, crimes against the peace, and a long list of criminal actions that occur in war—such as torture, abuse of prisoners, taking hostages, unlawful deportation, rape, pillaging, and poisoning. I do not here delve into the arguments and definitions of each and every war crime. The ICC's account includes several lists of criminal activities, and some of these lists include dozens of entries. However, it is clear that in order to demand that war crimes be prosecuted, there would need to be a common definition of what counts as a wrongful or criminal action in war. This raises a difficulty, of course, which is that even though war crimes are defined in scholarly arguments, as well as in treaties and international agreements, the legitimacy of those arguments and treaties is often not agreed to by those who are accused of war crimes. And the supposed crimes defined by those agreements are sometimes disputed. The dispute about torture provides a poignant recent example. This is a significant problem that can only be resolved by appealing to a larger theory that provides a detailed account.

However, the dispute about what counts as a war crime is often part of the problem of victor's justice. One obvious example concerns the question of torture. And this brings us to the first example: the American war on terrorism. Recall that American forces used torture during the war on terrorism. Torture was widely viewed at the time as illegal, immoral, and a war crime (despite the moral dispute). Yet no official of the US military or government was ever prosecuted internationally for war crimes. Eleven soldiers were prosecuted by the US military for what they did at Abu Ghraib prison. But no higher authority has been held responsible and punished for authorizing the use of torture, either within the United States or in an international tribunal. As Human Rights Watch concluded in a 2022 report on war crimes committed in the war on terrorism, including at Abu Ghraib in Iraq, Bagram Airfield in Afghanistan, and Guantanamo Bay in Cuba, "No US government officials have been held accountable for creating, authorizing, or implementing the CIA's secret detention and torture programs" (Tayler and Epstein 2022). The lack of accountability for crimes committed in the war on terrorism is not just a remnant of the Bush Administration. Human Rights Watch reports that both Republican and Democratic administrations have refused war crimes investigations at the ICC. According to HRW:

> Both the Trump and Biden administrations have sought to thwart any accountability for international crimes by US forces before the International Criminal Court (ICC). In 2020, Trump imposed unprecedented sanctions on ICC staff including the prosecutor at the time, after the court's judges authorized an investigation into alleged war crimes and crimes against humanity in connection with the conflict in Afghanistan that could have included abuses by US nationals. In April [of 2022], the Biden administration lifted the US sanctions against the court's members but made clear it continued to oppose the court's jurisdiction over US nationals and personnel in Afghanistan.
>
> (Tayler and Epstein 2022)

We should also note that the invasion of Iraq by American and allied forces has been widely described as criminal since it was a war of choice and a war of aggression. The crime of aggression is a violation of international law and also of the just war theory's considerations of *jus ad bellum*. The question of whether the invasion of Iraq was an act of aggression is perhaps more complicated than the authorization of torture in the war: arguments were made at the time about the justification of pre-emptive war, and there were purported threats of weapons of mass destruction (that proved to be bogus).

At any rate, George W Bush and other members of his administration who authorized the invasion of Iraq and the use of torture were never tried at the ICC. It is true that Bush and others were tried *in absentia* at a war crimes commission in Malaysia in 2012, and the ICC engaged in a preliminary investigation into war crimes committed by the United States in 2016 (Ridley 2012; The Guardian 2016). However, American authorities were never put directly on trial or punished. A similar problem occurred when Vladimir Putin authorized the invasion of Ukraine and Russian forces committed war crimes. In 2023, the ICC issued arrest warrants for Putin and other Russian authorities for war crimes, including the forced deportation of Ukrainian children (International Criminal Court, 2023). However, it has not been possible to detain Putin and other Russian leaders for trial or to punish him or the Russian forces who are accused of committing war crimes. And even if Russia were defeated in this war, it is unlikely that Putin would be extradited or punished—given what I said above about the way that global and regional superpowers have a kind of impunity even in defeat. Moreover, accusations of war crimes can set off a cascade of reactions and reprisals. In response to the arrest warrant, Russian leaders initiated legal proceedings against magistrates of the ICC, and former Russian President Dmitry Medvedev threatened missile strikes on the Court in The Hague (Jochecová 2023).

While the United States has not threatened military strikes on the ICC, it did move to resist and discredit the Court, as indicated in the above quote from Human Rights Watch. In this regard, it is worth noting the language of the Trump Administration's Executive Order (of June 2020) that authorized official resistance to The Hague Court, including sanctions against any person who assists the Court in prosecuting American military or political personnel.[2] The Executive Order declares that the ICC has claimed "illegitimate assertions of jurisdiction over personnel of the United States." The Order states that the United States has consistently rejected the ICC's claims of jurisdiction. It further states,

> These actions on the part of the ICC, in turn, threaten to infringe upon the sovereignty of the United States and impede the critical national security and foreign policy work of United States Government and allied officials, and thereby threaten the national security and foreign policy of the United States.

It is also worth noting that, as the war on terror proceeded, President Trump pardoned convicted war criminals from Iraq and Afghanistan. The pardons included three American service members whose crimes included intentionally shooting civilians and mutilating corpses. Trump pardoned these soldiers in 2019 (Zafar 2019). In 2020, Trump pardoned four private Blackwater contractors who were accused of opening fire on civilians in Iraq in 2007. At least one author (Ford 2020) has suggested that in pardoning war criminals, President Trump himself committed war crimes by failing to exercise proper "command responsibility."

And so we see that despite plausible accusations made against President George W. Bush and members of his administration regarding war crimes (crimes of aggression and the crime of torture), there was no official investigation or prosecution of the matter (Haas 2009; Holtzman 2012). War criminals have even been pardoned by American officials, which may in fact be another corollary war crime that will not be prosecuted or punished.

In this case, the questions of administering justice after war and of ending wars justly run aground on the reality of "victor's justice" (and on the more complicated account that I've called "superpower impunity"). There are also difficulties that stem from the concrete real-world difficulty of establishing consensus about what counts as a war crime, who has jurisdiction to prosecute war crimes, and what the punishment for such crimes ought to be. This example shows that the strong often do what they want with impunity. And when wars end, strong states escape punishment. The example of the United States invasion of Iraq and the use of torture during the war on terrorism provide a reminder of the fact that strong states like the United States will resist any attempt to prosecute war crimes among their personnel. And as we have seen, Russia has also resisted the efforts of the ICC.

An optimal solution to this problem would be for states like Russia and the United States to join with the international community in supporting the ICC and submitting to its jurisdiction. A less optimal solution would be for these strong states to administer justice to themselves. However, as we have seen, given the realities of superpower impunity and the perpetual problem of victor's justice, neither of these solutions is likely. Thus, in the current geopolitical world, the problem of victor's justice will persist, and it will be unlikely that wars involving those parties will end justly.

Now let us turn to a second example: the Second World War example. It is fairly obvious that American and allied forces committed war crimes in that war, which were not punished—as Robert S. McNamara recognized in the quote with which we began. This assessment is shared by many of the leading scholars who discuss war crimes. Among these is Jeff McMahan, who defines war crimes as follows: "Ideally, therefore, the category of war crimes should include all forms of morally wrong action in war that inflict serious harms on their victims" (McMahan 2013). Appealing to his own revisionist interpretation of the just war distinction between *jus in bello* and *jus ad bellum*, McMahan reminds us, however, of the difficulty of delineating what counts as a *morally wrong action in war*. Those fighting on the unjust side have a different kind of moral culpability than those fighting on the just side, and even those who fight on the just side may commit war crimes. Moreover, this description of moral evaluation is exceedingly difficult to apply when we consider mitigating circumstances (such as the ignorance of the average soldier, the duress and anxiety of war, and the understandable excuse of following orders). As McMahan suggested in *Killing in War* (2009), the discussion of war crimes is "varied and complex" and

> the simple account according to which unjust combatants who fight within the rules are excused while war criminals are not is too simple to be sustainable. It is revealing about our attitudes in general that we sometimes do take combatants who have committed war crimes to be fully excused, or even justified, and not just in cases involving extreme duress, invincible ignorance, or insanity.
>
> (McMahan 2009, 128)

McMahan reminds us of the difficulty of judgment by describing the case of Paul Tibbets, who led the mission that dropped the atomic bomb on Hiroshima. This was a war crime by most accounts. Instead, Tibbets was hailed as a hero. As McMahan states, "Tibbets's act is the most egregious war crime, and the most destructive single terrorist act, ever committed, even though it was committed in the course of a just war" (McMahan 2009, 129). This is among the examples that McNamara was concerned with when he wondered whether the United States was responsible for war crimes in the Second World War—and it provides a poignant example of the problem of victor's justice.

This example might be expanded upon to include a consideration of the ultimate responsibility for the decision to use the atomic bomb, which rested with President Harry S. Truman (the US President associated with the phrase "the buck stops here"). Truman justified this in a straightforward utilitarian fashion as a matter of saving lives (with a thumb on the scale for saving American lives). In a radio address after the bombing, Truman explained that he authorized the bombing "in order to shorten the agony of war, in order to save the lives of thousands and thousands of young Americans" (quoted in Malloy 2012, Chapter 4). However, the debate about Truman among moral philosophers has tended to suggest that Truman was guilty of war crimes. Elizabeth Anscombe called Truman a murderer for his decision, and John Rawls suggested that Truman was motivated by anti-Japanese bias and that his decision to drop the bomb was a moral failure and a sign that Truman was a failed statesman (Anscombe 1981; Rawls 1999; for discussion, see Fiala 2023 and Fiala 2008).

The example of Tibbets and Truman reminds us how difficult it is to apply the just war theory and corresponding notions in international law in an impartial and neutral fashion. Indeed, the Second World War is often viewed in the popular imagination as a paradigm example of a just war. But it did not end justly. McMahan also reminds us that there are pragmatic considerations that also matter, including both the fact that there is no neutral international court that could prosecute war crimes without creating the problem of victor's justice and the risk of escalation that occurs when a state or its military is concerned that if it loses it will be prosecuted for war crimes (McMahan 2013; McMahan 2009, Chapter 4). We might add here, a point made at the outset of this section, that there are remaining disputes about what exactly counts as a war crime and about how, where, and by whom such crimes should be prosecuted.

3 Conclusion: Contingent Pacifism and the Problem of the Just War Myth

One of the vexing problems here is to distinguish between what we might call "ordinary" or "non-criminal" warfighting and war crimes broadly construed. As noted, the Rome Statute that founded the ICC includes a long list of war crimes. Consider one example from the Rome Statue following the Geneva Conventions of 1949: "Extensive destruction and appropriation of property, not justified by military necessity and carried out unlawfully and wantonly." One should ask, what counts as "extensive destruction," "military necessity," and "wanton-ness"? In the background here is some notion of proportionality as defined by the general concept of *jus in bello*. Instead, pacifists will argue that the very idea of military necessity is flawed and that all destruction in war is wanton and therefore wrong. Michael Walzer has explained pacifism as the idea that "war is a criminal act" (Walzer 2004, ix). For this reason, Walzer rejects pacifism—because he believes that it must remain morally possible to fight wars.

In opposition to this, pacifists have insisted that war is in fact criminal. The Dalai Lama once said:

> Since armies are legal, we feel that war is acceptable; in general, nobody feels that war is criminal or that accepting it is criminal attitude. In fact, we have been brainwashed.
>
> (Dalai Lama n.d.)

Full-fledged pacifists may nod in agreement with my overall analysis since they view all war as wrong. As an example, we might consider Pope Francis, who has said that war itself is a crime. In January 2024, the Pope said, speaking of the wars in Ukraine, Palestine, and Israel:

> Let us pray that those who have power over these conflicts may reflect on the fact that war is not the way to resolve them, because it sows death among civilians and destroys cities and infrastructure. In other words, *today war is in itself a crime against humanity. Let us not forget this: war is in itself a crime against humanity.*
>
> (Francis 2024)

We should also note that realists may simply accept the fact that all war is, in a sense, criminal—and argue that for that reason we must get on with it and make sure we win. This was Ernest Hemingway's assessment of the American war against Germany. Writing in 1945 at the end of the Second World War, Hemingway understood that the American war was a war waged without restraint against the German people. He said that waging war any other way was "playing with dolls" (Hemingway 1946, xv). What this means is that, in a sense, all war is criminal. He concluded,

> An aggressive war is the great crime against everything good in the world. A defensive war, which must necessarily turn to aggressive at the earliest moment, is the necessary great counter-crime. But never think that war, no matter how necessary, nor how justified, is not a crime. Ask the infantry and ask the dead.
>
> (Hemingway 1946, xv)

We can see here, in brief, the larger problem of justifying war. Realists will contend that even if war is criminal, we must win; pacifists will argue that all war is criminal; and just war theorists (and the evolving ideas of international law) hold that there are some things within a war that are criminal while avoiding the conclusion that war itself is criminal.

My own view, as a kind of hybrid pacifist, is that we ought to work toward the abolition of war and affirm the idea that war is morally deficient while at the same time allowing that some forms of war-fighting are obviously criminal (Fiala 2022). However, I worry that it is often difficult to distinguish between better and worse forms of war-fighting. And I suggest that we often wax mythological in our thinking about war. Obvious and egregious war crimes remain unaddressed—as in the case of Tibbets and Truman—due to the problem of victor's justice. In following the mythological application of the just war theory, we think that just wars are easily fought and that wars can end justly.

The nearly ubiquitous fact of victor's justice creates a fundamental problem for the idea that any war can end justly. This problem is typical: it happens often. And even in cases that are viewed as paradigmatic examples of just war-fighting (such as the American and Allied cause in the Second World War) and as paradigmatic examples of the prosecution of war crimes (such as the war crimes tribunals held after the Second World War), there is the appearance of victor's justice and superpower impunity, which ought to make us skeptical of the judgment that this supposed paradigm was indeed a just war or that it ended justly. Nonetheless, the belief that those paradigmatic tribunals were in fact just remains part of the mythology surrounding war: what I have described before as "the just war myth" (Fiala 2008). The myth results from a political and ideological application of the just war theory, which tends to hold that just wars are easy to fight, that good guys tend to win the wars they fight, and that "we" are the good guys who fight justly and win because "we" are good. This is mostly false. Just wars are not easy to fight—and very few wars actually live up to the standards of the just war theory. It is not true that good guys win (nor that when the good guys win, it is because of their goodness that they win). Nor is it true that "we" are the good guys who fight justly and win and who end wars justly.

Many scholars who discuss just war theory are aware of the fact that real wars often fail to live up to the standard of the theory. This view has led Larry May and others (including myself) to articulate a position known as "contingent pacifism." In his book, *War Crimes and Just War* (May 2007), May points out that most attempts to ban certain weapons and to criminalize certain forms of warfighting may leave us with a kind of "contingent pacifism." May has developed this idea in considerable detail in his more recent book, *Contingent Pacifism* (May 2015),[3] where he links it to ideas found in John Rawls' *A Theory of Justice*, where Rawls suggested, "the possibility of a just war is conceded but not under present circumstances" (Rawls 1971, 382). The problems that lead to contingent pacifism are many. They include the fact that principles of *jus ad bellum* and *jus in bello* are often violated by all parties involved in a war. Here, I add that the problem of victor's justice also gives us reason to doubt that wars will live up to ideas found in the emerging area of concern known as *jus post bellum* (justice after war).

May has also recognized this problem of victor's justice. One reason he supports the idea of prosecuting war crimes *during* the war is that once the war is over, it is more likely that victor's justice will occur. He also suggests that war crimes trials ought to be conducted by neutral international tribunals. He explains:

> After war has ended, mounting a war crimes trial poses serious difficulties for reconciliation. It is hard for the vanquished side not to see war crimes trials as "victor's justice." And it is harder yet for the victorious side to put their heroic soldiers on trial after war's end. Indeed, it is hard for the victorious side to think of their soldiers as anything but heroes. It is for this reason, among others, that there has been a recent trend

> toward holding *post bellum* war crimes trials in neutral states before international tribunals.
>
> (May 2012, 77)

However, May recognizes that in reality, the problem of victor's justice remains a significant concern. In replying to the worry that war crimes trials are "skewed by victor's justice," May says:

> Recent history has shown that the tendency of war crimes trials for *jus in bello* violations to be show trials is getting higher. And there is no good reason to think that things will get better when *jus ad bellum* trials begin. Indeed, the determination that a state has engaged in aggressive war is so fraught with political considerations that it is very unlikely that anything like an objective judgment can be reached that does not favor the victor.
>
> (May 2012, 81–82)

May offers suggestions for how to avoid this problem (by employing neutral, impartial tribunals and the like). Yet his admission here, and the ubiquitous reality of victor's justice and superpower impunity, shows us that this is at present a kind of hopeful wish. *Jus post bellum* could be attained, and wars could be ended justly if victor's justice were not a problem. However, since it is a problem, the idea risks becoming wishful thinking, which can again be brought back into an ideological usage in a further iteration of the just war myth.

The problem of victor's justice represents a significant impediment to ending wars justly and gives us reason to be skeptical of real-world applications of the idea of justice in war. It can lead us to affirm a kind of contingent pacifism, which holds that we ought not to support wars that will result in failures to hold war criminals accountable. To remedy this problem, Rodin (2007), May, and others propose that an expanded remit for the ICC could be part of the solution. Supplementing this is the idea that war-fighting nations should also prosecute their own soldiers for war crimes—as discussed in May (2014).

Both proposals are useful. However, the facts on the ground point toward two fundamental problems. The ICC is limited in its power and scope, considering the fact that the United States, Russia, Israel, and China have not ratified the Rome Statute and claim that they are not subject to the jurisdiction of the Court. Furthermore, the United States and other superpowers often fail to prosecute their own unjust warriors (or pardon them, as in the Trump example). With these examples on the table—and in light of the prior discussion of victor's justice after the Second World War—let me return in conclusion to my basic argument:

1 For a war to end justly, war crimes must be prosecuted, and victor's justice must be avoided.
2 Victor's justice is common.
3 Therefore, most wars do not end justly.

Notes

1 I am thankful to David Chan for a critical comment he made here and for a paper he delivered at the 2024 meeting of the Society for Philosophy in the Contemporary World where he discussed ethical challenges posed by superpowers ("Conspiring for Restraint in War: An Alternative to Just War, Realism, and Pacifism").
2 See Trump Executive Order June 11, 2020. Accessed February 20, 2024 at: https://www.federalregister.gov/documents/2020/06/15/2020-12953/blocking-property-of-certain-persons-associated-with-the-international-criminal-court.
3 For discussion, see Fiala 2014.

References

Anscombe, G. E. M. 1981. *Ethics, Religion, and Politics*. Minneapolis: University of Minnesota Press.
Bass, Gary J. Bass. 2004. "Jus Post Bellum." *Philosophy & Public Affairs* 32(4): 384–412.
Bellamy, Alex J. 2008. "The Responsibilities of Victory: Jus Post Bellum and the Just War." *Review of International Studies* 34(4): 601–625.
Dalai Lama. n.d. "The Reality of War." Accessed February 2024. https://www.dalailama.com/messages/world-peace/the-reality-of-war
Elshtain, Jean Bethke. 2004. "The Just War Tradition and Natural Law." *Fordham International Law Journal* 28(3): 742–755.
Ferstman, Carla and Mariana Goetz, eds. 2020. *Reparations for Victims of Genocide, War Crimes and Crimes against Humanity: Systems in Place and Systems in the Making*, 2nd Revised Edition. Leiden: Brill.
Fiala, Andrew. 2008. *The Just War Myth: The Moral Illusions of War*. Lanham, MD: Rowman and Littlefield.
Fiala, Andrew. 2014. "Contingent Pacifism and Contingently Pacifist Conclusions." *Journal of Social Philosophy* 45(4): 463–477.
Fiala, Andrew. 2022. "War Crimes in Ukraine: Pacifists Should Support War Crimes Tribunals." *Only Sky (October)*. https://onlysky.media/afiala/war-crimes-in-ukraine-pacifists-should-support-war-crimes-tribunals/
Fiala, Andrew and Jennifer Kling. 2023. *Can War Be Justified? A Debate*. New York: Routledge.
Ford, Stuart. 2020. "Has President Trump Committed a War Crime by Pardoning War Criminals?" *American University International Law Review* 35(4): 757–820.
Francis (Pope). 2024. Remarks following the Angelus Prayer, January 14, 2024. Accessed February 19, 2024. https://www.vatican.va/content/francesco/en/angelus/2024/documents/20240114-angelus.html
Haas, Michael. 2009. *George W. Bush, War Criminal? The Bush Administration's Liability for 269 War Crimes*. New York: Praeger.

Hemingway, Ernest. 1946. "Introduction" for *Treasury for the Free World.* New York: Arco Publishing.
Holtzman, Elizabeth 2012. *Cheating Justice: How Bush and Cheney Attacked the Rule of Law and Plotted to Avoid Prosecution and What We Can Do About It.* Boston: Beacon Press.
International Criminal Court. 2023. "Situation in Ukraine: ICC Judges Issue Arrest Warrants against Vladimir Vladimirovich Putin and Maria Alekseyevna Lvova-Belova." March 17, 2023.
Jochecová, Ketrin. 2023. "Russia Blasts Back at ICC Over Putin Arrest Warrant." *Politico*, March 20, 2023. Accessed February 19, 2024. https://www.politico.eu/article/putin-russia-icc-criminal-case-moscow-ukraine-war/
Johnson, James Turner. 2006. "The Just War Idea: The State of the Question." *Social Philosophy & Policy* 23(1): 167–195.
Kellogg, Davida E. 2002. "Jus Post Bellum: The Importance of War Crimes Trials." *Parameters* 32(3), doi:10.55540/0031-1723.2108
Lucas, George R. 2013. "Forgetful Warriors: Neglected Lessons on Leadership from Plato's *Republic*." In *The Ashgate Research Companion to Modern Warfare*, edited by Buckley and Kassimeris. Burlington, VT: Ashgate.
Malloy, Sean L. 2012. "Harry S. Truman and the Decision to Use the Atomic Bomb." In *A Companion to Harry S. Truman*, edited by Daniel S. Margolies. New York: Wiley Blackwell.
May, Larry. 2007. *War Crimes and Just War.* Cambridge: Cambridge University Press.
May, Larry. 2012. *After War Ends: A Philosophical Perspective.* Cambridge: Cambridge University Press.
May, Larry. 2014. "War Crimes Trials during and after War." In *Law and War*, edited by Austin Sarat, Lawrence Douglas, and Martha Merrill Umphrey. Stanford, CA: Stanford University Press.
May, Larry. 2015. *Contingent Pacifism.* Cambridge: Cambridge University Press.
McMahan, Jeff. 2009. *Killing in War.* Oxford: Clarendon Press.
McMahan, Jeff. 2013. "War Crimes and Immoral Action in War." In *The Constitution of the Criminal Law, Criminalization*, edited by R.A. Duff et al. Oxford: Oxford University Press.
Morris, Errol. Director. 2003. *The Fog of War: Eleven Lessons from the Life of Robert S. McNamara.* Radical Media & Sen Art Films.
Orend, Brian. 2001. *Michael Walzer on War and Justice.* Toronto: McGill-Queen's University Press.
Rawls, John. 1971. *A Theory of Justice.* Cambridge, MA: Harvard University Press.
Rawls, John. 1999. "Fifty Years after Hiroshima." In *Collected Papers.* Cambridge, MA: Harvard University Press.
Ridley, Yvonne. 2012. "Bush Convicted of War Crimes in Absentia." *Foreign Policy Journal*, May 12, 2012. Accessed February 19, 2024. https://www.foreignpolicyjournal.com/2012/05/12/bush-convicted-of-war-crimes-in-absentia/
Rodin, David. 2007. "The Liability of Ordinary Soldiers for Crimes of Aggression." *Global Studies Law Review* 6(3): 591–607.
Rome Statute of the International Criminal Court. 2021. Accessed August 12, 2024. https://www.icc-cpi.int/sites/default/files/Publications/Rome-Statute.pdf
Scheid, Anna Floerke. 2016. "Just War Theory and Restorative Justice: Weaving a Consistent Ethic of Reconciliation." *Journal of Moral Theology* 5(2): 99–115.

Steffen, Lloyd. 2012. *Ethics and Experience: From Just War to Abortion*. Lanham, MD: Rowman and Littlefield.

Tayler, Letta and Elisa Epstein. 2022. "Legacy of the 'Dark Side'." *Human Rights Watch*, January 9, 2022. Accessed February 19, 2024. https://www.hrw.org/news/2022/01/09/legacy-dark-side,

The Guardian. 2016. "US Army and CIA may be Guilty of War Crimes in Afghanistan, Says ICC." November 15, 2016. Accessed February 19, 2024. https://www.theguardian.com/law/2016/nov/15/us-army-and-cia-may-be-guilty-of-war-crimes-afghanistan-says-icc

Vitoria, Francisco de. 2006. "On the Law of War." In *The Morality of War*, edited by Larry May, Eric Rovie, and Steve Viner. Upper Saddle River, NJ: Prentice Hall.

Walzer, Michael. 2004. *Arguing About War*. New Haven, CT: Yale University Press.

Walzer, Michael. 2006. *Just and Unjust Wars: A Moral Argument with Historical Illustrations*, 4th edition. New York: Basic Books.

Williams, Robert E. and Dan Caldwell. 2006. "Jus Post Bellum: Just War Theory and the Principles of Just Peace." *International Studies Perspectives* 7(4): 309–320.

Wringe, Bill. 2006. "Why Punish War Crimes? Victor's Justice and Expressive Justifications of Punishment." *Law and Philosophy* 25(2): 159–191.

Zafar, Noor. 2019. "Trump's War Pardons Are Sabotaging the Military Justice System." *ACLU*, December 13, 2019. Accessed February 20, 2024. https://www.aclu.org/news/national-security/trumps-war-pardons-are-sabotaging-the-military-justice-system

4 Bodies that Are "Ready-to-Politics": A Feminist Approach to *Jus Ex Bello*

Jennifer Kling

Wars end.[1] Sometimes they end well, or justly, and sometimes they end poorly, or unjustly, with a so-called "victor's peace." We know these different endings when we see them, and yet the question of how to end a war justly is difficult: what conditions must warmakers and warfighters meet, when they stop warring, to ensure that they are doing so in the right way, at the right time, and in the right manner? In this chapter, I follow Bat-Ami Bar On in arguing that war is fundamentally opposed to politics (Bar On 2008). As Bar On argues, politics is properly understood as the practice of people relating across differences to collaborate on the creation and maintenance of structures, institutions, policies, procedures, and social conditions that are conducive to everyone living a flourishing life. This feminist, relational approach—inspired by Hannah Arendt—contends that while politics is irreducibly agonistic, it is not antagonistic (contra Clausewitz), because underlying the contention is a kind of friendship, or good will, toward others that manifests in the use of rationality, words, and persuasion to rule rather than coercion, violence, and force.

Following this line of thought, wars end justly when the space of politics is reconstituted such that communities of people—both within and across borders—are in good relation with each other. And as feminism teaches us, the conditions of possibility for the space of politics to emerge are not only conceptual but also social, material, and embodied. The move from warring to politicking occurs when the *body*—both the so-called body politic and the individual body—is no longer "ready-to-fight," but rather, to coin a phrase, ready-to-politics.[2] Bringing this bodily shift about is difficult, as is well-documented by Bar On, Susan Brison, bell hooks, and other feminist scholars who argue for the importance of lived experience and embodiment to relationality. The actual space of politics is always fragile and is especially at risk, during this transition phase, of disintegrating back into coercion, violence, and force. Recognizing both its fragility and its embodiment, though, gives us a tracking concept to tell when wars are ending and when they have ended well. When social, material, and embodied

DOI: 10.4324/9781003454144-6

mini-spaces of politics start to emerge, it is a sign that the war is beginning to end justly; when those sparks flare, hold, and spread throughout and across societies, such that people are in good relation with each other "in the here and now," as Kim TallBear puts it, we can tell that the war is finished ending and has ended justly (TallBear 2019).

In addition to providing a robust tracking concept, this feminist conceptualization of *jus ex bello* helps us to see the conditions that warmakers and warfighters should strive to generate in ending wars. They ought to work to bring about the social, material, and embodied, as well as the conceptual, conditions of possibility for the space of politics to be reconstituted. This work is difficult but necessary for ending wars justly, rather than creating desolation and calling it peace.

1 The Nature of Politics

My discussion of *jus ex bello* begins with a description of a conceptual fight about the nature of politics, exemplified by Carl von Clausewitz and Bat-Ami Bar On.[3] This might seem unrelated, but it is in fact deeply connected because, without a conceptual understanding of politics and war's place within it, it is difficult to dig into the specifics of *jus ex bello*, which is about the (necessarily political) shift from war to peace. If we take up one traditional view of politics, *jus ex bello* is about shifting from one means to another while keeping the same end; but if we take up a particular feminist relational view of politics, *jus ex bello* is about shifting ends entirely. Let me explain.

One tradition of thought holds that politics is the power to dominate, that is, the ability to seize and control people, territory, and resources. This view is encapsulated by 19th-century Prussian general Clausewitz's (in)famous claim that "war is not merely an act of policy but a true political instrument, a continuation of political intercourse, carried on with other means" (Clausewitz 1976, 87). On this understanding, politics is an arena in which nonviolent means (like economic incentives) and violent means (like war) are all used toward the same end, which is to compel others to do as one wills.[4] The end of politics is dominion and domination, according to Clausewitz, and war is simply a different means to that same end. War *is* politics, just via violent means. Such violence is not the only political means, of course, but it is always in the background of this conception of politics as a fight for dominion and domination, because war is—according to this tradition of thought—one of the ultimate means of domination.

On this view, war and politics are inextricably intertwined: political violence can be oppressive, progressive, revolutionary, or some combination thereof, but it is inevitably business as usual. Whether a state goes to war or sues for peace, it is still engaging in, as Clausewitz might put it, political intercourse, because it is ultimately striving to compel others to do as it wills. This is a simple gloss of a complex theoretical picture; still, for our purposes, it is sufficient because it enables us to see that on this understanding of politics, *jus ex bello* is about how to switch well or justly from one political instrument or means (war) to another (peace) while maintaining the same political end (domination).

By contrast, Bat-Ami Bar On, inspired by and following Hannah Arendt, argues that politics is the practice of people relating across differences to collaborate on the creation and maintenance of structures, institutions, policies, procedures, and social conditions that are conducive to everyone involved living a flourishing life. This approach contends that while politics is irreducibly agonistic, it is not antagonistic (contra Clausewitz), because underlying the contention is a kind of friendship, or good will, toward others that manifests in the use of rationality, words, and persuasion to rule rather than coercion, violence, and force. The end of politics, according to Bar On, is the "enormous plurality of humanity" being able to meet in the public sphere and decide together to act in concert regarding matters of common concern and public significance (Bar On 2008, 143). It is the materialization of human freedom through inclusive civic engagement; people come together and, through a complex mix of rational persuasion and discourse, public reason and deliberation, and pragmatic collaboration, cooperation, and compromise, are able to make collaborative decisions about how their society/societies should function without dominating each other.

Notably, this applies both domestically and internationally: within borders, politics occurs when decisions about the particular shape and character of domestic institutions, policies, procedures, and social conditions are made collaboratively and in common. Across borders, politics occurs when decisions about the particular shape and character of regional and global structures and institutions are similarly made collaboratively and in common. Such collaborative decision-making, underlaid by a general approach of good will toward others, is not easy, especially in situations where people are divided in a multiplicity of ways (by borders, religions, cultures, beliefs about what constitutes a flourishing life, etc.). This is why a common regional structure, often proposed in this tradition as a political collaboration across particular borders, is the taking up of a respectful "live and let live" mentality and approach to one's international neighbors.[5] Such a non-dominative approach to others—both others within a society and across societies—is neither the norm nor straightforward, of course, but to say this is simply to acknowledge that politics, properly understood as the practice of coming together in the public sphere to make decisions together about matters of public (domestic, regional, international, and global) concern, is hard to do at all, let alone do well.

On this view, violence and thus war are excluded from the space of politics. As Arendt puts it, pulling from the ancient Greek view that she reimagines for modernity, "to be political, to live in a *polis*, meant that everything was decided through words and persuasion and not through force and violence" (Arendt 1958, 26–27). Force and violence, particularly war, are "prepolitical ways to deal with people" that necessarily undermine political freedom, because political freedom (the end of politics, for Bar On, following and elaborating on Arendt) is democratic action in the public sphere (Arendt 1958; Bar On 2008). Once violence comes into the mix, proponents of this view say, politics is no longer occurring, strictly speaking, because violence and agonistic democratic engagement are antithetical. Following this line of thought, war is first about switching ends—from political freedom to domination—and then using the means to hand. War is the *failure* or *outside limit* of politics, not politics by other means.[6]

Now, neither Arendt nor Bar On is a pacifist; both admit that there is not a political solution to every problem, in particular the problem of fascism. Arendt, in particular, writes that violence, although never politically legitimate, may be justified in two contexts: in response to extreme injustice and in order to open up the space for politics (Arendt 1969, 52, 64, 79). This is because, on the one hand, violence is sometimes the right response to horrors such as the victimization of the innocent, and on the other hand, violence has a certain kind of effectiveness. It can make things happen in the immediate sense, such as knocking away the adversary that is actively destroying any possibility of politics at the domestic and/or international levels (Arendt 1969, 80). However, even when violence is necessary, as Arendt suggests it may be in response to resolutely anti-political fascist regimes such as Nazi Germany or Stalinist Russia, it should never be conflated with, or confused for, being politics itself (Arendt 1969, 53). The two are conceptually and materially distinct.

Bar On similarly claims that there are times when people are (uneasily) justified in using violence to protect themselves and their families. However, she grapples with the historically grounded concern that defensive violence, regardless of how we attempt to circumscribe and limit it, always has the potential to "run amok" and devolve into oppressive violence that destroys the conditions that make talking to each other, and relating across differences, possible (Bar On 2002b, 155). It is germane here that Bar On grew up in Israel and lived through and with the ongoing (at the time of writing) Israel/Palestine/Middle East military conflicts. The most likely outcome of violence, she concludes, is to produce a more violent world; it thus pollutes and corrupts politics, even when it does not destroy the possibility of politics altogether. So while violence may be justified, it is nevertheless anti-political in a strong sense, in that it goes against preserving the conditions that make talking to each other, and relating and collaborating across (moral, social, political, material, and geographical) differences, possible.[7]

Bar On acknowledges that these commitments sit uneasily with each other, and much of her work is about thinking through the ambiguity of violence and the impossibility of reducing the political to the ethical. Again, this is a simple gloss of a complex theoretical picture. Still, it is sufficient for our purposes, because it enables us to see that on this understanding of politics, *jus ex bello* is about switching **ends** altogether, from domination (war) to political freedom (politics). When we think of politics "agonally and democratically," as Bar On and Arendt encourage us to do, we recognize that ending wars justly is not merely a matter of people laying down their weapons in favor of other means but of taking up an entirely different relational project (Bar On 2008, 150). Wars end justly when the space of politics is constituted (or reconstituted) such that communities of people—both within and across borders—are in good relation with each other. At a conceptual level, this makes sense: but it still leaves us with some questions essential to a full characterization of *jus ex bello*, namely, what does this switching of ends look like, and how does such a transition occur?

2 The Move from Warring to Politicking

So far, I have outlined two contrasting views of politics—the first dominatory, the second relational—and have shown that each provides a different schematic understanding of *jus ex bello*. Here, I flesh out Bar On's and others' feminist approach to relating with others to provide a more complete picture of *jus ex bello*, one that includes not only its theoretical details but also how it operates as a robust tracking concept that helps us discern when wars are ending well. Abstractly, *jus ex bello* is when the conditions of possibility for the space of politics to arise are met; feminism can help us to see what those conditions are and how they operate.

Feminist approaches to politics teach us that the conditions of possibility for the space of politics to emerge are not only conceptual—people must have (at least implicitly) the *concept* of democratic agonal engagement for politics proper to even possibly occur—but also social, material, and embodied. The move from warring to politicking proper, then, is only possible when our embodied selves are no longer "ready-to-fight" physiologically and psychologically, but rather ready-to-politics. The materiality of our bodies matters, Bar On and others emphasize, because it is that materiality that sets the conditions of possibility for what actions we see as meaningful and as possible, and thus what actions we are able to undertake and what relations we are able to build, foster, and maintain. We relate to each other through our lived experiences and our embodiment.

For example, as a woman, I walk through the world as a body that is constantly under physical threat; as a result, I relate to others with similar threatened bodies, and dissimilar threatening bodies, in certain ways. Some actions are meaningful and possible for me when I am in the presence of those who are also threatened bodies, that are not available when I am in the presence of those who are threatening bodies. The specifics of this can be difficult to describe, precisely because our embodiment provides an experiential event horizon for actions, so to speak, beyond which we cannot see and so struggle to imagine.[8] It is difficult to explain to men the visceral ways in which I feel threatened when I am walking at night and a group of men comes up behind me. I resolve this fear, which I not only know intellectually (data; statistics; anecdotes from others; and personal experience) but also know feelingly (coursing adrenaline; tense muscles; faster steps; and shortness of breath) by not walking alone at night. I could resolve this fear in other ways, of course, but my point here is not what I choose to do in response to living in a patriarchal world.[9] The point, rather, is that my embodiment—my concrete situatedness as a body in a world with a particular sociopolitical character—changes what is possible and sensical for me in terms of relating with others, just as your embodiment does for you. More broadly, our relations, both with ourselves and with others, are always *relations-through* our embodiment and our materiality in our sociopolitical world[10]; thus, when thinking about the conditions that must be met for politics to possibly occur, we need to think about what our bodies are able and ready to do.

Drawing on this point, in concert with the relational understanding of politics outlined above, we can develop a feminist approach to *jus ex bello*: it is when people's bodies are able to and ready to politics that they have switched their end, that they have moved from *jus in bello* through *jus ex bello*, and are ready to embark on *jus post bellum*. *Jus ex bello* marks out and describes this transition (briefly: *jus post bellum* is when politics **does** occur; *jus ex bello* is when the **conditions of possibility** for politics to occur are met). By contrast, when people's bodies are ready-to-fight, the conditions of possibility are such that the space of politics cannot arise. Only war and violence can arise. This is because, as Sarah Clark Miller argues, discussing Bar On's work,

> it is not possible to draw a sharp distinction between the ready-to-fight body and the violent body. Any supposedly sharp distinction between the potential and the actual violent body is necessarily murky, and, it turns out, morally and politically vexed.
>
> (Miller 2023, 4)

Bodies that are ready-to-fight are poised to be violent, if not already violent; they are not poised to relate with others across (moral, social, political, material, geographical) differences to collaborate on collective actions to take regarding matters of public (domestic, regional, international, and global) concern and significance. As Bar On writes, "the ready-to-fight body is a practice-habituated body" that "is schooled...so that it could act violently as quickly as possible" (Bar On 2002b, 152). This is not quite so simple as Aristotle's point that we are what we repeatedly do, but it is related in that the materiality of our bodies burdens us through its habituation to particular pathways of action and reaction. When our bodies are constructed as ready-to-fight—when we so construct them—violent actions, relations, and ways of living are foregrounded, and nonviolent and pacifist others are foreclosed. Not deterministically so, but enough so such that certain actions, relations, and ways of living do not even arise or become apparent to us as realistic or sensical possibilities.[11]

Importantly, the construction, reproduction, and maintenance of ready-to-fight bodies is not merely an individual project; as Bar On explains, habituating one's own body to act violently is often a national project (as in her case, growing up in Israel), a social project (as in her case, joining a feminist antirape group), a family project (as in Sarah Clark Miller's case, learning martial arts with her queer child), and/or a cultural project (as in Simone de Beauvoir's case, embracing violence as a response to the denigration of femininity) (Bar On 2002b, 149–51; Miller 2023, 5; de Beauvoir 1961, 308–10). It is, moreover, a reasonable response to the violent bodies that surround people both in war and in other oppressive systems. When the world is threatening, it makes sense, at both a visceral and social level, to make your body an "implement of violence" in turn (Bar On 2002b, 152; Miller 2023, 5–6). However, this construction of the body as ready-to-fight in response to the presence of other violent bodies is morally and politically ambiguous at best; one of Bar On's crucial points is that becoming ready-to-fight in a violent, oppressive world is likely necessary and never innocent. She holds this ambivalence throughout her work, writing that

> A feminist cannot merely celebrate the...construction of her own or other violent women bodies. She must concern herself with quite complex questions about the possibility that as women's bodies become habituated to violent action, they may act in [inhumane and destructive] ways...This is a possibility that cannot be dismissed as too marginal to worry about, not in light of the extensive evidence regarding the enormity of past and present abusive or cruel violence in which women, too, have partaken. Women have acted violently not merely because they are not in control but also because, like men of the same socioculture, they also can find something attractive about violence.
>
> (Bar On 2002b, 164–65)

Violence purports to offer a solution to the violence that surrounds women at all times and that surrounds all people caught in a war. It is attractive for this and many other reasons: as Bar On and Arendt both discuss, sometimes violence—especially defensive and protective violence—is instrumentally successful. However, it is also in Bar On's words "seriously troubling," (Bar On 2002b, 152, 165) because the configuration of one's body as violent, as ready-to-fight (whatever else it is), is also at the same time antithetical to the emergence of politics properly understood, because a ready-to-fight body cannot, or is at least highly unlikely to, be vulnerable, humane, and productive of action in the way that the space of politics requires.[12]

As bell hooks writes,

> bodily anger and rage, in the body…leads us to…push away what is most longed for—companionship and understanding. It is a denial of the humanness of others, as well as a denial of your own humanness. Anger is…a wall that separates you from others, as effectively as it were concrete, thick, and very high. There is no way through it, under it, or over it.
>
> (hooks 2004, ch 3)

hooks emphasizes the materiality and embodiment of emotional attitudes such as anger and rage (she also discusses fear and despair similarly in other work) to draw out the point that our somatic, limbic, and psychological systems are all intertwined, such that it does not make sense to separate out what we can do conceptually from what we are doing (explicitly or implicitly) physiologically and psychologically. The conditions of possibility are at once conceptual, social, material, *and* embodied. If my body is ready-to-fight, although I may be able to conceptually (in the abstract, as it were) grasp the need to relate with others across differences, I will either not be able to do it, or at best will struggle to do it in the here-and-now, because my concrete situatedness—my habituated body embedded in the material social world—will not allow for it, either easily or at all. In Bar On's language, such visceral, bodily rage makes it impossible for the space of politics to arise, because the embodied conditions of possibility for politics, for making myself vulnerable by revealing my unique self in the public (domestic, regional, international, and global) sphere with others, are simply not there.

As Susan Brison (2003) asks in a variety of ways throughout her work, how can I meaningfully relate to others if my body is always ready to defend and attack? The short answer is: I cannot. I may be able to approximate genuine vulnerability and so political action. But in reality, I am always on guard, ready to justify violence or other fabrications to attain my pre-determined—aka nonpolitical, on Arendt's view—ends (of safety, of domination, of protection, etc.).[13] Again, such guardedness is reasonable in a world marked by and saturated in violence. However, it is not conducive to politics understood relationally. Politics proper is a collaborative generative space marked by freedom and plurality; the whole point of it is that it is not predictable in its outcomes. When we do politics, we cannot have a finished product in view. However, to inhabit that unpredictable, uncertain space, a person's somatic and limbic systems have to be de-escalated in terms of stress, alarm, and violent reflexiveness, facilitating their openness to trusting themselves, others, and the process. So, to make the shift to the space of politics, people must engage in a *bodily* shift, and that requires very difficult material, social, psychological, and relational shifts over time.

Now, the space of politics is fragile as well as embodied; following Kim TallBear, it is marked by "an explicitly spatial narrative of *caretaking relations*" that "requires us to pay attention to our relations and obligations here and now" (TallBear 2019, 25, emphasis in original). TallBear argues that a feminist, indigenous approach to politics is one that views politics as a "relational web framework…that focuses here, not then" (TallBear 2019, 25–26). This echoes Arendt and Bar On, with the added explicit elements of spatiality and temporality as well as embodiment, materiality, and sociality. The space of politics can only emerge when there is literal as well as figurative space for it, and when people are able, as their whole embodied unique selves, to engage in caretaking relations—both thick and robust in the domestic case and (potentially) thinner and more attenuated in the international case—in the present with an eye to continually cooperating and collaborating as the future comes into being as the present. Importantly, TallBear is clear that this does not equate to ignoring or disregarding the past; rather, to be in good relations with others is to simultaneously recognize and acknowledge the past and *not* allow it to dictate the present and the future (TallBear 2019, 32–34). It is to be able to build community with others—to act rather than react—via the collaborative creation of social and political structures in communal spaces of practice in the here and now. But to do that, we must avoid the "inherently eliminatory dreaming" that TallBear argues is both a feature and a legacy of the trauma of settler colonialism, and that Bar On argues is a feature of rising fascism, wherein people strive to create (to fabricate, in Arendt's language) literal and political exclusionary spaces that match their imagined past or imagined future (TallBear 2019, 26; Bar On 2019, 413–17). In this imagined past or future, the "other" is not present, so there is no need to be in good relations with them. Given the calamitous present, especially in wartime, it is both tempting and understandable for people to focus on—and dream of—there and then, not here and now; but this is incompatible with their "*actively relat[ing]*" with others in the concrete situated present, with making the necessary accommodations and ceding literal and figurative spaces so that politics proper can occur and continue (TallBear 2019, 29–32, emphasis in original). Bluntly, Russians (and so Russia) cannot engage politically with Ukrainians (and so Ukraine) while they dream of a future and a past wherein Ukrainians (and so Ukraine) do not exist.

The space of politics, when fully conceived of in a feminist relational register, is thus "quite fragile and cannot be made otherwise" because it depends not only on the configuration and maintenance of bodies that are ready-to-politics but also on an embodied, material, spatial acceptance of the present as marked by human plurality, of people relating well across their (moral, social, political, material, geographical) differences in the here and now rather than muting or striving to eliminate those differences to survive (Bar On 2002a, 197). At the best of times, this fragility makes doing politics difficult. And given the heretofore discussed concomitant features of war, namely the "subjectifying effects of soldiering," militarization, and being ready-to-fight that Bar On and others outline (Bar On 2008, 144), to make the *transition* from war to politics (or, as we might say, from war to peace) is an especially fraught process. Any space of politics that is established is at risk of disintegrating back into coercion, violence, force, and domination. It is hard to "do politics" today with the people and communities who were trying to kill you yesterday, and that difficulty is not only conceptual but also embodied. However, by determining through feminist analysis that the conditions of possibility for the space of politics to arise are both fragile and embodied in particular ways, we have filled out a schematic understanding of *jus ex bello* such that we now have a robust tracking concept for the occurrence of *jus ex bello*.

3 Tracking *Jus Ex Bello*

At this point, we know what to look for to tell whether a war is ending well. When social, material, and embodied mini-spaces of politics start to emerge, it is a sign that the war is beginning to end justly. Good examples of mini-spaces of politics are local, regional, and cross-border mutual aid networks; democratic community centers; transformative justice collectives; self-organizing special interest and consciousness-raising groups/circles; solidaristic social clubs; and transnational/international protest and activism movements.[14] When they occur, develop, and sustain themselves in the midst of a war, such material, social, present-focused spaces of practice are both the *result* of some people making the shift from being ready-to-fight to being ready-to-politics, and can help *create* the conditions for other people to start to engage in that same bodily shift away from being ready-to-fight and toward being ready-to-politics. The appearance of such spaces of practice is thus the beginning of *jus ex bello*, insofar as these mini-spaces prefigure the collaborative, cooperative, free, agonistic-but-not-antagonistic, pluralistic engagement that is characteristic of politics proper and antithetical to domination and violence.

While my focus in this chapter is *jus ex bello*, it is essential to notice that anti-oppression scholars, in particular Black feminist theorists, philosophers of race, and cosmopolitan and anarchist political thinkers, have argued that such spaces of practice are essential for overcoming oppression in societies, and indeed in a global community, marked by domination and subordination. As social theorists and activists Heidi R. Lewis, Dana Maria Asbury, and Jazlyn Andrews discuss in their volume focused on the experiences of women of color educators, artists, activists, scholars, and other intersectional and transnational feminist "friends in the struggle," such spaces are necessary to encourage, allow, and address "the always advantageous but sometimes contentious contours of solidarity" (Lewis et al. 2021, n.p.). They argue that anti-domination, pro-liberation community- and movement-building requires, in Audre Lorde's words, "new patterns of relating across difference" that recognize and honor people in all their concrete situatedness and embodiment (Lorde 2007, n.p.).

Importantly, such new relational patterns require spaces of practice that are not ameliorative—it is not about the creation of "safe spaces" as US conservatives use the term—but rather are political in Arendt and Bar On's sense. As Donatella della Porta puts the point, writing about transnational activism movements, it is about "actually constructing a global public sphere" wherein people can "intense[ly] participate in conversations, protest...and [justice] campaigns beyond...and between borders." Such campaigns "have multiplied...over the last decades" with the advent of global understandings of oppression and injustice; there has been a concomitant rise in building transnational/international solidarity movements (Porta 2009, 264). When we see the cultivation of such spaces of practice and associated new embodied patterns of relation, it is a sign that people are pushing back against domination and subordination, *whether it is occurring in the form of war or via some other means*, and are striving for political freedom. Liberationist movements within and across societies that are marked by structural and overlapping systems of domination can thus be (I think helpfully) read as attempts to bring about *jus ex bello* and, eventually, *jus post bellum*. This is part of why they are often opposed by the powers that be: as Howard Zinn puts it, "they'll say we're disturbing the peace, but there is no peace. What really bothers them is that we are disturbing the war" (Zinn 1971, 2).

As W.E.B. Du Bois argues, to build inclusive, democratic societies that recognize all members as sources of moral value and interpretation, subcommunities and associations within the dominatory society must be formed that respect people's "right of diversity" and so develop people's abilities to engage in honest, contentious yet productive conversations about justice, oppression, freedom, and other matters of public concern and significance (Du Bois 1915, n.p., 2004, 25). Tellingly, Du Bois notes that respecting people's right of diversity is not only about acknowledging their "maximum of freedom to be, to move and to think," but also about accepting their "cut of vest...curl of hair...[and] color of skin" (Du Bois 1915, n.p.). Building mini-spaces of politics is conceptual and intellectual, to be sure, but it is also social, material, and essentially embodied. These "pockets of democratic community," as Leland Harper and I call them in other work when interpreting Du Bois (Harper and Kling 2022, 57), can then spread outwards, as people from one association join other sub-communities and groups within the society, such that eventually the whole political community can be rightly regarded as engaging in politics proper.[15] Whether such pockets of democracy arise as a war is winding down or as a response to structural oppression, they are the same in the sense that they both signify the beginning sparks of politics proper.

The example that Du Bois gives of a civic association doing this work is the Black church during the post-US Civil War period, which not only fostered democratic discussion among its members but also advocated for "improved public infrastructure and redistributions of social and political power," such as the creation of public school systems, which would benefit *all* citizens (Harper and Kling 2022, 57–58) (and, not coincidentally, this would also work to habituate the majority of people as ready-to-politics). Insofar as the US Reconstruction-era Black church was both a political space of practice and fostered the conditions of possibility for other political spaces of practice to emerge and develop, it was a sign of *jus ex bello*, of hope that the US Civil War might be ending well. Of course, the United States did not achieve *jus post bellum* after the Civil War; the Reconstruction era is a complicated history that, while it had elements of *jus ex bello*, such as the Black church and other spaces of politics proper, eventually devolved into the Jim and Jane Crow era.[16] As mentioned above, *jus ex bello* is always fragile and at risk, either of falling back into war or failing to bring about *jus post bellum*. Nevertheless, the presence and development of such mini-spaces of politics is how it starts, and how we recognize its beginning.

Du Bois focuses largely, though not exclusively, on the domestic United States; thus, his analysis—and by implication, mine—might not seem *apropos* to war, which often occurs across borders and thus across, rather than within, societies. In response, it is important to bear in mind two points. First is the existence and growth, as discussed above, of regional, transnational, international, and global mini-spaces of politics. While people across borders rarely share a constitutional framework, they are nevertheless sometimes able to reach across their differences (moral, social, political, material, geographical) and recognize each other as friends in the struggle. For example, the Alliance for Middle East Peace (ALLMEP) is a coalition of over 160 inter- and intra-border organizations working toward building and maintaining a just peace in Israel, Palestine, and surrounding countries.[17] These organizations, which bring people together through their shared embodied experiences of and desires to escape from violence and war, are precisely the kinds of associations that foster the conditions of possibility for politics proper to occur both within and across borders. Thus, we should recognize them—like the domestic civic associations that Du Bois describes—as the sparks of *jus ex bello*, as attempts to help transition people and communities on opposing sides of that long-running conflict from being ready-to-fight to being ready-to-politics.

This leads to the second point, which is that in both civil and international military conflicts, ordinarily and for the most part, the bulk of the people in all of the societies involved are deeply affected by said wars. It is an oddity of the United States that it can fight wars without the US population being affected very much, if at all. Almost everywhere else in the world, many, if not most, people are caught up in and strongly affected by any wars and military conflicts in which their countries are involved.[18] For most of the globe, wars don't happen "over there;" they happen here, in our fields, towns, cities, streets, houses, and lives. As author and social activist Fannie Hurst put the point in 1941, "We [the general populace] may not be interested in this war, but it is interested in us" (Griswold 1941, n.p.).[19] Both Bar On and Arendt are working within this understanding: globally, war is very much an intrusive, embodied, material national reality that leads the bulk of affected populaces to be ready-to-fight. So when we consider the advent of *jus ex bello*, we must pay attention not only to what is happening across borders but also to what is happening domestically, regardless of whether the war in question is civil or transnational. When mini-spaces of politics begin to be established throughout the societies that are at war, with the potential to facilitate the populaces' shift from being ready-to-fight the Other to being ready-to-politics with the Other (whoever the Other happens to be in any particular case), it is the recognizable start of *jus ex bello*.

On this theory of *jus ex bello*, peace treaties or the restoration of order—in the sense of negative peace—do not signify by themselves that war has ended, in the sense of switching ends. Rather, they signify the cessation of direct, large-scale physical hostilities, which is what most people think of when they think of the end of a war (i.e., when they think of *ex bello*). However, insofar as peace treaties and the restoration of order are both compatible with maintaining the end goal of domination, neither of them is sufficient for *jus ex bello*. Order may be necessary for *jus ex bello* in that it is difficult to be ready-to-politics in chaos. Yet it is not sufficient, as we learn from the Chinese just war tradition (Sawyer 2007). Order involves the implementation of a rule-based sociopolitical system where it is both possible and likely that the bulk of the populace will follow the rules, either because they view those rules as authoritative, or because they are sufficiently afraid of the penalties for breaking the rules, or because they are unwilling to cause upset, etc. However, order is not sufficient for having a harmonious society; for that to occur, the system's rules must be conducive to individual and societal flourishing, understood as material, cultural, and spiritual well-being (Li 2006). Ending a war well, then, essentially involves aiming at what the Confucian tradition might recognize as harmony, at the ideal of both individuals and body politics reconfiguring to be ready-to-politics rather than ready-to-fight.

Ultimately, *jus ex bello* is about switching ends, or changing aims, from domination to political freedom, and that shift is social, material, and embodied. We see it not in the restoration or production of order, or in a straightforward return to so-called normal patterns of behavior, except insofar as the society's normal patterns of behavior are properly political. In the likely event that they are not, *jus ex bello* has not occurred simply because large-scale physical hostilities have stopped. Rather, we see *jus ex bello* in the establishment of spaces of politics throughout and between societies, and when the bulk of the affected populaces are psychologically and physiologically ready-to-politics, such that people are in good relation, to use TallBear's phrase, with each other in the here and now. With this tracking concept elaborated, we are able to distinguish sharply, in both theory and practice, between the occurrence of *jus ex bello* and the political desolation or détente that some would call peace.

4 Generating *Jus Ex Bello*

In addition to enabling us to track the occurrence of *jus ex bello*, the feminist conceptualization I have argued for here also provides normative guidelines for how to generate *jus ex bello*. Abstractly, warmakers and warfighters should strive to create the conditions of possibility for the space of politics to be either constituted or reconstituted (depending on the history of the societies in question). More specifically, meeting the conditions of *jus ex bello* will involve building material and social, as well as conceptual, spaces that foster the growth of webs of relations that can enable the necessary bodily shifts. I have discussed some particular examples of such spaces above, although it is important to note, in line with the feminist emphasis on concrete situatedness and sociopolitical embeddedness, that the sorts of spaces warmakers and warfighters should seek to bring into existence must be simultaneously those that foster good webs of relations and that are authentic to—that is, recognized by—the particular societies in question. As political scientists have noted, you cannot "astro-turf," so to speak, particular civic and other associations into societies with no history of such groups (Byman 2003). On the other hand, many theorists reject the idea of a "clash of civilizations," wherein societies are *so* different that they cannot recognize in each other anything to relate to at all; the complexity of the world, in combination with humanity's shared features (such as our material sociality), suggests that cross-societal recognizable spaces of politics are possible and indeed are historically existent (Bottici and Challand 2010; Midgley 2021). If nothing else, people are able to recognize analogues of their own society's spaces of politics. A mosque is not a Buddhist temple, and a New York dinner party is not a Tehran book club, but members of each society are able to recognize the other society's space as one wherein politics could potentially occur (although they may argue that such a space, while recognizable, is not "for them"). Bearing these points in mind, the spaces that warmakers and warfighters should strive to bring about must be sensitive to, and at least somewhat grounded in, the societies in question. So meeting the conditions of *jus ex bello* is fraught with pitfalls both theoretically and historico-practically. Still, warmakers and warfighters should endeavor to build, either directly or indirectly, such spaces as I have described, because doing so will allow for and encourage—although it cannot guarantee—the transition, within both the warring and warred-upon populations, from bodies that are ready-to-fight to bodies that are ready-to-politics.

One consequence of this is that warmakers and warfighters need to pay close attention to actions within wars that alternatively foreclose or leave open shifting the conditions of possibility later.[20] For instance, the prevalent use of human shields in contemporary conflicts may traumatize everyone involved to the extent that they are never able to reconfigure themselves away from violence and toward politics. This is because our somatic, limbic, and psychological responses are not completely under our conscious control.[21] As Brison notes, "a person's bodily sense of self is fundamentally altered by trauma," such that while "survivors of trauma [may] create meaning and remake themselves," the self that emerges is fundamentally different than the previous self and may or may not always be on guard in certain unalterable ways (Brison 2022, 313). This is precisely why building material, social, embodied spaces that foster good relational webs is critical to *jus ex bello*; Brison argues that it is "with the help of empathetic others" who are "understanding listeners" and supportive of the survivor's narrative reconstruction of themselves and their sociopolitical world "that recovery of the sense of self is possible" (Brison 2022, 313). So while war is indelibly traumatic in a wide variety of ways, it would behoove warmakers and warfighters to a) avoid those military actions that are highly likely to make it difficult if not impossible for warzone survivors to reconfigure their whole embodied selves as ready-to-politics, and b) work to build the material and social conditions necessary for survivors to enter into good (domestic, regional, international, and global) relations with others in the here and now.

In thinking through creating the conditions of possibility for the space of politics to arise, it is necessary to consider not only those civilians trapped in warzones but also those who are sent to warzones by their respective political entities.[22] Civilians often become habituated to violence through their entrapment and subsequent involuntary traumatization, or alternatively as a (at least partially) deliberate response to their violence-saturated and violence-haunted lives. (Recall here that ordinarily, war is an intrusive, material national reality for many, if not most, civilians in societies that are at war.) Warfighters, in partial contrast, both configure themselves, and are explicitly produced by their military institutions, as violent bodies that are physiologically and psychologically ready-to-fight. As a result, they often—like many civilian survivors of war—struggle to "move past" the war once large-scale physical hostilities have ceased (Litz 2014). Statistically, military veterans are more prone to violence in the face of interpersonal, familial, and social and political disagreement (Garske 2011; McCarroll et al. 2004; Rentz et al. 2006; Chamberlain et al. 2003; Litz 2014). This suggests that veterans, like other war survivors, require support in transitioning from warring to politicking. Helpfully, the approach to *jus ex bello* that I have developed here provides both an analysis of this issue and recommendations for how to help: veterans need material, social, and embodied opportunities to reconfigure their bodies away from violence and concomitantly take up an "ethico-political stance" (to borrow one last time from Bar On) oriented toward being in good relations with others in the here and now (Bar On 1998, 45).

Finally, it is important to distinguish between ready-to-fight bodies, ready-to-politics bodies, and exhausted bodies.[23] On some readings of World War I, the war ended because everyone was simply too tired to continue, rather than there being any significant shift in the relevant material, social, and embodied conditions of possibility such that politics proper was able to emerge (Mock et al. 2018). If this is correct, then the interwar period between World War I and World War II ought not be read as a proper peace but rather as a détente or pause before the next round of direct large-scale hostilities. The shift from warring to politicking that I have argued is the core of *jus ex bello* never fully occurred, although arguably mini-spaces of politics proper did arise and develop during the interwar period. Accepting this, we might say instead that the conditions for *jus ex bello* were partially met at the tail-end of World War I, but that the process faltered and eventually devolved back into antagonistic relations focused on domination rather than agonistic relations grounded in good will that were productive of political freedom.

The reasons for this devolution are varied and complex, and I will not attempt to enumerate them here; nevertheless, it occurred at least in part because many people in 1918 were simply exhausted rather than newly ready-to-politics. Reconstituting the space of politics such that wars end well, or justly, is difficult, and it is made more difficult by the fact that exhaustion and a willingness to engage in politics proper can often look very similar. However, the feminist approach to *jus ex bello*, because of its close focus on embodiment, enables us to draw this distinction on the one hand and, on the other hand, emphasizes the importance of materially and socially configuring spaces of practice such that people are able to make the bodily shift away from exhaustion, if that is where they are psychologically and physiologically as direct large-scale hostilities are winding down, and toward being ready-to-politics.

Overall, this picture of *jus ex bello* comes out of a feminist take on the relational understanding of politics. When we carefully consider what needs to happen to go from war to peace, we recognize that it is not merely a matter of switching our means (from war to other instruments of domination) but rather of switching our ends (from domination to political freedom). Furthermore, this shift cannot occur apropos of nothing; it involves shifting the material, social, and embodied conditions of possibility that either enable or prevent the emergence of the space of politics. For people to be in good relations with others in the here and now, such that political action can occur within and across borders, requires the production of bodies that are ready-to-politics, not ready-to-fight. Contra Helen Stacy, *jus ex bello* is not about "mopping up" well when military maneuvers have by and large ended (as quoted in May 2012, 3). Rather, it is about putting the concrete resources in place, or noticing and encouraging them when they spontaneously arise, that enable and empower people to embark, as their whole embodied selves, on an entirely different sort of ethico-political project. War starts to end where and when politics begins.

Notes

1 Many thanks to David Chan, Kiran Bhardwaj, Colin Lewis, and the participants at the "Ending Wars Justly: Theory and Applications" symposium at the 2024 Central APA for their many helpful thoughts and comments.
2 The discussion of bodies that are "ready-to-fight" comes from Bar On (2002b, ch 7).
3 The two traditions I discuss here are also analyzed in Frazer and Hutchings (2008). Their focus is on the broad relationship between violence and politics, while mine is on war and specifically *jus ex bello*.

4 There is a large discourse regarding the nature and definition of violence; for the purposes of this chapter, I am working with a relatively standard definition from Western just war theory, whereby "violence" connotes the use of potentially overwhelming physical and/or kinetic force. For a deeper discussion of what violence is, see Kling and Mitchell (2021).

5 This may not appear to be a political structure, but it is, insofar as it is collaboratively decided upon and implemented and provides a framework and guidelines for a variety of inter- and intra-societal interactions, both present and future.

6 It is a genuine philosophical question whether the limit of something is contained within the thing itself or is outside of or separate from that thing. Both Bar On and Arendt, throughout their philosophical work, argue that, in the case of politics and war, the limit is not part of the very thing it limits.

7 One consequence of this is that not all so-called politicians are actually doing politics; those who call for and embody the end, or goal, of domination are not *real* politicians, although that is the name we have for them. Only those whose interactions regarding matters of public concern and significance are undergirded by good will toward all others, what Martin Luther King, Jr. would call *agape*, are actually engaging in politics proper (King, 1957).

8 This is one of the core insights of what is sometimes called feminist epistemology or, alternatively, standpoint epistemology. For two foundational texts in this area, see Collins (1990) and Young (1990).

9 The question of how to respond to a patriarchal world in both theory and practice is a core concern for feminists and a subject of deep and contentious debate.

10 This is a broad feminist point; Susan Brison (2003, 2022) provides one articulation of it.

11 Pacifists have long pointed out that, in a world habituated to violence, pacifism is derided as foolish, idealistic or unrealistic, nonsensical, or otherwise detached from the "real world." Such derision, pacifists argue, is at least in part the result of people's habituation—through individual action and social and political enculturation—toward violence and away from peacebuilding. For more on this point, see Holmes (2013) and Fiala (2018).

12 Arendt distinguishes between action and fabrication as two different modes, the first political, the second not. Fabrication is instrumental and so always constrained by a pre-set end; in this sense, violence is always fabrication. (Part of the trouble with violence, for Arendt, is its innate tendency to spill over the constraints set by the end which initially justifies it: violence begun for a purpose always runs the risk of overwhelming that purpose.) By contrast, action is what humans do when they are engaging in politics proper; it is what happens in the public sphere when the plurality of humanity comes together to freely decide, through cooperation, collaboration, and public reasoning, how to respond to matters of public concern and significance. Action is distinctive of human beings, Arendt argues, because it is when we interrelate with others in this way that we disclose and affirm our unique identities. In doing politics, which can only be done with others, we as a plurality *act*: we bring about the unexpected, the improbable, the unanticipated, and so freedom appears. For Arendt, politics is about engaging the faculty of action, not fabrication; hence, her view that politics and violence are antithetical. Those who argue that violence is integral to politics have mistaken fabrication for action (Arendt 1958, 1969). For further discussion, see Frazer and Hutchings (2008).

13 For more on fabrication, see Note 12.

14 For excellent primers on the particulars of such practices, see, among others, Kaba (2021) and Porta (2009).
15 There is no guarantee that such a spread will happen; *jus ex bello* is always fragile and at risk of falling back into war. However, the conditions of possibility for such a spread include the existence of such pockets of democracy as are described here, wherein people can become ready-to-politics at both the domestic and international levels.
16 For two comprehensive historical accounts of the Reconstruction era, see Foner (1988); White (2017). For a discussion of Black politics during that time period, see Hahn (2003).
17 https://www.allmep.org/about-us-allmep/.
18 Thanks to Dragan Stanar for drawing my attention to this important point.
19 This quote is commonly misattributed to Leon Trotsky, due to Michael Walzer paraphrasing Trotsky's comment about the dialectic in his (Walzer's) landmark *Just and Unjust Wars*: "War is most often a form of tyranny. It is best described by paraphrasing Trotsky's aphorism about the dialectic: 'You may not be interested in war, but war is interested in you'" (Walzer 2006, 29). Walzer's reformulation of Trotsky's comment to be about war, rather than the dialectic, has subsequently been taken up as a quotation by Trotsky. However, this attribution is inaccurate; the earliest version of the quotation about war is from Fannie Hurst, as cited in the *Cleveland Plain Dealer* in 1941.
20 Thanks to Elad Uzan for pushing me to consider this point.
21 We can indirectly impact our bodily systems through various mental and somatic techniques, as Buddhist, Confucian, and Stoic philosophers, among others, have long noted; still, the point stands that our bodily responses, especially those born out of trauma, are never fully under conscious lock. Ta-Nehisi Coates discusses this vividly (Coates 2015).
22 Thanks to Andrew Fiala for pushing me to consider this point.
23 Thanks to Raphael Sassower for raising this point.

References

Arendt, Hannah. 1958. *The Human Condition*. Chicago: University of Chicago Press.

Arendt, Hannah. 1969. *On Violence*. New York: Harcourt Brace.

Bar On, Bat-Ami. 1998. "Everyday Violence and Ethico-Political Crisis." In *Daring to Be Good: Essays in Feminist Ethico-Politics*, edited by Bat-Ami Bar On and Ann Ferguson, 45–52. New York: Routledge.

Bar On, Bat-Ami. 2002a. "Ruin, Repair, and Responsibility." *International Journal of Philosophical Studies* 10 (2): 195–207.

Bar On, Bat-Ami. 2002b. *The Subject of Violence: Arendtean Exercises in Understanding*. New York: Rowman & Littlefield.

Bar On, Bat-Ami. 2008. "The Opposition of Politics and War." *Hypatia* 23 (2): 141–54.

Bar On, Bat-Ami. 2019. "But Is It Fascism?" *Journal of Social Philosophy* 50 (4): 407–24. https://doi.org/10.1111/josp.12322

Bottici, Chiara, and Benoit Challand. 2010. *The Myth of the Clash of Civilizations*. New York: Routledge.

Brison, Susan J. 2003. *Aftermath: Violence and the Remaking of a Self*. Princeton, NJ: Princeton University Press.

Brison, Susan J. 2022. "Outliving Oneself: Trauma, Memory, and Personal Identity." In *Feminist Philosophy of Mind*, edited by Keya Maitra and Jennifer McWeeny, 313–29. Oxford: Oxford University Press. https://doi.org/10.1093/oso/9780190867614.003.0018

Byman, Daniel. 2003. "Constructing a Democratic Iraq: Challenges and Opportunities." *International Security* 28 (1): 47–78.

Chamberlain, Heather, Valerie Stander, and Lex L. Merrill. 2003. "Research on Child Abuse in the U.S. Armed Forces." *Military Medicine* 168 (3): 257–60.

Clausewitz, Carl von. 1976. *On War*. Edited and translated by Michael Howard and Peter Paret. Revised 1984. Princeton, NJ: Princeton University Press.

Coates, Ta-Nehisi. 2015. *Between the World and Me*. New York: One World.

Collins, Patricia Hill. 1990. *Black Feminist Thought: Knowledge, Consciousness, and the Politics of Empowerment*. New York: Routledge.

de Beauvoir, Simone. 1961. *The Second Sex*. New York: Bentam.

Du Bois, W. E. B. 1915. "The Immediate Problem of the American Negro." *The Crisis* 9 (6): n.p.

Du Bois, W. E. B. 2004. *The Souls of Black Folk*. New York: Taylor & Francis.

Fiala, Andrew. 2018. *Transformative Pacifism: Critical Theory and Practice*. London: Bloomsbury Academic.

Foner, Eric. 1988. *Reconstruction: America's Unfinished Revolution, 1863–1877*. 1st ed. New York: Harper & Row.

Frazer, Elizabeth, and Kimberly Hutchings. 2008. "On Politics and Violence: Arendt Contra Fanon." *Contemporary Political Theory* 7 (1): 90–108. https://doi.org/10.1057/palgrave.cpt.9300328

Garske, Gregory. 2011. "Military-Related PTSD: A Focus on the Symptomatology and Treatment Approaches." *Journal of Rehabilitation* 77 (October): 31–36.

Griswold, George Z. 1941. "6,000 Here Assail Hostage Slayings." *Cleveland Plain Dealer*, November 17, 1941.

Hahn, Steven. 2003. *A Nation under Our Feet: Black Political Struggles in the Rural South, from Slavery to the Great Migration*. Cambridge, MA: Belknap Press of Harvard University Press.

Harper, Leland, and Jennifer Kling. 2022. *Racist, Not Racist, Antiracist: Language and the Dynamic Disaster of American Racism*. New York: Lexington Books.

Holmes, Robert. 2013. *The Ethics of Nonviolence: Essays by Robert L. Holmes*. New York: Bloomsbury.

hooks, bell. 2004. *The Will to Change: Men, Masculinity, and Love*. New York: Atria Books.

Kaba, Mariame. 2021. *We Do This 'Til We Free Us: Abolitionist Organizing and Transforming Justice*. New York: Haymarket Books.

King, Jr., Martin Luther. 1957. "Loving Your Enemies." *The Martin Luther King, Jr., Research and Education Institute*, November 17, 1957. https://kinginstitute.stanford.edu/king-papers/documents/loving-your-enemies-sermon-delivered-dexter-avenue-baptist-church

Kling, Jennifer, and Megan Mitchell. 2021. *The Philosophy of Protest: Fighting for Justice Without Going to War*. Lanham, MD: Rowman & Littlefield International.

Lewis, Heidi R., Dana Maria Asbury, and Jazlyn Andrews. 2021. *In Audre's Footsteps: Transnational Kitchen Table Talk*. Berlin: Edition Assemblage.

Li, Chenyang. 2006. "The Confucian Ideal of Harmony." *Philosophy East and West* 56 (4): 583–603.

Litz, Brett T. 2014. "Resilience in the Aftermath of War Trauma: A Critical Review and Commentary." *Interface Focus* 4 (5): 20140008. https://doi.org/10.1098/rsfs.2014.0008
Lorde, Audre. 2007. "Age, Race, Class, and Sex: Women Redefining Difference." In *Sister Outsider: Essays and Speeches*, 114–123. Berkeley, CA: Crossing Press.
May, Larry. 2012. *After War Ends: A Philosophical Perspective*. Cambridge: Cambridge University Press.
McCarroll, James E., Robert J. Ursano, Zizhong Fan, and John H. Newby. 2004. "Classification of the Severity of U.S. Army and Civilian Reports of Child Maltreatment." *Military Medicine* 169 (6): 461–64. https://doi.org/10.7205/milmed.169.6.461
Midgley, Mary. 2021. "Trying Out One's New Sword." In *The Moral Life: An Introductory Reader in Ethics and Literature*, edited by Lewis Vaughn and Louis P. Pojman, 7th ed. Oxford: Oxford University Press.
Miller, Sarah Clark. 2023. "On Justifying Violent Self-Defense." *APA Studies on Feminism and Philosophy* 22 (2): 3–6.
Mock, Geoffrey, Peter Feaver, Adriane Lentz-Smith, and Erdağ Göknar. 2018. "How the Trauma and Struggles of World War I Helped Shape the Modern World." *Duke Today*, November 8, 2018. https://today.duke.edu/2018/11/how-trauma-and-struggles-world-war-i-helped-shape-modern-world
Porta, Donatella Della, ed. 2009. *Democracy in Social Movements*. New York: Palgrave Macmillan.
Rentz, E. Danielle, Sandra L. Martin, Deborah A. Gibbs, Monique Clinton-Sherrod, Jennifer Hardison, and Stephen W. Marshall. 2006. "Family Violence in the Military: A Review of the Literature." *Trauma, Violence & Abuse* 7 (2): 93–108. https://doi.org/10.1177/1524838005285916
Sawyer, Ralph D. 2007. *The Seven Military Classics of Ancient China*. New York: Westview.
TallBear, Kim. 2019. "Caretaking Relations, Not American Dreaming." *Kalfou* 6 (1): 24–41. https://doi.org/10.15367/kf.v6i1.228
Walzer, Michael. 2006. *Just and Unjust Wars: A Moral Argument with Historical Illustrations, Fourth Edition*. New York: Basic Books.
White, Richard. 2017. *The Republic for Which It Stands: The United States during Reconstruction and the Gilded Age, 1865–1896*. New York: Oxford University Press.
Young, Iris Marion. 1990. *Throwing Like a Girl and Other Essays in Feminist Political Theory*. Bloomington: Indiana University Press.
Zinn, Howard. 1971. "Disturbing the War." Presented at the Boston Common Peace Rally, May 5, 1971. https://www.howardzinn.org/collection/disturbing-the-war/

5 Endless War and the Ideologies of War

Cheyney Ryan

A specter haunts modern war: the specter of endlessness. Its threat is an ideological one. The political arrangements of Western modernity have always championed themselves as ones of peace. This has been fundamental to their legitimacy. "Civilized" societies are said to be ones that maintain peace *within* themselves and promote peace *outside* of themselves by bringing, if not imposing, peace on the less "civilized" world. Let us call this Western modernity's *Peace Narrative*. This Peace Narrative has always allowed for war; indeed, it has often been a *justification* for war. For it holds that peace can only be achieved through war, specifically through "civilized" wars: wars fought in a "civilized" manner for "civilization", ending in the triumph of a "civilized" – hence peaceful – world. World War I was famously the "war to end all wars". Hence war-as-ending-war has been a recurring motif of the Peace Narrative. The power of that narrative is evidenced in how consistently it is recycled in times of crisis, such as America's post-9/11 "War on Terror".

Thus, the prospect of truly endless war challenges this long-standing picture. This is how I diagnose the preoccupation of many today with the problem of endless war. At bottom, it suggests that war cannot end war any more than crime can end crime. It obliges us to fundamentally rethink our perspective on war, specifically the conception of "civilized" wars that have promised to end or dramatically constrain war while achieving nothing of the sort.

1 The Night Side of Modernity

There are two ways to approach the problem of endless wars.

One is the micro approach, which focuses on an actual war and the problems posed by its apparent endlessness. America's war in Afghanistan is an example. Or, it focuses on hypothetical cases, on a hypothetical "war X" and the problems of "X's" apparent endlessness. This basically anecdotal approach characterizes current just war theory; its preference for bite-sized cases fits with the aspirations of many for an impact on "real-world"

DOI: 10.4324/9781003454144-7

policymaking. Philosophers have recently focused on the problem of "how wars end". This is the concern of *jus ex bello*, when wars must end, and *jus post bellum*, what should happen after they end (Chiu 2017; Orend 2000). To this might be added the problem of *jus ad aeternitatem* – what happens when wars never end?

Another approach is the *macro* one. It looks at war generally, or the type of war characteristic of an era, and asks why it lends itself to chronic endlessness. This is the approach that says: If you step back from any specific war of the 20th century, like World War II, what you see is an era of constant war, whose particular "wars" are distinguished from one another only arbitrarily. What does this say about war in our time, and what is its import for war's place in society and its culture? These are the questions addressed in such works as Mary Dudziak's *War Time: An Idea, Its History, Its Consequences* (Dudziak 2013). Pursuing this macro approach means pursuing what might be called the *Big Picture*. This essay adopts the macro/Big Picture approach. It draws on my recent book, *Pacifism as War Abolitionism*, though nothing I say presumes familiarity with this work or agreement with it (Ryan 2023). My claim is that the problem of endless war is not just a policy matter for governments. It must be approached more broadly and deeply as a problem endemic to Western modernity, meaning those economic/political arrangements and their ideologies that triumphed in Western Europe in the 17th century and have defined the world ever since.

Here is the specific problem that I have in mind:

The story of Western modernity has been fundamentally one of war: war that has been a distinctively *European* affair. Sociologist Michael Mann puts it thus:

> Over the second millennium AD, *Europeans were probably more warlike than the inhabitants of any other continent.* Europeans were from Mars. Rough statistics of global wars are available from 1494, better ones from 1816. European wars dominated both periods. Although these data may undercount early nineteenth-century wars in Latin America and precolonial wars in Africa, a contrast with East Asia is on firmer ground. This region saw a 300-year period of peace between the 1590s and 1894, broken only by barbarian incursions into China and five fairly small two-state wars. During the preceding 200 years, China was only once at war, with Vietnam. In Japan, firearms were banned for two centuries from 1637 onward. In contrast, the European powers were involved in interstate wars in nearly 75 percent of the years between 1494 and 1975, and *no twenty-five-year period was entirely free of war.*[1]

Such unrelenting warfare has posed significant economic/political challenges. I shall focus on the *ideological* challenges posed by it – specifically, to the self-conception of Western modernity. Its legitimating ideology has been one of peace, yet its reality has been a story of perpetual war. How are we to reconcile the self-conception with the reality?

Numerous strategies have been used to address this problem. Mainstream political philosophy/just war theory has simply ignored it by ignoring the whole question of why European modernity has been so warlike. Reading Walzer's *Just and Unjust Wars*, you would never know that it was written amidst one of the most warlike centuries in human history (Walzer 1977). Otherwise, the denial strategy has been construing constant war not as reflecting Western "civilization's" fundamental character but as reflecting the intrusion of premodern/"savage" elements into "civilization's" otherwise peaceful core. Thus, World War II is portrayed as a giant historical hiccup, reflecting the premodern "tribalism" of Nazism. And exorcising this "tribal"/ "primitive"/"uncivilized" element is something that can only be achieved by war, thus sustaining the conception of modernity's wars as wars for peace.

Some years ago, sociologist Zygmunt Bauman maintained that the Holocaust should not be viewed as some massive aberration from an otherwise "civilized" order. Rather, it should be viewed as revealing what "civilization" has always been about. He writes, "The etiological myth deeply entrenched in the self-consciousness of our Western society is the morally elevating story of humanity emerging from pre-social barbarity." However, "[t]he world of the death camps and the society it engenders reveals the progressively intensifying night side of Judeo-Christian civilization" – which will persist until modernity and its self-conceptions are fundamentally challenged (Bauman 2002, 12). I claim that the same holds for the reality of endless war. It reveals the extent to which war is *baked into* our very institutions and ideologies, the extent to which modernity has been driven by what I and others have termed the *war system*, and how that will continue until the system is fundamentally challenged.

My discussion proceeds as follows.

The next section places the problem of endless war in the context of America's "War on Terror" and the prominence of the Peace Narrative at its inception. I adopt an admittedly polemical if not snarky tone in reflecting on a particularly bombastic example of "wars-for-civilization-as-wars-for-peace" ideology. This leads me to some tentative remarks on what might be termed the politics of the war-narrative and how the whole question of constructing meaningful war narratives involves the question of their proper endings, with specific reference to those who have served in endless wars and are challenged to create a coherent story of their experiences.

Section 3 steps back to place the problem of endless war in its larger social/historical context. This section is more schematic, addressing the notion of civilized war that has informed the ideology of the modern war system while stressing its complexity in terms of the different types of war involved and the different types of entities that have waged war, specifically states and empires. It suggests how today's problem of endless war speaks to a larger legitimation crisis that war faces. The final section concludes with some remarks on how the widespread defection of ordinary people from participating in war today relates to the meaninglessness that war requires when the enterprise seems to be endless.

2 "Why We Fight"

Today's anxiety about endless war is best understood against the background in which prominent voices recently proclaimed that history had "ended" and that the only wars still to be fought were wars that would end all war. To see how this perspective crashed and burned, let us return to the dire – but also heady – moments following 9/11.

Pursuing the "Bad Guys"

"One day, this war will end", the authors of "A Letter from America" (on "Why We Fight This War") confidently proclaimed.

> When it does – and in some respects even before it ends – the great task of conciliation awaits us. We hope that this war, by stopping an unmitigated global evil, can increase the possibility of a world community based on justice. But we know that only the peacemakers among us in every society can ensure that this war will not have been in vain.[2]

This letter [hereafter: *The Letter*] was published on February 12, 2002, five months after the 9/11 events, and meant to defend – indeed, champion – America's "War on Terror". Its authors, all "high-powered" academics according to the *Chronicle of Higher Education*, included such "celebrated scholars" as Jean Elshtain, Michael Walzer, Robert Putnam, and Theda Skocpol (Ruark 2002). Its tone was strikingly reminiscent of 1914's "Manifesto of the Ninety-Three" ["To the Civilized World"] where "high-powered" German academics championed the Kaiser's cause in World War I ("Have faith in us! Believe, that we shall carry on this war to the end as a civilized nation, to whom the legacy of a Goethe, a Beethoven, and a Kant is just as sacred as its own hearths and homes").[3] Like that "Manifesto", "A Letter from America" alternated between imperiousness, preachiness, and pomposity:

"We say to you forthrightly …", "We solemnly say with one voice …", "We are united in our conviction …"—and, "The great task of conciliation awaits us …".

With such words, the authors "pledged" to defend the "universal moral truths" which, they insisted, America's war against "unmitigated global evil" was ultimately about. Such truths were "accessible to all people" except, presumably, America's "enemies". Chief among those "universal moral truths" was that "Killing in the name of God is contrary to faith in God". By contrast, *The Letter* assured us that killing in the name of "universal moral truths" was not just defensible but *imperative* at times – like now.

It was not exactly a call to arms. On the contrary, like the statements emanating from the White House, *The Letter* fastidiously avoided any calls for sacrifice, such as those in the "Why We Fight" pronouncements of World War II. It especially refrained from urging anyone to actually become one of the soldiers tasked with doing the killing and dying. It spoke from the standpoint of what Edward Luttwak has termed "post-heroic warfare": the widespread refusal of ordinary citizens to fight in wars, no matter how cosmic the stakes (Luttwak 1995). Nor was there any mention of what, specifically, eradicating "unmitigated evil" would involve by way of explicit military actions for concrete military goals. Such mundane matters might have muddied the pristine clarity of the cause: a war against Evil waged by The Good – with the blanks to be filled in later.

What should we say about this remarkable document?

Its Olympian tone exemplified that heady moment of American liberal triumphalism between the end of the Cold War and 9/11. Its posture was that of unalloyed, unquestioned power; the confidence of its voice expressed not just the triumph of a particular narrative but the triumph of the narrative itself in the End of History. After all, America had the most powerful military in the history of the earth: who could doubt its ability to win this war or any war? History had ended, capitalism had won, and the fiddles were tuning up all over the globe celebrating the triumph of "Western liberal democracy as the final form of human government" (Fukuyama 1989). The only worry, for some, was whether the American people were truly up to the task. Would they take up the liberal-man's burden, or did they "lack the guts to do it" (in the words of another "celebrated scholar", Niall Ferguson (2002, 418)?

All this fortuitously coincided with what Michael Walzer had several years earlier termed "The Triumph of Just War Theory" (Walzer 2002). However, just war theory's triumph proved a Pyrrhic victory. In its better moments, the just war tradition has been one of humility, insisting, for example, that "war aims be made clear, that criteria for what is to count as success in achieving those aims be publicly articulated, and that negotiated settlement never be ruled out of court by fiat". These are in fact the words of Elshtain, in an earlier characterization of it (Elshtain 2001, 9). So understood, it stood in sharp *contrast* to an ethic of Holy Wars, of wars of "Good over Evil". However, no sooner had just war theory triumphed than humility was cast aside and it was enlisted in just such a Holy War against an "Axis of Evil" – with no specific aims stated, hence no specific criteria of success identified, and an enemy unworthy of negotiation, only extermination. It was, in fact, a ticket for quagmire, which is where the triumphant liberal project landed in the debacles of Iraq and Afghanistan.

War's Ends and War's Endings

Famous last words: "One day, this war will end", *The Letter's* authors had proclaimed (Ruark 2002). What happens when the "War on Terror's" Polish cavalry charge, with its numerous "Operations" – "Enduring Freedom", "Iraqi Freedom", "New Dawn", "Inherent Resolve", "Freedom's Sentinel", etc. – proves unwinnable in part because, for all its magniloquent rhetoric, its specific aims were never defined? Almost a million people have been directly killed in these conflicts, indirect deaths have been almost five million, and 38 million have been displaced in conflicts ranging over 78 countries.[4]

What happens when the reality of all this sinks in and, for all the blustering about "eradicating evil", the citizenry finds itself tired of the whole sordid endeavor?

Not one of *The Letter*'s authors ever paused to revisit its clarion call for moral certainty and its blind belief in the efficacy of war. Reflection on it all has mainly come from those who were charged with doing the actual fighting and who have been fated ever since to live in the gap between the grandiose rhetoric and the grim reality. Iraq veteran Phil Klay writes of how

> Talking about American wars [has] increasingly becomes like talking about Schrödinger's cat. Outside the closed black boxes of our military involvement overseas, the American public remains blissfully at peace until an American dies, and it turns out we were at war all along.

A character in Vietnam vet Tim O'Brien's stories admits, "'It just came to me,' he whispered. 'The moral, I mean. Nobody listens. Nobody hears nothing.'" (O'Brien 1997, 176)[5] The question it raises, Klay asks, is "How to speak meaningfully of a conflict that has lasted so long, and at such a low ebb that most Americans can pretend it isn't happening?" (Klay 2022, xv)

"How to speak meaningfully…" – the larger topic here, of how endless war threatens the very possibility of meaningful speech, has been a theme in Western culture at least since World War I. One problem is the lack of a meaningful audience. Alienated from the larger community, veterans experience themselves as speaking *only* to themselves; their speech is rendered a Wittgenstein-type "private language" that lacks any criteria distinguishing the true and the false. This is how I make sense of Tim O'Brien's reflections on the challenges of telling a "true" war story. "In any war story, but especially a true one, it's difficult to separate what happened from what seemed to happen. What seems to happen becomes its own happening and has to be told that way".

> The pictures get jumbled; you tend to miss a lot. And then afterward, when you go to tell about it, there is always that surreal seemingness, which makes the story seem untrue, but which in fact represents the hard and exact truth as it seemed.

The result is a set of double-binds.

> In many cases a true war story cannot be believed. If you believe it, be skeptical. It's a question of credibility. Often the crazy stuff is true and the normal stuff isn't because the normal stuff is necessary to make you believe the truly incredible craziness. In other cases you can't even tell a true war story. Sometimes it's just beyond telling.
>
> (O'Brien 1997, 176)

Phil Klay has stressed the sense of *fraudulence* in any attempt to speak meaningfully of endless war.

> Though I continue to tell stories about Iraq, I sometimes fear this makes me a fraud. I feel guilty about the sorrow I feel because I know it is manufactured, and I feel guilty about the sorrow I do not feel because it is owed, it is the barest beginning of what is owed to the fallen.
>
> (Klay 2022, 6)

The source of it all is the sense of chronic *incompleteness*. O'Brien concludes, "You can tell a true war story by the way it never seems to end. Not then, not ever". No story can match the full details of war, which includes how events are experienced and remembered; hence, the attempt to pin down anything like "the final and definitive truth" can never end, especially as they engage matters we are fated to never understand – like death. Something like this thought is found in Leo Tolstoy, who in *War and Peace* rejected the possibility of putting war into anything like a coherent narrative. Any attempt to tell the history of a particular war or war generally "necessarily falsifies it" (Tolstoy 2006, Book 9, Chapter 1). Another way to frame the problem is as the *kind* of narrative to which war is subject and the kind of narrative that war requires in order to have the kind of meaning it is presumed to have. Tolstoy's claim that the story of war lacks any meaning might be restated as the story of war is an *epic* one, epic narratives being ones in which individuals and groups are basically the playthings of larger social forces. Most importantly, they have no real end, in the sense of a *conclusion* – of what all the events have been leading towards;

they end only in the sense that they *stop*. What Tolstoy is denying, then, is that the story of war constitutes a *drama*, that is, the type of narrative in which individuals and groups rise above their circumstances to clash around fundamental interests or values – and which does have a proper end that gives coherence and meaning to the full narrative.

The struggles of veterans on the personal level to construct a meaningful narrative of their war experiences suggest the extent to which a proper ending is a prerequisite for such meaning. Absent such an ending, the point of what they did remains ever elusive. What I want to suggest is that the same problem arises on the political level where the endings of wars remain problematic. There is no standpoint from which a meaningful narrative of war can be constructed – with the upshot that the enterprise becomes increasingly alienated from the larger community, no matter how much it is told that ultimate stakes are involved.

To pursue this thought further, let me turn to some broader reflections on the topic of "ending wars" by exploring the ideologies that have surrounded it and still surround it.

3 Ending Wars and the War System

Not all discussions of this topic are *per se* ideological, but any discussion of it should be mindful of the ideological purposes to which such discussions can and have been put. I begin with a sketch of my skeptical framework. It will be quite schematic, if not crude. Some of what I say is addressed at greater length in my *Pacifism as War Abolitionism*.

The Tasks of Ideology

The starting point is that war must be understood not as a series of discrete events but as a system. Call it the war system. One reason for approaching it as a system bears especially on the topic at hand. It is that whether or not wars are constituted *as* discrete events, that is, as possessing "beginnings" and "endings", is *itself* an artifact of the larger system. Consider, for example, that war was a constant feature of the Middle Ages, but it was not an era of individual "wars"; hence, the story of the Middle Ages is not told around its wars.[6] By contrast, the fact that wars are now constituted as discrete events, in ways to be described shortly, and we frame our "history" around the story of those wars – all of this is an artifact of the modern war system, one that emerged circa 1500, coalesced circa 1700, and is intimately connected with the emergence of the modern state as the agent that wages wars. The modern war system may be approached on two levels: how it is *constructed*, practically, and how it is *configured*, ideologically. The first pertains to the principal institutions that define their actions, and the second to the principal ideas that inform those institutions. While the study of the war system is the study of both, my focus in this essay is the war system's ideology.

That ideology has been complex and changing. However, its principal concern throughout has been its *legitimizing* function. The same is true for the ideologies of other social practices like capitalist exploitation or racial/gender oppression. That legitimizing function has been *twofold*, one more theoretical and the other more practical.

On the one hand, legitimizing war has been a matter of *justifying* it so that it gains widespread social acceptance. The problem of justification has traditionally arisen from the fact that war is the collective exercise of an action – killing – that society otherwise condemns. One challenge is distinguishing war from murder. This challenge has taken different forms depending on how the critique of murder has been framed; for example, is it framed in the language of the sacred (violating the sacredness of human life) as in earlier times, or is it framed in the language of rights (infringing on the rights of persons) as in modern times? For Christianity, the initial problem was reconciling war with Jesus's injunction to "Turn the other cheek". This remained a concern for the first just war theorists, though their framework eventually became fully rights-focused. Another challenge is the fact that war is *collective* killing. The question here is whether this collective enterprise can be carried out with sufficient organization, discipline, etc. I have framed this as whether war can be waged *responsibly*, in addition to being waged *justly* (as the question of killing asks).

On the other hand, legitimizing war has been a matter of *motivating* it, so that people will engage in it. This problem arises from the simple fact that people generally don't want to fight in wars. Whenever significant numbers of soldiers have been needed, it has required massive amounts of coercion. However, coercion has never been enough, especially in societies that have prided themselves on their *non*-coercive character. Motivation always involves a number of elements, both cognitive and emotional. On the whole, though, motivating participation in war has principally been a problem of *meaning*. Dwight Macdonald once characterized war as "the maximum of physical devastation accompanied by the minimum of human meaning".[7] So the challenge is one of endowing purpose and dignity on the activities that war involves. Only by doing so can those engaged in war *care* enough about what they do so as to fight and die for it.

Together, these provide a framework for approaching the ideology of the war system. Roughly, the question of justification approaches war from the "outside", as it were, from the third-person perspective. Its enterprise is one of *arguments*, typically juridical ones. This is the focus of contemporary just war theory, with its intimate relationship to the laws of war. The question of motivation approaches war from the "inside", as it were, from the first- or second-person perspective of how war is experienced. It involves the cultural sphere, as distinct from the juridical one; its realm is the imaginative as distinct from the argumentative. In modern war, meaning in war has been principally a matter of the available narratives about "why we fight" that have been intimately connected with nationalism. For example, in the United States, the meaning of military service has been intimately connected with notions of what it means to be an "American".

Ideologically, *legitimation crises* have occurred when war is seen as having lost its justification, or logic, and/or is experienced as having lost its motivation, or meaning.

The Challenge of Legitimacy

The ideology of the modern war system arose in response to the legitimation crisis at the dawn of modernity. This resulted from a conjunction of factors: the chaotic emergence of the modern state, the disruptive impact of nascent market/capitalist relations, and the breakdown of the medieval religious synthesis. It was all part of what historians have termed the "General Crisis" of the 17th century, with its serious ecological dislocations as well.[8] These culminated in the era of constant warfare in the 16th–early 17th centuries. In his *The Struggle for Stability in Early Modern Europe*, Theodore Rabb characterized the early 17th century as involving a wholesale reorientation of society on multiple levels and suggested that the decisive factor in the transformation was "the revulsion against the brutal excesses of the Thirty Years War", a revulsion that ultimately provoked a "return to stability" in the mid-17th century (Rabb 1975, 118, 124). The depth of this revulsion was symbolized in popular images of the "Beast of War" devouring all in its path. The challenge to war's legitimacy arose from the twin perceptions that the destructive powers of war had dramatically increased, in contrast to the more limited powers of earlier times, while control over those powers had all but disappeared, in contrast to what was seen as the more orderly arrangements of earlier times.

The crisis engendered several responses, whose broad outlines have continued to define different responses to war ever since.

The more radical response construed the problem as one of the demonic, in images evoking "The Sorcerer's Apprentice". Society had conjured up powers beyond its control, indeed powers to which society itself was now enslaved. The only solution lay in slaying the "Beast of War": fundamentally reconstructing our arrangements and reconfiguring our ideas to dispense with all powers associated with war. This was anticipated in the earlier writings of Erasmus; it was concretized in the religious movements like Anabaptism of the Radical Reformation. Its prophetic-type orientation endured in the tradition of visionary pacifism, such as William Blake (Erdman 2011, 3–19).

The more conservative response was not to reject all war but to *relegitimize* it. To this end, it sought to reconstruct arrangements and reconfigure ideas so as to tame the "Beast of War", that is, to leave a place for war such that war would be controlled and constrained so as not to overwhelm everything around it. The upshot was the modern war system, which coalesced in conjunction with the other two pillars of modernity: the modern state system and the modern capitalist system. The ideological transformation was consolidated in the Enlightenment. It can be understood this way. The medieval ideology of war had portrayed and recommended it as an inherently *Christian* endeavor, with all the overtones that "Christian" evoked. The modern ideology of war portrayed and recommended it as an inherently *civilized* endeavor, with all the overtones that "civilized" evoked. Legitimation crises for the medieval ideology of war arose when people came to perceive/experience the (allegedly) Christian nature of war as in fact demonic. Legitimation crises for the modern ideology of war have arisen when people come to perceive/experience the (allegedly) civilized nature of war as in fact "savage".

Wars, States, and Empires

I have characterized civilized war as war fought for civilization in a civilized manner. However, both notions need unpacking. Most importantly, the notion of civilized war has actually involved *two* types of wars, reflecting the fact that the wars of Western modernity have been fought by two types of institutions: states and empires. One type of war I call *war, proper*. We might specify them as wars *of* civilization – wars within Europe and between European states. The other I call *hostilities*. These are truly wars *for* civilization, as they have been wars by European empires to impose civilization on the non-civilized world.

War, Proper – or Wars of Civilization

War, proper, is how wars between civilized peoples have been construed. Such wars are discrete events, bound by rules, constituted by distinct battles, with finite beginnings and ends, and akin to civil strife insofar as their aim is ultimately reconciliation – which the mutual recognition of the adversaries *as* civilized makes possible.

This is the picture of civilized war that coalesced in the 18th century among Enlightenment thinkers. It underwent significant modifications with the rise of nationalism in the 19th century, but its basic structure has remained in place. It was part of a larger picture of European society as the cradle and exemplar of civilization, of a sort that could be considered a single community. Thus Voltaire:

> For some time now it has been possible to consider Christian Europe, give or take Russia, as "une espèce de grande republique" – a sort of great commonwealth – partitioned into several states, some monarchic, the others mixed, some aristocratic, others popular, but all dealing with one another; all having the same basic religion, though divided into various sects; all having the same principles of public and political law unknown in the other parts of the world.

Their civilized status was exemplified in how they fought.

> Because of these principles the European [states] never enslave their prisoners, they respect the ambassadors of their enemies, they jointly acknowledge the preeminence and various rights of [legitimate rulers], and above all they agree on the wise policy of maintaining an equal balance of power between themselves so far as they can, conducting continuous negotiations even in times of war, and exchanging resident ambassadors or less honourable spies, who can warn all the courts of Europe of the designs of any one, give the alarm at the same time and protect the weaker.
>
> (Voltaire 2002, 131)

There are two thoughts here. One is that civilized wars are fought with *decorum*. "Although European nations fight frequent wars", Voltaire wrote,

> in the midst of these dissensions, they generally observe so much decorum and politeness, that it often happens, that a Frenchman, an Englishman, and a German meeting, seem to be natives of the same city.[9]

Adam Ferguson spoke of how they "mingle ... politeness with the use of the sword".[10] Thus civilized war was characterized by certain formalities: declarations of war, to officially mark the beginning of conflicts, and formal negotiations – often lengthy – to resolve them. The latter were crucial in specifying what the war had actually been about. Declarations of war were statements of war aims, but these were best understood as terms for negotiation; this is why the very notion of unconditional acquiescence to another's war aims was excluded by just war principles. The negotiations concluding a conflict specified which of those aims would be accepted and which rejected by mutual agreement. The reason for such decorum was, as Kant noted, so that trust could be maintained between the parties required for a true resolution (Kant 1983).

This leads to the second thought, that civilized wars are fought for *balance*. Europe's status as a civilized society was identified with its maintenance by a balance of power between its elements, one that sustained diversity among unity. The Scottish historian William Robertson declared it "the great secret of modern politics".[11] David Hume agreed in his famous essay on the topic. "The maxim of preserving the balance of power is founded so much on common sense and obvious reasoning, that it is impossible it could altogether have escaped antiquity", and concluded, "the ancients were entirely ignorant of the balance of power" because "the Romans never met with any such general combination or confederacy against them" (Hume 1994, 155). The importance of the balance of power is illustrated by considering the role of self-defense in civilized war.

Self-defense has always played an important role in war. However, that role has varied depending on the different types of war. The Enlightenment conception of war, proper, between European powers generally conceived of wars as negotiating strategies. Starting a war against another country was like initiating a lawsuit in court; war aims had to be declared in the same way plaintiffs in a lawsuit stated their demands. The right to defend oneself in war was like the right to defend oneself in court; hence, it was ill-conceived as akin to the right to self-defense in criminal law. For example, the question of who started the fight, so central to the criminal-law model, had little bearing on the justice of a war. The typical European war involved boundary disputes around where the territory of one state began and another ended. These wars typically involved dynastic succession, making them akin to property disputes in civil law: who was the rightful owner, and how far did that ownership extend? The crucial point is that the resolution of such disputes always involves attention to the balance of power, leading to situations so odd to modern eyes that the loser in a conflict could be rewarded territory they previously did not possess so as to maintain that balance of power. Just war thinking has always conceived of war as a form of law enforcement, but the meaning of this has depended on the type of law taken as a model.

Each type of war has been associated with a generic narrative. Let us identify war, proper with the "civiliz*ed* narrative". Wars were expected to occur in Europe but with two caveats. As noted, those wars were expected to be limited ones in both their impact and duration. And they were expected to be part of a larger process – call it "progress" – involving the slow disappearance of war to the point of its abolition. European wars were expected to abide by the demands of "Reason"; the civilizing effect of such "Reason" meant the expectation that with its continued spread, war would become a thing of the past. War reflected the persistence of primitive elements within civilized society, whose role was increasingly marginalized. This was the theory, at least. Note that only with this as the assumption can one explain the profound shock that World War I or the Holocaust generated.

Hostilities – or Wars for Civilization

However, war, proper has always existed alongside another type of war between the European world, specifically its empires, and the non-European world. My term for this is *hostilities*. A paradigm case is America's so-called "Indian Wars" (circa 1609–circa 1890). As they are construed, hostilities are not a discrete event but an ongoing condition that waxes and wanes, answering to few rules, if any, constituted by skirmishes rather than battles, with vague beginnings and even vaguer endings. This is partly because hostilities have no *specific* aims but only a general *object*, which I address momentarily. The negotiations that end a war, proper mark the point at which the conflict has been concluded. However, hostilities are "concluded" only in the sense that they stop, and generally with the presumption that they may start up again.

What are hostilities about?

In reality, the purposes of imperialist wars have been crude ones, principally economic exploitation and military advantage. However, their ideology has been one of social/moral elevation. Sociologist Michael Mann notes that empires have been characterized by "mission statements" that endow their expansion with "a higher moral tone":

> Few people like to think of themselves as being simply rapacious. This was a "civilizing mission" given a racial slant because it was conducted by the "Anglo-Saxon Race," spreading "Commerce, Civilization and Christianity" – nineteenth-century signifiers of freedom. Violence was unavoidable, it was said, because the natives were at "endless war" with each other, unable to provide order... The colonists claimed natives were "savage," "bloodthirsty," and war-prone, despite the fact that although Ethiopian and Zulu Empires and the Sokoto Caliphate had intermittently used "scorched earth" tactics, most African chiefs, in a context where they could rarely utterly defeat their rivals, preferred diplomacy and ritualized low-level conflict to all-out.
>
> (Mann 2012, 36–37)

Note then how wars for civilization have been wars to end war by ending the conditions of "natives" fighting "endless wars". Those conditions have been construed as outside history, proper. Thomas Hobbes configured them as a "state of nature" constituting a "state of war" as containing "no arts, no letters, no society" – and "no account of time" (Hobbes 1651, Chapter XIII). Hence, they were outside the realm of narrative, meaning that wars for civilization were conceived as drawing the non-civilized world into a common narrative.

"Self-defense" acquires a different meaning in hostilities, closer to its meaning in criminal law. Self-defense in war, proper, may be likened to the more limited meaning of self-defense as repelling an immediate attack. Self-defense in hostilities involves a more expanded meaning of securing one's long-term survival against an ongoing threat. The "Indian Wars" were a case in point. Especially in their earlier phases, the very existence of Native Americans was portrayed as an existential threat to Euro-American society. This threat was configured in racial terms, but something like this perspective had informed Christian attitudes toward Muslims. Wars for civilization were wars in defense of civilization. Ironically, this is how Adam Ferguson regarded Britain's efforts to quash the American Revolution, holding that defeat in America would herald the collapse of Britain's Empire and its commercial civilization (just as surely as barbarian invasion heralded Rome's fall).[12] The impulse of hostilities thus construed is explicitly genocidal: its aim is not reconciliation with an adversary but the total elimination of the enemy. This meaning of self-defense is also implicit in wars for civilization construed as wars for civilizing the uncivilized. Consider the "Indian Wars" as exercises in "pacification". Their stated aim was not to destroy Native Americans as a people but to transform Native American society so as to "civilize" it in ways that might not end all conflict with them but would transform any such conflict into "civilized" war, proper rather than "savage" "wars of extermination", in Kant's words.

How are hostilities waged?

Hostilities have persistently been configured as ones in which, to defeat the savage, the forces of civilization must become like the savage. The whole idea of adversaries abiding by mutual respect is thrown out the window. A fundamental premise of wars between the civilized is that actions in war are not criminal ones *per se* (I have noted the importance of distinguishing the killing in war from murder). However, the adversaries in wars for civilization are criminals, as Ferguson stressed in his remarks on how the rebels in the American colonies needed to be treated. "Subjects in Rebellion incur a Personal Guilt and may be distressed not only in order to distress their Community but likewise in order to Punish Their Crime".[13] That is the "civiliz*ing* narrative", which has been much studied with notions like the "myth of the frontier".[14]

Blurring the "Civilized" and the "Savage"

So, one may conceive this picture of civilized war as constructed around a set of binaries: wars of civilization and wars for civilization, or war, proper and hostilities, reflecting the deeper distinction between the civilized and the non-civilized/savage, itself identified with the European world and the non-European world. I have noted that war, proper was regarded as a constitutive element of the European community. We may think of this full set of distinctions as defining the *global* community as Europe has conceived it – with special reference to its imperial projects. I posed the question of how Western modernity's ideology could be one of peace, but its reality has been one of ongoing war. We see that an answer has been to relegate ongoing war to the non-European world, rendering it to a great extent out of sight and out of mind; and portraying the persistence of war within Europe as reflecting residual premodern/extra-European "savage" elements.

It follows, then, that problems arise for this picture when the binaries on which it rests are blurred. The view that I have argued for elsewhere holds that the story of Western modernity is one where these binaries are periodically blurred due to the logic of states and empires. For example, the crimes of World Wars I and II are often characterized as Europeans treating one another as they had traditionally treated non-Europeans; that is, treating each other as "savages", via "savage" means. In my parlance, wars within Europe have degenerated from wars, proper into hostilities. Note, however, that the conflicts were provoked by conflicts outside of Europe, specifically conflicts between European empires or, as with Germany and Japan in World War II, states aspiring to empires – in the name of "survival". Something like the same logic occurred in previous hyper-wars, the Thirty Years War and the Napoleonic Wars. The rhythm is that relations between European states in Europe abided by civilized standards for a time, but eventually their imperial conflicts outside of Europe returned to Europe itself, unraveling the international order until the depth of the crisis compelled the powers that be to reconstitute it. The impulse to reconstitute a stable order invariably involved reestablishing the legitimacy of war itself, as with the 17th-century crisis.

This is how I understand our current historical situation. In particular, it is how I would place the "Letter from America" discussed at the outset. The events of 9/11 did not happen out of the blue. They were the end product of American actions in the Middle East, the most important being the upshot of the first Iraq War and America's continuing support for Israel's treatment of the Palestinians. The "Letter from America" took itself as endorsing yet another "war for civilization" that – by "ending evil" – would presumably diffuse the conditions of war generally. However, it did just the opposite, by the logic I have just described. The upshot of the "War on Terror" was to undermine the international legal order that had provided stability within the civilized world since World War II (while the rest of the world remained consumed in conflict). It did this most dramatically by undermining the more limited conception of self-defense previously held and replacing it with a more expanded conception of self-defense that I have identified as always central to the imperialist project. This is the analysis that Oona Hathaway has offered in several significant articles

(Hathaway 2023). Now war has returned to Europe with Russia's invasion of Ukraine, which the Russian government constantly justifies by appealing to the new standards of self-defense established by America's "War on Terror".

4 War without Meaning

I conclude with some words on where this leaves us.

Legitimation crises occur when either war's justification or war's motivation are rendered problematic. However, a notable fact about today is how justification and motivation have become unhinged. War is generally regarded as fully justified, often in the most cosmic terms – witness the "Letter from America". But hardly anyone is motivated to fight it anymore. I have elsewhere termed this the "Great Defection" and related it to what I've called the "Chickenhawk Syndrome" – adamant justifications for going to war alongside adamantine refusals to fight it oneself (Ryan 2009). Apparently, even self-defense fails to fully motivate even when the stakes seem obvious. Note the constant stories about the difficulties of mobilizing Ukrainian citizens to fight against Russia (Méheut 2024; Khurshudyan and Khudov 2024; Harmash 2024).

Proponents of war seem mystified by this. Edward Luttwak subtitled a recent book review "The reasons we started fighting and why we won't stop". In it, he canvassed considerations he found persuasive for why war should be accepted as a permanent and not entirely unfortunate feature of our social order. Humanity would remain, in his words, a "battleground". Yet in conclusion, he could not

> resist noting that, in the West, there seem to be fewer and fewer warriors who are actually willing to fight. A few months ago the Italian defence and foreign ministers both declared that Italy will not send even one soldier to serve in Ukraine under any circumstances.
>
> (Luttwak 2024)

My own view is that the situation is perfectly understandable if we consider that the motivation to fight comes from the meaning that persons find in doing so, but the endless nature of modern war has rendered war increasingly devoid of meaning.

Notes

1 Mann 2012, 23–24 (Italics mine). See also McNeill 1982.
2 "What We're Fighting For: A Letter from America; February 13, 2002", Avalon Project. https://avalon.law.yale.edu/sept11/letter_002.asp.

3 "Manifesto the 93", https://web.tohoku.ac.jp/modern-japan/wp-content/uploads/Manifesto-of-the-93.pdf.
4 The figures are from the Watson Institute for International and Public Affairs Cost of War Project. https://watson.brown.edu/costsofwar/figures#:~:text=Human%20Toll%3A%20905%2C000%20%2D%20940%2C000%20Direct,reverberating%20effects%20of%20these%20wars.
5 See also Viet Thanh Nguyen. 2015. "On True War Stories". In *(Re)Collecting the Vietnam War*, special issue of *Asian American Literary Review* 6 (2): 140–145.
6 On war as conceived as battles, see Nolan 2017.
7 McDonald (1957, 96), cited in Fussell 1989, 142.
8 Trevor-Roper 1959. See also Parker 2017.
9 Voltaire 1859, 253, cited in Buchan 2011, 67.
10 Ferguson 1767/1995, 190, cited in Buchan 2011, 68.
11 Robertson 1759, 173, cited in Deudney 2007, 152.
12 Ferguson 1776, 59, cited in Buchan 2011, 68.
13 Ferguson 1995, 561, cited in Buchan 2011, 68.
14 See the writings of Richard Slotkin, starting with Slotkin 2024.

Bibliography

Bauman, Zygmunt. 2002. *Modernity and the Holocaust.* Cornell University Press.

Buchan, Bruce. 2011. "Civilized Fictions: Warfare and Civilization in Enlightenment Thought." *Alternatives: Global, Local, Political* 36 (1): 64–71.

Chiu, Yvonne. 2017. "War's Endings and the Structure of Just War Theory." In *The Ethics of War*, edited by Saba Bazargan and Samuel C. Rickless. Oxford University Press.

Deudney, Daniel. 2007. *Bounding Power: Republican Security Theory from the Polis to the Global Village.* Princeton University Press.

Dudziak, Mary. 2013. *War Time: An Idea, Its History, Its Consequences.* Oxford University Press.

Elshtain, Jean Bethke. 2001. "Just War and Humanitarian Intervention." *American University International Law Review* 17 (1): 1–12.

Erdman, David. 2011. *Blake: Prophet Against Empire.* Dover.

Ferguson, Adam. 1767/1995. *Essay on the History of Civil Society.* Cambridge University Press.

Ferguson, Adam. 1776. *Remarks on a Pamphlet Lately Published by Dr.Price...* T. Cadell.

Ferguson, Adam. 1995. "Notes on the Enquiry into General Sir William Howe's Conduct in the American War, 10 May 1779." In *Correspondence of Adam Ferguson, Volume II, 1781–1816*, edited by V. Merolle. William Pickering.

Ferguson, Niall. 2002. *The Cash Nexus: Money and Power in the Modern World, 1700–2000.* Basic Books.

Fukuyama, Francis. 1989. "The End of History?" *The National Interest*, no. 16: 3–18.

Fussell, Paul. 1989. *Wartime: Understanding and Behavior in the Second World War.* Oxford University Press.

Harmash, Olena. 2024. "Ukraine's Parliament Cracks Down on Draft Dodgers." *Reuters*, May 9. https://www.reuters.com/world/europe/ukraines-parliament-cracks-down-draft-dodgers-2024-05-09/

Hathaway, Oona. 2023. "How the Erosion of U.S. War Powers Constraints Has Undermined International Law Constraints on the Use of Force." *The Harvard National Security Journal* 14: 336–366.
Hobbes, Thomas. 1651. The Leviathan.
Hume, David. 1994. "Of the Balance of Power." In *Political Essays*, edited by Knud Haakonssen. Cambridge University Press.
Kant, Immanuel. 1983. Perpetual Peace and other Essays on Politics, History, and Morals. Translated by Ted Humphrey. Hackett.
Khurshudyan, Isabelle and Khudov, Kostiantyn. 2024. "As Mobilization Rules Kick In, Some Ukrainian Men Pay to Flee, Dodging Draft." *Reuters*, July 17. https://www.washingtonpost.com/world/2024/07/17/ukraine-mobilization-draft-dodgers-russia
Klay, Phil. 2022. *Uncertain Ground*. Penguin.
Luttwak, Edward. 1995. "Toward Post-Heroic Warfare." *Foreign Affairs* 74 (3): 109–122.
Luttwak, Edward. 2024. "Battle Grounds: The Reasons We Started Fighting, And Why We Won't Stop." *Times Literary Supplement*, July 19. https://www.the-tls.co.uk/politics-society/politics/why-war-richard-overy-book-review-edward-luttwak
"Manifesto the 93." https://web.tohoku.ac.jp/modern-japan/wp-content/uploads/Manifesto-of-the-93.pdf
Mann, Michael. 2012. *The Sources of Social Power: Volume 3, Global Empires and Revolution, 1890–1945*. Cambridge University Press.
McDonald, Dwight. 1957. *Memoirs of a Revolutionist*. Farrar Strauss.
McNeil, William. 1982. *The Pursuit of Power: Technology, Armed Force, and Society since A.D. 1000*. University of Chicago Press.
Méheut, Constant. 2024. "As Ukraine Expands Military Draft, Some Men Go Into Hiding." *New York Times*, June 21. https://www.nytimes.com/2024/06/21/world/europe/ukraine-war-draft-dodgers-conscription.htm'.
Nolan, Cathal. 2017. *The Allure of Battle: A History of How Wars Have Been Won and Lost*. Oxford University Press.
O'Brien, Tim. 1997. "How to Tell a True War Story." In *Postmodern American Fiction: A Norton Anthology*, edited by Paula Geyh, Fred G. Leebron and Andrew Levy. W. W. Norton.
Orend, Brian. 2000. "Jus Post Bellum." *Journal of Social Philosophy* 31 (1): 117–137.
Parker, Geoffrey, 2017. *Global Crisis: War, Climate Change and Catastrophe in the Seventeenth Century*. Yale University Press.
Rabb, Theodore. 1975. *The Struggle for Stability in Early Modern Europe*. Oxford University Press.
Robertson, William. 1759. *The History of Scotland*, 2nd ed. Legare Street Press.
Ruark, Jennifer. 2002. "Celebrated Scholars Release a Letter Supporting War on Terrorism." *Chronicle of Higher Education*, February 22. https://www.chronicle.com/article/celebrated-scholars-release-a-letter-supporting-war-on-terrorism/
Ryan, Cheyney. 2009. *The Chickenhawk Syndrome: War, Sacrifice, and Personal Responsibility*. Roman and Littlefield.
Ryan, Cheyney. 2023. *Pacifism as War Abolitionism*. Routledge.
Slotkin, Richard. 2024. *Regeneration Through Violence: The Mythology of the American Frontier, 1600–1860*. Open Road Media.
Tolstoy, Leo. 2006. *War and Peace*. Penguin.

Trevor-Roper, Hugh. 1959. "The General Crisis of the Seventeenth Century." *Past and Present*, 16 (1): 31–64.
Voltaire, M. 1859. "'Preliminary Discourse' to Fontenoy." In *The Henriade With the Battle of Fontenoy*, edited by W. Wight. Derby and Jackson.
Voltaire, M. 2002. *L' Histoire du regne de Louis XIV*. Cited in Phillip Bobbitt, *The Shield of Achilles: War, Peace, and the Course of History*. Knopf Doubleday.
Walzer, Michael. 1977. *Just and Unjust Wars*. Basic Books.
Walzer, Michael. 2002. "The Triumph of Just War Theory (and the Dangers of Success)." *Social Research* 69 (4): 925–944.
Watson Institute for International and Public Affairs Cost of War Project. n.d.. https://watson.brown.edu/costsofwar/figures#:~:text=Human%20Toll%3A%20905%2C000%20%2D%20940%2C000%20Direct,reverberating%20effects%20of%20these%20wars
"What We're Fighting for: A Letter from America, February 13, 2002," Avalon Project. https://avalon.law.yale.edu/sept11/letter_002.asp

Part II

Reflections on Ukraine and Afghanistan

6 Ending Wars and the Problem of Moral Hazard

Elad Uzan

1 Introduction

The conflict between Ukraine and Russia—which began in 2014 with the annexation of Crimea, escalated with the invasion of eastern Ukraine in 2022, and is ongoing as of this writing in July 2024—represents one of the most significant geopolitical crises of the 21st century. Russia's aim is to absorb within its borders territories globally recognized as part of Ukraine. Ukraine's struggle, then, is to defend its sovereignty, territorial integrity, and the rights of its citizens against unjust aggression.

Since the moment of Russia's escalation, Ukraine has faced significant moral and political pressure to compromise on its just goal of self-defense, on the theory that doing so might enable a lasting peace. Such pressure has only increased as the war has ground on, producing, by summer 2024, an apparent stalemate.[1] The moral question underlying Ukraine's decision—to give up or to continue fighting—is whether the state has a duty to end the war before fully achieving its just war aims. In other words, is Ukraine obligated to compromise?

The answer might seem an obvious "yes," because surely drawing war to a close has many good effects, above all sparing lives. However, compromise is a complicated matter. Often it is necessary to end a war, but it must be approached cautiously to avoid undermining the very principles that justified the use of force in the first place. This is particularly relevant in the context of resisting aggression or invasion, in which the primary justification for the use of force is self-defense in hopes of establishing a just and stable peace. Peace, in this context, is understood not merely as the absence of conflict but as a state in which justice prevails, allowing societies to flourish without fear of future aggression. An unjust peace, in contrast, potentially rewards the aggressor and sets the expectation that aggression will be met with retreat. Not only the principle but also the norm of justice is diluted. The result is potentially the cultivation of moral hazard.

DOI: 10.4324/9781003454144-9

Still, there are strong moral reasons to pursue a compromise peace, and so we should attempt to understand them and weigh them against the countervailing reasons above, which counsel against compromise. What are these moral reasons to pursue compromise peace? First, as noted above, any peace—just, unjust, or compromise—reduces the direct harm of the war, which may be great and may affect countless people, including civilians not liable to harm and the soldiers of the defending military, who, though combatants, have done nothing to forfeit their right not to be harmed.[2] Furthermore, war causes political emergencies, which may result in harm to civil liberties and erode the accountability of political and military leaders. These outcomes are obviously best avoided, which is a goal served by peace. Finally, a compromise peace may be the best available method to achieve at least some of a war's just goals. In the case of Ukraine, a weaker power defending itself against a much stronger one, a compromise peace might enable the retention of sovereignty and at least partial territorial integrity against the real possibility that continued war would lead to the annihilation of the state. Given the power imbalance between Russia and Ukraine, then compromise may be the best possible result for Ukraine.

The key question, then, is whether the humanitarian benefits of ending the war outweigh the injustice and the long-term consequences of compromising on justice, such as the consequence of emboldening aggressors. Should Ukraine compromise on its just goals, or would the downsides of doing so outweigh the benefits? Put more strongly, is Ukraine morally obligated to compromise or to keep going?

According to traditional just war theory, just combatants are never obligated to compromise: as the predicates of the war are just, and the means of fighting it necessary and proportionate, a defender may continue fighting until victory is achieved.[3] However, revisionist just war theorists argue that a just war should be ended short of victory when this is the lesser evil—when conceding to unjust aggression is less harmful, all things considered, than continuing to defend against it unto the aggressor's defeat.[4]

Although the second position has its adherents, it is under-theorized—little attention has been paid to what it would mean for compromise to be the lesser evil. This chapter fills in the gap, exploring the ethical considerations that might obligate just defenders to end conflicts through compromise. Specifically, the chapter examines the moral hazard associated with prematurely ending a just war, which increases along with the scale of concessions to the aggressor. In the case of Russia, concessions would involve securing wrongful gains, potentially emboldening the Russian state to pursue future acts of aggression and encouraging others to do the same.

The chapter argues that any compromise—whether understood as obligatory or optional—must be carefully structured to avoid rewarding aggression and should ensure that the benefits of peace outweigh the moral costs, thus maintaining justice. In particular, it is argued that compromise is morally permissible to the extent that it has the real potential to ensure long-term stability. Broadly, the chapter offers a framework for determining the circumstances under which a state, in particular Ukraine, might seek compromise peace and how it can do so without undermining moral principles. This framework incorporates parameters for balancing the extent of concessions and the likelihood of achieving lasting peace. I also argue that the degree of international support for any particular instance of compromise is morally relevant. While my focus is on Ukraine, my aim is to develop a broadly applicable framework for assessing the complex ethical and strategic considerations in ending wars through compromise.

2 Compromise and Moral Theory

The concept of compromise is often taken for granted but in fact is full of subtlety. In particular, it must be carefully differentiated from related ideas like consensus and concession.

Consensus and compromise both aim to resolve disagreements but differ in fundamental ways. According to Bellamy and Hollis, consensus is reached when all parties find their final agreement to be as good as or better than their initial positions, implying the achievement of common ground.[5] In contrast, compromise involves all parties retaining their original positions and accepting an outcome worse than they had hoped for. Compromise does not resolve the initial disagreement and is morally inferior to consensus because it requires that all parties give up some demands and that at least some morally just demands go unmet.[6]

While compromise is not necessarily a path to consensus, it can be an essential step in conflict resolution, particularly when consensus is unachievable. Compromise can thus be seen as a pragmatic tool to manage disagreements and mitigate conflicts when a fully just and mutually satisfactory agreement cannot be reached. While compromise does not achieve the ideal of consensus, it provides a practical means to achieve stability and prevent further conflict.

As for concessions, all compromises involve concessions, but compromise is not reducible to concessions. This is because compromise demands a particular *kind* of concession: namely, a concession that must be mutual. This is distinct from a one-sided concession, where only one party makes sacrifices. In the case of war, mutual concession has the potential to result in lasting peace. One-sided concessions, in contrast, are more likely to result in fragile peace by encouraging further aggression and fostering resentment on the part of the conceding party, which gives up its moral rights. For example, the Treaty of Westphalia, a compromise, achieved lasting peace, while the Munich Agreement, a one-sided concession, provoked further conflict.[7]

Compromise can be categorized as either nonmoral or moral, depending on what the parties relinquish in order to resolve their disputes. Nonmoral compromise involves sacrificing interests, typically material ones, without violating moral convictions. For example, coalition governments often require parties to sacrifice some legislative goals without endorsing policies they find morally objectionable, thus allowing them to maintain their convictions. Moral compromise is more complex and may require parties to perform acts they consider morally wrong. Such compromises are unlikely to be morally justifiable unless highly valuable compensation is offered or unless no other options exist.[8]

Compromises might also be pragmatic or principled. Here, compromises are differentiated by their motivations rather than by the substance of the concession.[9] Pragmatic compromise arises when continuing the conflict is no longer in the parties' interests so that their desire to end the conflict outweighs their reasons to continue it. There may be pragmatic reasons to accept a moral compromise: compromises to end just wars often fall into this category, in which the unjustly attacked party gives up its morally just goals due to the high military, economic, or diplomatic costs of war. However, it seems, pretheoretically, that there might also be principled moral compromises. In the case of such a compromise, the just goal could be achieved, but in light of moral considerations such as minimizing harm to civilians, the just side accepts the moral cost of not achieving its goal. This kind of compromise acknowledges the moral weight of reducing suffering, even if it means not fully realizing a just objective. Thus, principled compromises are motivated by ethical values and the desire to uphold humanitarian principles, rather than mere strategic interests.

Scholars from various disciplines, including political philosophy, political science, and international relations, debate whether moral compromises—that is, the acceptance of less than fully just outcomes—can ever be principled or whether they are always pragmatic. Some political philosophers, such as Simon Căbulea May, argue that moral compromises are justified only on pragmatic grounds—that is, they are justified only by the parties' interests.[10] Others, like political theorist Daniel Weinstock, contend that moral compromises can also be principled, reflecting values such as concern for others, mutual understanding, and respect for diverse ethical points of view.[11]

I accept, as it is pretheoretically reasonable, that principled moral compromises exist. The stakes here revolve around the justification and legitimacy of moral compromises in war, which might aim to minimize loss of life and other harms. If moral compromises are only pragmatic, they may be viewed as necessary evils. However, if they can be principled, they might be seen as morally commendable actions that align with deeper ethical commitments, even in the face of conflict.

The rest of this chapter focuses on principled moral compromises to end war. These are moral compromises because they violate the moral principle that wrongful acts should not be rewarded. They are principled compromises because they seek to comply with the moral principle of minimizing human suffering. I choose to address principled moral compromises because they, specifically, speak to the condition of an unjustly attacked party that is morally required to end war short of victory—that is, principled moral compromises are not only fraught but also are not contemplated by the just war tradition and so benefit from explication. Then too, Ukraine finds itself in the position of considering a principled moral compromise.

Below I detail in turn the potential wrongs of principled moral compromise, possible justifications for it, and whether it is justified in order to conclude a defensive war. We will see that it can indeed be justified, assuming certain stringent conditions are met.

3 Moral Hazard, Premature Peace, and Compromise

From the standpoint of justice, a compromise peace is always premature in the sense that the just goal is left unachieved. Premature peace can have serious consequences. In particular, moral hazard arises when the premature cessation of hostilities allows an aggressor to secure wrongful gains.[12]

Moral hazard involves rewarding the aggressor's unjust actions, which undermines the principles of justice and international law. Moral hazard also weakens deterrence, which relies on the idea that unjust actions will be met with significant consequences. If an aggressor is allowed to gain from their aggression, the deterrent effect is nullified. This can lead to a more unstable international environment in which states are more willing to engage in aggressive actions, knowing that the risk of significant retaliation or punishment is reduced.

Objections to moral hazard can thus be framed in both consequentialist and deontological terms. Act-consequentialists would argue that rewarding present aggression increases the likelihood of future aggression and may lead to more military conflicts. Rule-consequentialists would suggest that accepting unjust moral compromises as a general rule would undermine the permissibility of all just wars. Deontologists would oppose moral hazard as unjust in itself, as it violates the principle that no one should benefit from wrongdoing and also involves trading goods such as territory or peace that the aggressive party does not have the right to receive.

Even if one is an act-consequentialist and disregards rule-consequentialist or deontological objections to moral compromises, many moral compromises in war are unjustified. Consider again the Munich Agreement of 1938.

In an effort to avoid war, Britain and France allowed Nazi Germany to annex the Sudetenland, a region of Czechoslovakia with a significant ethnic German population. This concession was made under the policy of appeasement, with the hope that it would satisfy Hitler's expansionist ambitions and secure peace in Europe. However, the opposite occurred. The Munich Agreement emboldened Hitler, reinforcing his belief that the Allies would not militarily oppose his further territorial ambitions. This miscalculation led to the invasion of Poland in 1939 and the onset of the Second World War.[13] While the agreement might have seemed justified at the time based on the existing conditions and the desire to prevent war, its eventual outcomes highlighted the inherent risks and moral hazards of such compromises.

The Munich Agreement was not a principled moral compromise but rather a pragmatic one driven by the immediate desire to avoid conflict. It failed to consider the broader ethical implications and long-term consequences of rewarding aggression. The miscalculation lay in believing that conceding to Hitler's demands would lead to lasting peace, when in fact it only strengthened his resolve and paved the way for further aggression. This example illustrates the danger of pragmatic moral compromises which lack a solid ethical foundation and fail to address the underlying injustices.

Another unjustified moral compromise was the Treaty of Brest-Litovsk, signed between Soviet Russia and the Central Powers during the First World War.[14] The treaty marked Russia's exit from the war but at the cost of significant territorial concessions to Germany, Austria-Hungary, and the Ottoman Empire. While the treaty provided a temporary peace that enabled the consolidation of the Bolshevik government, the harsh terms of the treaty contributed to internal unrest and weakened the Soviet state. Additionally, the treaty did not bring lasting peace to Europe. Instead, it shifted the focus of German military efforts to the Western Front, prolonging the overall conflict. This case illustrates how premature peace, achieved through significant concessions, can undermine the stability and security of the conceding nation without resolving the broader conflict.

On the other hand, despite the existence of moral hazard, a compromise can be a lesser evil as compared to continued conflict. This may hold true even for rule-consequentialists or deontologists, in particular when the moral costs of a compromise peace are outweighed by the benefits. History provides many examples in which, although one party was the aggressor and war was necessary to achieve the just goal of defeating aggression, the war itself seems retrospectively not worth the cost, as it also did to many contemporaries. The paradigmatic example is the First World War, which, in hindsight, appears to have been too catastrophic to justify its goals, even if the post-war aims—such as the establishment of national self-determination for states within the Austro-Hungarian Empire and beyond—were justifiable in themselves. The devastation and loss of life during the war ultimately overshadowed the just goals that were intended to be achieved, illustrating how compromise, even with its moral hazards, might sometimes be the more ethical choice.

Legends and myths often illustrate the perils of an unreasonable unwillingness to compromise. The story of Helen and the Trojan War, for instance, can be seen as a narrative about the catastrophic consequences of a failed compromise. While, in the Homeric context, Helen's abduction by Paris represents a wrong done to her husband Menelaus and to the divine order—a wrong that justifies defensive war—the war itself escalates into a prolonged conflict driven by pride, honor, and fate. The *Iliad* thematizes the potential for, and ultimate failure of, compromise. This narrative underscores a broader theme present in many myths and stories about war: the recognition of the dangers inherent in both the lack of compromise and the wrong kind of compromise as forms of hubris.

Another, lesser-known, example comes from the annals of Rajasthan.[15] In this case, we see how moral compromise might be justified, even though it rewards aggressors. The narrative follows General Alauddin Khalji as he invades the city of Chittoor. The general is so smitten by the beauty of Padmini, queen of Chittoor, that he offers to spare the city if she is surrendered to him. When this proposal is refused, he scales down his demands first to merely seeing Padmini and finally to seeing only her reflection in a mirror. All these demands are refused; the residents of Chittoor chose mass suicide in a hopeless battle over submission. Here, moral compromise seems a reasonable alternative to the devastation of war.

The story is legendary, but it illustrates something that seems intuitively right: that moral compromise, even one that courts a degree of moral hazard, can be the morally best option when it is the lesser evil. Whether in fact compromise is the morally best option depends on whether the significant moral costs incurred—such as rewarding aggression, failing to achieve the just goal, undermining deterrence, and destabilizing the international order—are outweighed by the benefits of partially achieving the just goal, which in the case of war will always include preventing loss of life. As a first approximation, we can say that principled moral compromise in war is justified only when the cost of continuing the war is high (as in the First World War) or the cost of the moral compromise is low (as in the case of Queen Padmini).

What then of Russia's war against Ukraine? Is there a conceivable compromise that minimizes bad effects and maximizes good effects? Such a compromise peace would be morally acceptable, but it may not be achievable. In the rest of this chapter, I explore how we might identify the compromise that incurs minimal costs and maximizes benefits. I proceed in two stages. First, I examine in greater detail the specific costs and benefits associated with a compromise peace in the Ukraine-Russia War—for instance, the potential consequences of rewarding Russia for its aggression on the one hand, and, on the other, the potential for saving lives by reaching a compromise. Second, I explore strategies to minimize costs and maximize benefits. With these strategies applied, I aim to determine the morally best compromise peace: the one that yields the greatest benefits while incurring the lowest possible costs.

4 Evaluating Ukraine's Path to Compromise

The immediate cessation of hostilities in Ukraine is a humanitarian imperative, aimed at saving lives and preventing further harm. However, we ought to be concerned not only with reducing harm right now but also with lasting peace, so it is important that any concessions made in the name of saving lives be compatible with long-term stability. This is not always the case. Clearly, the fastest way to stop bloodshed right now is to give up the defense and accede to Russia's demands. However, this course of action maximizes moral hazard, rewarding aggression and thereby weakening deterrence. The result is likely to be a brief respite followed by a later resumption of Russian aggression. A negotiated settlement that achieves some of the war's just goals might actually provide a better path to long-term peace.

Let us step back for a moment and consider the realities of the situation, which determine as well the moral costs and benefits that will attend any compromise. The war in Ukraine has caused the deaths of thousands of civilians and military personnel. For instance, the city of Mariupol has faced relentless bombardment, resulting in catastrophic loss of life and severe injuries among those who escaped death.[16] By ending the war sooner, Ukraine could halt the violence and prevent further loss of life, injury, and long-term disability. In short, stopping the fighting would significantly reduce the war's human toll in the immediate term.

There is also hope that ending the war will reduce long-term suffering. Millions of Ukrainians have been displaced, forced to flee their homes and live in precarious conditions either within Ukraine or as refugees. Ending the war could bring much-needed relief to these individuals by allowing them to return home and resume a semblance of normal life. The ongoing conflict has also disrupted access to essential services such as healthcare, education, transportation, electricity, and clean water. Hospitals have been destroyed or repurposed for military use, schools have been closed, and basic infrastructure has been heavily damaged. In the Donbas and elsewhere, residents have faced chronic shortages of food, water, and medical supplies.[17] Were the war to end, these services could be restored, and with them the quality of life that all Ukrainians have a right to enjoy.

Finally, by prioritizing peace even at the expense of its moral rights, Ukraine can begin the extensive work of reconstruction. International aid and investment, often contingent on a stable and peaceful environment, can be mobilized to support these efforts. For instance, the European Union and other international bodies have expressed a willingness to provide substantial financial aid for Ukraine's reconstruction.[18] These resources could be deployed to rebuild homes, schools, hospitals, and other critical infrastructure and to repatriate exiles.

Relatedly, a compromise end to the war, even if it involves some concessions, would allow Ukraine to redirect its resources from military expenditure to development. This would facilitate economic recovery and improve living conditions. For example, rebuilding heavily damaged cities would not only provide homes for displaced residents but also would stimulate local economies by encouraging hiring in construction and related industries.

However, as great as the benefits of a compromise peace could be, the moral costs of a compromise peace could also be very high. If Ukraine were to agree to peace terms involving significant territorial or sovereignty concessions to Russia, then Russia's aggression would effectively be validated. This sets a dangerous precedent that might encourage not only Russia but also other states to pursue their aims through similar unjust means, undermining international law and norms.

As of June 2024, Ukraine's war aims are to regain full sovereignty over its territories, restoring pre-2014 borders by reclaiming Crimea, Donetsk, Luhansk, Kherson, and Zaporizhzhia. These objectives have been articulated by various Ukrainian officials. For instance, President Volodymyr Zelensky has repeatedly emphasized Ukraine's commitment to regaining control over these regions, underscoring the nation's determination to restore its pre-2014 borders.[19] If Ukraine were to concede to Russia's demands—such as by conceding full sovereignty over the annexed territories of Crimea, Donetsk, Luhansk, Kherson, and Zaporizhzhia and by withdrawing from efforts to join the EU and NATO—it would not only embolden Russia to pursue further aggressive policies but also send a message to other states that similar tactics might be successful. Indeed, Ukraine would signal that aggressive territorial expansion can be retroactively legitimized. For years now, Ukraine has officially insisted that it has been wronged. To back down is to accept otherwise.

The potential consequences are difficult to overstate. Rewarding Russian aggression in Ukraine could encourage further Russian activity in separatist regions of Georgia, which Moscow has backed since the early 2000s. The perception of weakened international resolve against territorial aggression could also embolden China to act on its ambitions in Taiwan. More generally, as states come to feel less secure, the global order will become increasingly fragmented and unstable.

A compromise peace might also wrongly compel the victim—Ukraine—to play an active role in its own diminishment. Furthermore, the humiliation and moral costs involved in willingly surrendering to an aggressor cannot be overlooked. It is one thing to be coerced, quite another to consent to coercion, even under duress. Doing so registers to the victim as cooptation. This dynamic is demoralizing, with long-term detrimental effects on the victim's national morale and international standing.

Additionally, compromise can undermine the principles of justice that Ukraine is justly fighting for. Ukraine rightly seeks not only territorial integrity but also vindication of its right to self-determination, sovereignty, and security from aggression. Conceding to Russia, an unjust aggressor, is a betrayal of these rights and of the principle of justice Ukraine aims to uphold.

What is more, if Ukraine were to agree to a peace deal that grants amnesty to Russian officials and separatist leaders responsible for war crimes, this would undermine all efforts to hold perpetrators accountable. The conflict has seen numerous reports of human rights violations, including war crimes, such as torture, extrajudicial killings, and bombings of civilian areas.[20] Granting immunity to those responsible as part of a peace agreement would not only deny justice to the victims but also would weaken the international legal framework designed to prosecute and thereby deter such crimes. This could lead to a culture of impunity.

Finally, a compromise peace could weaken the legitimacy of the Ukrainian government in the eyes of its citizens. Many Ukrainians see the conflict as a fight for national sovereignty and justice, and a peace deal that sacrifices these principles could lead to domestic unrest and a loss of public trust in the state. This internal instability could further weaken Ukraine's ability to resist future aggression and undermine its efforts to build a stable, democratic society.

Thus, while the pragmatic approach to ending conflict might sometimes necessitate compromise, it is crucial to weigh these compromises against the potential moral hazards and long-term repercussions. The challenge lies in balancing the immediate benefits of peace against the broader principles of justice and the potential for encouraging future aggression.

The lesson for Ukraine is clear: any peace agreement must be carefully crafted to avoid numerous pitfalls, not just minimizing the injustice of the compromise peace itself but also ensuring that the peace is truly peaceful: a long-term, stable condition of nonaggression, not merely a postponement of the conflict and inducement to further war.

We have seen that, in the abstract and in the particular case of Ukraine, compromise is complicated. "Peace now!" is a fine and agreeable slogan, but the concessions made in achieving it are hugely consequential, not least because they can themselves undermine peace. Given this, we would be well served to think more carefully. If there is a duty to reach a compromise peace in order to minimize suffering, the peace in question cannot be just any peace. It must be a sustainable one. I turn next to the ethical framework that can help us assess whether a given proposed compromise peace is this sort of peace.

5 Evaluating Compromise Peace and Concessions

A compromise peace exists if, when moral costs are minimized and moral gains maximized, the moral gains are worth the costs. This is the only sort of compromise that a defender can be obligated to pursue. In this section, I define crucial factors that affect the stringency of the duty to reach a compromise peace. I then evaluate how these factors affect the duty of Ukraine to end the war through compromise. I define these factors as follows:

- **Extent of Concessions:** Concessions may include the compromise of territorial integrity, political autonomy, and military capabilities; relinquishing rights to compensation for the harm caused by war; and forgoing accountability for those responsible for unjust war and unjust actions in war. Where concessions are too few, aggressors will not likely agree to peace. Where they are too great, they make for a more unjust peace and incentivize aggression by rewarding unjust actions.
- **Likelihood of Lasting Peace:** This refers to the probability that the peace agreement will lead to a stable and enduring resolution of the conflict. A morally acceptable compromise is structured in a way that addresses the root causes of the war and includes mechanisms to enforce compliance by all parties. Most likely, a morally acceptable compromise will therefore address sources of grievances and will include security arrangements to prevent the outbreak of further war, as well as economic incentives that promote lasting peace. Where these elements are lacking, the likelihood of lasting peace is diminished, increasing the injustice of compromise.
- **Degree of International Support:** Strong international support can provide legitimacy to a compromise peace agreement, ensuring that both parties adhere to its terms. It may also include explicit or implicit assurances of security for the parties, thus deterring future aggression. International support influences the other two factors: it can help to minimize the extent of concessions (reducing injustice but also thereby making the proposed peace less palatable to the aggressor) while maximizing the likelihood of lasting peace.

Let us analyze how these factors interact to define Ukraine's duty to reach a compromise peace with Russia and end the war. This duty will be most compelling where the compromise involves the least cost—that is, where Ukraine gives up the least of its just goals. For instance, relinquishing demands for international trials of Russian war leaders such as President Vladimir Putin would be a relatively small concession. Arguably, Ukraine must be willing to make this concession if doing so would assure lasting peace. A higher-cost compromise would see Ukraine ceding territory and giving up its efforts to obtain NATO and EU membership, both of which provide valuable guarantees of security and autonomy.

As of this writing, protection from prosecution seems unlikely to move Russian leaders, who believe they are on a path to military victory, and, in any case, they at least act as though they are immune from international tribunals. Ukraine might then consider further concessions, seeking again to ensure they are as minimal as possible. For example, Ukraine might consider allowing limited autonomy for the Donetsk and Luhansk regions, provided that this autonomy does not compromise its overall sovereignty or invite further Russian interference. This concession could help deescalate the conflict, reducing the immediate loss of life and displacement of civilians, without granting Russia a substantial strategic advantage. However, larger concessions, such as ceding Crimea or agreeing to a permanent Russian military presence in eastern Ukraine, could severely undermine Ukraine's sovereignty and would signal to other aggressors that territorial expansion through force yields rewards, leading to further instability in the region and beyond. As ever, the extent of concessions must be calibrated to balance immediate humanitarian benefits against long-term risks to justice and the global order.

Ukraine's willingness to compromise should depend on the quality of international backing it receives. Ultimately, the highest justification for compromise peace comes from the durability of the resulting peace, so security guarantees are crucial. Given this, Ukraine should be willing to concede more—likely bringing about peace more quickly—if pledges of support are both credible and robust. For instance, the provision by outside powers of peacekeeping forces and substantial economic aid packages, alongside ongoing maintenance of diplomatic pressure and sanctions against Russia, would blunt the negative effects of concessions by helping to enforce Russian compliance with the peace agreement while better assuring that Ukraine can deter future aggression. Admission to the EU and NATO would also provide substantial assurance. In essence, Ukraine could be justified in ceding territory if it can be reasonably assured that it will not be forced to do so again.

That said, the more international backing Ukraine receives, the less willing Russia may be to compromise. Analysts debate whether Russia's avowed grievances are pretextual, but one way or another, Vladimir Putin has argued unfailingly that Ukraine is a legitimate target because it is a stalking horse for the "collective West." International backing, especially if it is limited to the support of Western powers, might be seen to confirm this allegation. President Putin's political standing at home will be diminished if the war ends with Ukraine cosseted by the very states he claims are committed to Russia's downfall. International support, therefore, must be arranged carefully, with the interests of Russian leadership in mind.

Having said that, international involvement can also increase Russia's willingness to compromise, making compromise less costly for Ukraine. For example, Russia may agree to renounce territorial gains in exchange for immunity to Russian leaders backed by international guarantees. To avoid the arrangement becoming a form of blackmail, where Russia selectively decides which ill-gotten gains to keep, international players must establish clear and enforceable conditions. These could include international oversight and phased lifting of sanctions tied to specific actions by Russia, ensuring compliance and accountability. Additionally, economic and political pressures from international actors, such as sanctions and diplomatic isolation, can further incentivize Russia to adhere to the terms of the compromise.

To illustrate, and in order to explore the range of possible compromises that could theoretically lead to a stable and lasting peace, suppose that China—Russia's major protector—joins the sanctions camp, so that economic pressure might finally be robust enough to cause real pain within Russia. In such a situation, Ukraine could offer a nominal concession—like allowing formal Russian representation in Crimea—enabling Russia to save face in return for its withdrawal in hopes of escaping sanctions. Additionally, Ukraine could afford to offer a greater degree of compromise without being perceived as weak. Ukraine might even offer autonomy for the Russian population in Crimea or other regions while demanding not just a stable peace but a resolution to the historical conflict with Russia. Both of these options seem morally acceptable as compromises, showing how international guarantees can facilitate a more favorable and sustainable peace agreement. Such support increases the likelihood that, despite the high costs of moral compromise, a principled moral compromise is possible in the Ukraine-Russia war.

All of the above considerations speak to the central matter: how likely a compromise peace is to endure. If there is a high probability that a negotiated settlement will result in lasting peace, the moral argument for compromise strengthens. For example, if diplomatic efforts indicate that Russia is genuinely committed to adhering to a peace agreement—for instance, if Russian leaders were to publicly welcome robust international monitoring and enforcement mechanisms—then a compromise would be more easily justified. However, if significant doubts exist regarding Russia's commitment to a peace agreement, the risks of moral hazard may outweigh the potential benefits of a compromise. In other words, Russia's willingness to negotiate is inversely related to the costs of compromise for Ukraine. Where costs are high, the moral justification for compromise diminishes, and with it the stringency of a possible moral obligation to compromise.

6 Mitigating Moral Hazard: Compensation Duties

One way to minimize the moral hazards of a compromise peace is for a just defender to be compensated by other parties, ensuring that it is not worse off overall despite allowing the aggressor unjust gains. True, the aggressor will be rewarded, which would tend to increase moral hazard. However, if the defender winds up strengthened vis-à-vis its enemy, then the aggressor is deterred from future attacks. This section examines how such a compensation scheme can thus make moral compromises feasible for defenders.

Of all the war aims claimed as just, compensation may be the most controversial.[21] There is little disagreement that liberating territory from invasion is a just goal; however, there is much disagreement about whether a just peace requires compensation paid by the aggressor. As a practical matter, though, compensation might enable lasting peace by improving a just belligerent's capacity to defend itself. And this could be achieved through foreign intervention. Of course, there are important differences between intervention by allies and intervention by an international body. Allied intervention typically involves support from countries with a direct interest in the conflict, often providing military aid, economic assistance, and diplomatic backing to the defender. Such support can bolster the defender's capacity to protect itself and deter future aggression. In contrast, intervention by an international body, such as the United Nations, aims to provide neutral and multilateral support. This form of intervention can include peacekeeping missions, economic sanctions against the aggressor, and humanitarian aid to affected populations. While both types of intervention can be crucial, they differ in their motivations and methods of support.

Let us set aside the controversy and stipulate that defenders are owed compensation by aggressors as part of a just peace. Even so, the value of long-term peace may prompt a defender to waive some or all of the compensation it is due, the better to secure the aggressor's willingness to compromise. This concession is morally easier to justify if the defender accepts compensation from alternative sources in return. For instance, the defender might accept some of the aggressor's unjust gains but secure additional advantages, such as gaining territory elsewhere through land exchange from a third party. The defender could also be compensated for their unjust losses through enhanced diplomatic status and foreign support for their armed forces. Though such outcomes are not entirely just, they are fairer than allowing the aggressor to keep ill-gotten gains without any compensation to the defender, and they could support the defender's capacity to protect itself, mitigating moral hazard.

Assuming Russia has an obligation to compensate Ukraine for damages caused by war, a potential compromise could involve Ukraine relinquishing its demands for direct compensation from Russia in exchange for equivalent economic support from the international community. This compromise could take various forms. For example, third parties could assist in strengthening Ukraine's armed forces, which could help offset any potential harm to deterrence capabilities that might arise from Ukraine forfeiting its compensation claims.

While direct historical parallels are challenging to draw, we can learn from instances in which international efforts facilitated recovery and stability. Following the First World War, the United States extended limited economic support to allies such as France and Britain, although the focus was on debt repayment rather than reconstruction. The absence of substantial aid in lieu of reparations contributed to economic hardship and political instability in Europe. In contrast, after the Second World War, the United States implemented the Marshall Plan, providing substantial aid to Western European countries, including former allies and adversaries, to rebuild their economies and stabilize the region. This plan, though primarily geopolitical in its origins, demonstrated how international support can play a crucial role in fostering long-term peace and recovery.[22] Similarly, in the context of Ukraine, while the situation involves defending sovereignty against aggression rather than a post-war recovery of allies, substantial international aid could serve as a mechanism to support reconstruction and stability, mitigating the need for direct compensation from Russia while addressing the humanitarian and economic needs of Ukraine.

However, if the international community shoulders the burden of compensation in lieu of Russia—particularly if Russia refuses to compensate, as is likely—this introduces a layer of moral complexity. It could be seen as requiring a moral compromise on the part of the international community, potentially leading to an unjust distribution of resources and creating a new moral hazard. In particular, Russia would be absolved of its responsibilities, potentially encouraging it and other aggressors to act with impunity, knowing that the international community might step in to cover the costs of their actions. Therefore, while this compromise might offer a pragmatic solution, it also necessitates careful consideration of the broader ethical implications and the potential for fostering further injustices.

7 Conclusion

To some observers, it is obvious that Ukraine should make significant concessions to Russia in order to end the bloodshed the latter initiated.

The logic underlying this argument is that Ukraine cannot win the war and so should cut its losses. This view holds intuitive appeal; however, it is unsound. Compromise, in fact, presents complex ethical considerations and cannot be invoked as a straightforward imperative wherever weaker states find themselves in conflict with stronger ones. Were this the case, the principle of self-defense itself would be vitiated. To make this claim is not to counsel in favor of futile war-making but simply to point out that there is much more at stake in any given compromise than harms in the here and now. Justice demands that victims possess rights.

Particularly vexing are the moral hazards involved in conceding to an aggressor. Compromise involves concessions, and concessions risk emboldening future violations of international law and norms and potentially encouraging further aggression. Yet, at the same time, these moral hazards are not overriding. They are a moral evil, but they must be weighed against the moral good of ending wars.

In this chapter, I have not sought to show definitively whether Ukraine should compromise in order to end the war with Russia. I have instead suggested that, given the right terms, doing so is justified and perhaps even obligatory—but only given the right terms. I therefore contest the traditional assumption that defenders are always justified in pursuing the full realization of their war goals while also recognizing that Ukraine faces no clear obligation.

Instead, I have tried to provide moral clarity as to the circumstances under which a compromise peace can be morally acceptable, even as it courts moral hazard and results in injustice to victims of aggression. To do so, I have proposed a framework for evaluating possible plans for compromise peace. Any plan should be assessed in terms of the extent of concessions, the likelihood of achieving lasting peace, and the quantity and quality of attending international support. These parameters provide a structured approach to analyzing the ethical considerations involved in ending wars. In reference to Ukraine, what I suggest is that a compromise peace can be just, but only if Ukraine's concessions do not significantly weaken its sovereignty and security, and only if compensation and international backing are sufficient to offset the moral costs of compromise while promoting sustainable conflict resolution.

Broadly, my framework suggests that there are conditions under which compromise can be justified, conditions especially likely to arise when the immediate humanitarian benefits of ending a conflict outweigh the long-term risks caused by moral hazard. However, the framework also recognizes that compromises cannot be justified when they severely undermine justice, sovereignty, or international norms. These are not abstract losses: they are losses that are likely to provoke further suffering.

For Ukraine, balancing pragmatic needs with principled considerations means securing robust global support and adequate compensation in light of concessions to Russia. A lasting peace that upholds moral principles and contributes to global stability is, in theory, possible. However, the associated burdens cannot be Ukraine's to bear alone. The prime movers of a just compromise will be Russia and third parties in a position to counter the costs and enhance the benefits of compromise.

Notes

1 Paton Walsh (2024); Ward et al. (2023).
2 It is widely accepted that merely posing a threat or participating in armed forces does not suffice for losing fundamental rights, as combatants fighting for a just cause, such as defending against genocidal attacks, should not be considered to have forfeited their rights. For assorted views, see McMahan (1994), 193–221; Rodin (20020; McPherson (2004); Fabre (2009); Fabre (2012).
3 The most important advocate of this view is Walzer (1977).
4 See Fabre (2015); Rodin (2015); Moellendorf (2015).
5 Bellamy and Hollis (1998). While this distinction originates from political science, its application in the ethics of war remains relevant: achieving a just peace requires careful consideration of the nature and implications of compromise.
6 Weinstock (2013).
7 Bellamy (1999).
8 Lepora and Goodin (2013).
9 Jones and O'Flynn (2012), 121.
10 Căbulea May (2013).
11 Weinstock (2013), 553. For a critical view on principled compromise, see Fumurescu (2003).
12 I use the term "moral hazard" not in its strict economic sense, but in Rodin's "extended sense." For Rodin, moral hazard signifies a situation in which an agent is rewarded for engaging in cost-producing or immoral behavior, thereby creating an incentive for similar actions by that agent or others in the future. See Rodin (2015), 693.
13 For a comprehensive study of the events surrounding the Munich Agreement of 1938, see Goldstein and Lukes (1999).
14 For a historical analysis of the Treaty of Brest-Litovsk, see Chernev (2017).
15 The story appears in James Tod's *Annals and Antiquities of Rajasthan*, first published between 1829 and 1832. This work remains a seminal reference on the history and culture of Rajasthan and the early colonial encounter in India. For further reading, see Tod (2023).
16 See a report by the Council on Foreign Relations, "War in Ukraine," and references there.
17 See the report by the UN Meetings Coverage Security Council (2024).
18 See the report by the European Parliament January (2024).
19 This commitment is detailed in the NATO report from July 9, 2024.
20 See the report by Human Rights Watch (2022).
21 Some argue that there are cases in which citizens can have duties to compensate the victims of their state's wrongdoing (see, for instance, Pasternak, 2011; Stilz, 2011). Saba Bazargan has developed a sophisticated account of compensatory duties,

according to which wrongs a state has committed in the recent past can affect proportionality calculations in the pursuit of just military goals against aggressors (see Bazargan, 2014). Seth Lazar argues that compensation can lead to overwhelming financial burdens for both just and unjust belligerents (see Lazar, 2012).

22 For a discussion, see Hogan (1987).

References

Bazargan, Saba. 2014. "Defensive Wars and the Reprisal Dilemma." *Australasian Journal of Philosophy* 93(3): 583–601.

Bellamy, Richard. 1999. *Liberalism and Pluralism: Towards a Politics of Compromise*. New York: Routledge.

Bellamy, Richard, and Martin Hollis. 1998. "Compromise, Consensus and Neutrality." *Critical Review of International Social and Political Philosophy* 1: 54–78.

Căbulea May, Simon. 2013. "Compromise." In *The International Encyclopedia of Ethics*, edited by Hugh LaFollette, 959–968. Chichester: Wiley-Blackwell.

Chernev, Borislav. 2017. *Twilight of Empire: The Brest-Litovsk Conference and the Remaking of East-Central Europe, 1917–1918*. Toronto: University of Toronto Press.

Council on Foreign Relations. "War in Ukraine." Accessed July 12, 2024. https://www.cfr.org/global-conflict-tracker/conflict/conflict-ukraine

European Parliament. 2024. "Multilateral Financial Assistance to Ukraine - January 2024." Accessed July 12, 2024. https://www.europarl.europa.eu/RegData/etudes/IDAN/2023/733763/IPOL_IDA(2023)733763_EN.pdf

Fabre, Cécile. 2009. "Guns, Food, and Liability to Attack in War." *Ethics*, 36–63.

Fabre, Cécile. 2012. *Cosmopolitan War*. Oxford: Oxford University Press.

Fabre, Cécile. 2015. "War Exit." *Ethics* 125 (2015): 631–652.

Fumurescu, Alin. 2003. *Compromise: A Political and Philosophical History*. New York: Cambridge University Press.

Goldstein, Erik, and Igor Lukes, eds. 1999. *The Munich Crisis, 1938: Prelude to World War II*. London: Routledge.

Hogan, Michael. 1987. *The Marshall Plan: America, Britain, and the Reconstruction of Western Europe, 1947–1952*. Cambridge: Cambridge University Press.

Human Rights Watch. 2022. "Ukraine: Russian Forces' Trail of Death in Bucha." Accessed July 12, 2024. https://www.hrw.org/news/2022/04/21/ukraine-russian-forces-trail-death-bucha

Jones, Peter, and Ian O'Flynn. 2012. "Can a Compromise Be Fair?." *Politics, Philosophy & Economics* 12(2): 115–135.

Lazar, Seth. 2012. "Skepticism about Jus Post Bellum." In *Morality, Jus Post Bellum, and International Law*, edited by Larry May and Andrew Forcehimes, 204–222. Cambridge: Cambridge University Press.

Lepora, Chiara, and Robert Goodin. 2013. *On Complicity and Compromise*. Oxford: Oxford University Press.

McMahan, Jeff. 1994. "Innocence, Self-defense and Killing in War." *Journal of Political Philosophy* 2: 193–221.

McPherson, Lionel K. 2004. "Innocence and Responsibility in War." *Canadian Journal of Philosophy* 34: 485–506.

Moellendorf, Darrel. 2015. "Two Doctrines of Jus Ex Bello." *Ethics* 125: 653–673.

NATO. 2024. "Relations with Ukraine." Accessed July 12, 2024. https://www.nato.int/cps/en/natohq/topics_37750.htm

Pasternak, Avia. 2011. "Sharing the Costs of Political Injustices." *Politics, Philosophy & Economics* 10(2): 188–210.

Paton Walsh, Nick. 2024. "The Rest of the World Wants the Ukraine War to Go Away. Putin Has Other Ideas." *CNN*, May 13, 2024. Accessed July 26, 2024. https://edition.cnn.com/2024/05/13/europe/russia-surging-on-frontlines-analysis-intl/index.html

Rodin, David. 2002. *War and Self-Defense*. Oxford: Oxford University Press.

Rodin, David. 2015. "The War Trap: Dilemmas of jus terminatio." *Ethics* 125: 674–695.

Stilz, Anna. 2011. "Collective Responsibility and the State." *Journal of Political Philosophy* 19(2): 190–208.

Tod, James. 2023. *Annals and Antiquities of Rajast'han*. New Haven: Yale University Press.

UN Meetings Coverage Security Council. 2024. "Escalating Attacks on Ukraine's Civilian, Energy Infrastructure Making Humanitarian Aid Delivery Even More Dangerous, Relief Chief Tells Security Council." Accessed July 12, 2024. https://press.un.org/en/2024/sc15695.doc.htm

Walzer, Michael. 1977. *Just and Unjust Wars*. 4th ed. New York: Basic Books.

Ward, Alexander, Paul McLeary, and Connor O'Brien. 2023. "Ukraine Can't Retake Crimea Soon, Pentagon Tells Lawmakers in Classified Briefing." *Politico*, February 1 2023. Accessed July 26, 2024. https://www.politico.com/news/2023/02/01/ukraine-crimea-russia-pentagon-00080799

Weinstock, Daniel. 2013. "On the Possibility of Principled Moral Compromise." *Critical Review of International Social and Political Philosophy* 16(4): 537–556.

7 Just War Continuation and Just War Exit in Afghanistan*

Jordy Rocheleau

1 Introduction

Just war theorists tend to hold that continuing a war is easier to justify than entering one. The term '*jus ad bellum*' – with its criteria of just cause, last resort, and so forth – is applied primarily to war's initiation. Insofar as the justice of continued recourse to war has been analyzed, it has been primarily under the rubric of *jus ex bello*, justice in *ending* a war (Moellendorf 2008). By suggesting that it is withdrawal from the conflict that needs justification, this terminology implies a presumption of continued war-waging, even when the *ad bellum*, just recourse conditions are no longer satisfied. In particular, it is suggested that just cause and last resort either are not necessary or have a lower threshold in war continuation.

This view seems to have gained support from the 2021 United States' withdrawal from Afghanistan and subsequent immediate Taliban takeover. The original justifying cause of defending against or punishing terrorism after the 9/11/2001 attacks was largely completed, with Al Qaeda dismantled in Afghanistan in the early years of the war. The focus of the intervention had long been stabilizing the new Afghan government, for the sake of the Afghanis as well as global security.[1] Absent prior US involvement, a new intervention in the war between the Afghan government and the Taliban probably would have been considered unjustified. Without the commission of atrocity crimes, intervention on the better side of a civil war is not normally considered just cause. Nonetheless, it seems common to think that the already-engaged United States would have been justified in continuing to help fight the Taliban and perhaps was obligated to do so (Bergen and Tillman 2023; Patterson 2022).[2] Legal scholar Nina Griscelli vividly charges that the United States withdrawal culpably "left Afghanistan

* The argument here is based on that of Chapter 7 of *New Interventionist Just War Theory: A Critique* (Rocheleau 2022).

DOI: 10.4324/9781003454144-10

open on the operating table" (Griscelli 2023). Former US National Security Adviser H.R. McMaster voiced a common view when he described Afghanistan as a "humanity problem on a modern-day frontier between barbarism and civilization" and criticized the Biden Administration for lack of will "to continue the effort in the interest of all humanity" (quoted in McKinley 2021). These judgments tend to presuppose that a war already underway can and should be continued for humanitarian purposes even if it is no longer a last resort and even if it does not meet the just cause threshold for intervention.

Against the above line of thought, I will argue that to be justly continued, a war must satisfy all the *ad bellum* criteria, including the standard threshold for just cause and last resort. I also discuss why Afghanistan does not provide a counterexample to my view. If any of the *ad bellum* criteria were no longer satisfied in Afghanistan, as seems likely, it was obligatory to end the war.

2 Why *Jus Ad Bellum* Applies Continuously

There is a common understanding of *jus ad bellum* as only applying to the initial decision to go to war, in contrast with *jus in bello*, which applies to actions throughout the conflict. For example, Brian Orend (2013) refers to *jus ad bellum*, *in bello*, and *post bellum* as "three phases, beginning, middle and end." Coppieters and Fotion's just war text (2008, 27) explicitly defines 'just cause' as meaning "that one has good reason for *starting* a war" (my emphasis). This terminology literally implies that the justice of recourse to war is only a matter of the initial decision to send forces into a conflict and that the status of a party's war as a whole cannot change over its course. My guess is that on reflection most thinkers would acknowledge that a war might become unjustifiable over time such that it should be rethought. However, since what is changed and being rethought in such cases is the justifiability of fighting for one's cause at all, or *jus ad bellum*, not the justice of particular *in bello* means (much less *jus post bellum*, which refers to justice *after* war is over), such change in status and rethinking do not accord with the letter of their theories. This one-off conception of just recourse is not only a failure of terminological precision but also directly affects normative analyses. For example, in his 2022 critique of "the Biden Administration's precipitous abandonment of Afghanistan," Eric Patterson quickly concludes that the US intervention had a just cause "to bring al Qaeda and its allies to justice and thwart future attacks" (2022, 63) after the 2001 terror attacks, without consideration of whether that cause still guided and morally justified the war 20 years later. This reflects a tendency to uncritically accept wars which were initially thought to satisfy *jus ad bellum* as justifiable to continue without further just recourse tests.

On the contrary, reflection shows that one needs just cause, proper authorization, and so forth, not only to start but also to justly keep fighting throughout. If one has achieved one's cause or adopted a new mission without just cause, as Walzer argued was the case in the Korean War (Walzer 1977, 117–119), one is no longer justified in killing for one's ends, regardless of means. Similar points are true for the other *jus ad bellum* criteria; a war that is no longer legitimately authorized or proportionate becomes unjust to continue prosecuting.[3] It might seem that last resort does not apply to war continuation, since it is impossible to avoid a war already underway.[4] However, new non-violent means of achieving one's cause could develop – indeed some sort of peace agreement must eventually be reached if a war is ever to end. Feasible alternatives should be chosen over war, such that the principle that a party should only wage war if there are no less violent means of achieving the cause applies continuously over time as well. In short, the logic of *jus ad bellum* is about the right to be at war, so its criteria must be satisfied throughout.

The idea that moral principles continue to apply over time, such that whatever is wrong to start is wrong to continue, seems straightforward. Admittedly, there are cases in which it appears to be morally permissible to continue with something at a reduced threshold of justification. Academic tenure is a classic case, as the rigorous criteria for meriting it are no longer applied to retention thereafter. Laws which permit someone to be "grandfathered in," having satisfied previous, perhaps less-exacting, rules, are also examples of discrepancies in standards over time. Such cases are exceptional, though, and limited to actions which are not inherently rights infringing. Presumptively rights-violating actions, paradigmatically violence, should be ceased as soon as there isn't an overriding reason to continue them. Moreover, in the rare cases where there is a presumed right of continuation or "grandfathering in," it is typically because there are practical benefits of permitting the ongoing status, and a demand for continual re-justification would do more harm than good. The value of academic freedom and job security arguably outweighs the harm of the occasional coasting professor. By contrast, a right to continue to wage war without justification would invite much harm with little corresponding benefit, as I argue in Section 6.

Admittedly, having already decided that a war is justified may give a practical presumption of continuing to wage it from day to day. Leaders need not constantly rethink their decisions. Absent good reasons to rethink a – presumably carefully undertaken – decision to go to war, heads of state are probably justified in assuming their wars will continue to be justified. However, any presumption of continued justice is immediately lost if changing conditions call the satisfaction of any *ad bellum* criteria into question.

In Afghanistan, there was good reason to rethink many of the criteria over the 20 years of intervention. After the early dismantling of Al Qaeda at Tora Bora, the primary justifying defensive cause for the invasion of Afghanistan was largely achieved. The shift to an ongoing mission focused on state-building was a dubious cause for continued intervention, particularly once the Taliban resurged to begin a civil war with the government. The long intervention yielded varying results and assessments of proportionality and likely success, mostly characterized by a downward trend (Malkasian 2021; Whitlock 2021). In terms of last resort, at various times, there were opportunities to negotiate peace with the Taliban (Malkasian 2021; Whitlock 2021). There was also an ongoing possibility of contingently withdrawing forces and re-intervening, or engaging in targeted operations, should Al Qaeda resurge or human rights violations become sufficiently grave (Miller 2011, 113–114). In sum, there was good reason to rethink the satisfaction of most of the *ad bellum* criteria over the course of the intervention. It was questionable whether any of them were satisfied in 2021, such that stopping the war against the Taliban and withdrawing most or all troops was probably obligatory.[5]

3 The Case for Presumed War Continuation Based on Acquired Duties

Although the view I articulate seems the most straightforward way of theorizing the justice of war over time, few thinkers have explicitly endorsed it.[6] Several thinkers have instead theorized the conditions for justly exiting or ending a war, which Moellendorf (2008, 2015) terms "*jus ex bello*."[7] Several of the factors in just war exit that Moellendorf endorses – just cause, proportionality, and likely success – are actually *jus ad bellum* principles, implying that they must be satisfied to *continue*, not exit, a war, in accord with my view. Summarizing this normative perspective, Moellendorf says that there is a basic *ex bello* principle of "all due haste," such that war should be exited as soon as the *ad bellum* criteria are no longer satisfied (2015, 669). However, he would balance this with a second *ex bello* principle of "costs minimization," which stipulates that "a war should be ended in a manner that minimizes ... the moral costs to civilians, the institutions of a just and peaceful social life, and the country's resources and infrastructure" (2015, 670). If one's war has a just cause but fails to meet other *ad bellum* criteria, Moellendorf requires the satisfaction of a third principle, "injustice mitigation[,] requir[ing] that the just cause should be realized as much as possible" before discontinuing the fight (2015, 670). Avoidance of such harms could entail fighting a war which violates *jus ad bellum*: "the path to peace in an unjust war might itself be unjust" (2008, 135). Since the minimization of harm or injustice implies that such wars would be proportionate, I take it that the wars in question would fail the *ad bellum* just cause or last resort tests. To the extent that just cause is required for continuation, Moellendorf offers a reduced threshold:

> if preventing a predicted future injustice may be a just cause for continuing a war, the principle of just cause in the doctrine of *jus ex bello* may include empirical forecasts and counterfactual claims that are not typically employed with respect to consideration of just cause in the doctrine of *jus ad bellum*.
>
> (2008, 133)

Moellendorf's *ex bello* principles would also allow last resort to be overridden since injustice mitigation applies especially in situations where options are "between decisive victory and surrender" (Moellendorf 2015, 670), seemingly where there are alternatives to war that could be expected to at least partially achieve one's (just) cause, arguably making war no longer a last resort. His *jus ex bello* principles would permit – or require – continuing a war which has acceptable alternatives if there is potential for a more just solution in the future.[8]

The case for presumed war continuation, or at least a lower threshold for continuation than initiation, seems to rest on a couple of arguments. The first, directly implied by Moellendorf's cost minimization and injustice mitigation principles, is that stopping the fighting and withdrawing forces involve new decisions with new foreseeable consequences, for which the withdrawer bears responsibility. If stopping a war and withdrawing forces would lead to significant harms, outweighing the moral costs of continued war, this gives reason to continue fighting. Socrates invokes a similar principle in the *Republic*, arguing that one ought not to return a sword to a crazed person, despite the return of property being *prima facie* obligatory (Plato 1996, 580). In Afghanistan, a Taliban takeover violating the rights of Afghanis, especially women and Taliban opponents, was a foreseeable result of withdrawal. One might think that, even if traditional just cause and last resort were lacking, minimization of costs would justify continued fighting.

A second argument is not one emphasized by Moellendorf, but I think it captures some of the sense of obligation not to abandon a war early or even perhaps when just war criteria do not appear to be met. This is that an occupying force acquires a particular obligation to remain to stabilize a territory following its overthrow of the previous ruling body. The duty to provide law enforcement and security until self-governance is feasible is enshrined in international law (Hague 1907, Article 43). Brian Orend defends the reconstruction of a defeated state as an occupier's *jus ex bello* duty: "the goal of justified post-war regime change is a minimally just political community" (2013, 221), a goal that may not be complete upon achieving one's just cause.

The duty to stabilize appears strongest for an *unjust* intervener, who would be obligated to repair the harm it has done. This "pottery barn" – "you break it, you buy it" – principle was used to justify an extended US occupation of Iraq (Rocheleau 2010). On the other hand, while a *just* intervener, arguably like the United States (at least initially) in Afghanistan,[9] lacks an inherent duty of reparation, it still has a duty to avoid harm to the civilian population.[10] To the extent that an intervention harms the innocent, there is arguably a duty of redress, even if the harms were unintended consequences of just acts of war. If one faultlessly causes harm to bystanders, say going into an uncontrollable skid in one's car, one would bear some responsibility to remediate the damage one caused. The responsibility to help is magnified if one is the only party available or the most capable of helping. Orend argues that "Reconstruction needs to take place within a secure context, and the war winner is clearly best positioned to provide this" (2013, 232). Although Orend's "post bellum" terminology technically would not apply to war continuation, his conditions for ending an occupation also appear to be conditions for ending an ongoing war. In Afghanistan, the United States and its allies initially won the war against the Taliban and Al Qaeda, so re-entry into – and continued combat in – the renewed civil war could be viewed as a matter of simultaneously *jus post bellum* and *jus ad bellum*. In any event, the idea that the United States acquired a duty to stabilize was clearly salient in justifications for continued military force and resistance to withdrawal.[11]

An intervener may also acquire other duties to inhabitants of the occupied territory in the form of gratitude for their assistance or fidelity to explicit or implied promises of assistance and protection. Afghans who had been fighting the Taliban alongside the United States felt abandoned and betrayed upon their partner's withdrawal (Malkasian 2021, 460). Moreover, while there was a desperate effort to evacuate friendly Afghanis before the final US withdrawal, the exit left behind thousands of supporters to whom the US acknowledged an obligation (Malkasian 2021; Griswold 2021). The failure to uphold these incurred duties was a major moral cost of the American exit.

Griscelli's metaphor of abandonment on the operating table combines the duties of acquired obligation, based on responsibility for risks to others, and avoidance of harm. She argues that international humanitarian and human rights law's protections of the innocent in war should be extended to "a duty of reasonable care to those [who would be] left behind," and that this was violated in Afghanistan (Griscelli 2023, 831). Conditions for war exit would again trump the duty to stop prosecuting a war which no longer met *ad bellum* requirements.

4 Why Competing Obligations Don't Justify Fighting without *Jus Ad Bellum*

While I accept that these obligations exist, I argue that they cannot justify continuing a war which lacks just cause or is not a last resort. Discharging one's duty of reparation or gratitude cannot justify the massive infringement of the rights to life and self-determination involved in war. The duty of non-maleficence generally takes priority over beneficently preventing harm. One is directly responsible for the harm one causes in a way that one isn't for the harm one fails to prevent. Drawing on a classic example, one would not be justified in forcibly harvesting organs in order to save the lives of those in need of transplants. In contradistinction to Socrates' example, the duty not to kill is not as easily overridden by harm prevention as the duty to return a weapon. Since war inherently infringes basic rights to life and liberty, it is war's continued prosecution, not its termination, which is primarily in need of justification.

Admittedly, responsibility for a threat to human rights gives rise to a duty to protect that goes beyond what one generally owes to third parties, as in Orend's duty to stabilize and Griscelli's duty to close up the surgical patient. However, such a duty cannot justify killing and sending people to their deaths if just cause or last resort is no longer present. Performing surgery does not normally kill bystanders; if completing a procedure would put lives in jeopardy, the presumption would tilt against it, regardless of one's *prima facie* obligations to one's patient. In Afghanistan, "closing" the war would have meant indefinite lethal intervention with uncertain results for many who would not consent. A requirement that a state must be in a decent condition before one can break off an intervention and leave would require continuing many dubious wars with costly results. Without a grave justifying cause and a lack of alternative resorts, ongoing war cannot be justified. Thus, the obligation not to continue an unjust war outweighs relational duties created by past entanglement.

Unlike gratitude or reparation, defending against threatened harm of a considerable magnitude may be able to justify continued war. However, *jus ad bellum* already provides a standard threshold for determining when defense of human rights is a just cause for war, which presumably would apply. Most commentators agree that only atrocity-level violations of human rights, involving large-scale killing of the innocent, can justify humanitarian intervention. This standard is legally enshrined in the United Nations' new Responsibility to Protect doctrine (ICISS 2001). It is beyond the scope of this chapter to defend this threshold, though I have elsewhere (Rocheleau 2022, chaps. 4–5). If, as some cosmopolitan individualist thinkers argue, any violation of human rights is a cause for war, intervention in Afghanistan would become much easier to justify, contingent on last resort and proportionality.[12] Though this lowering of the just cause bar might make my argument here less crucial to questioning the continued Afghan mission, it would not challenge my thesis that the *jus ad bellum* principles, however they are specified, apply continuously.

In Afghanistan, some would argue that Taliban rule amounts to an atrocity, and thus continued intervention to hold them back would meet a strict just cause threshold. This also would not challenge my continuous *jus ad bellum* thesis. Afghanistan is only a possible counterexample if one thinks that Taliban rule is not an atrocity that would justify starting a new war but is bad enough to justify continuing an ongoing intervention. On the substantive point of whether defeating the Taliban was a just cause, I would note that there was little or no discussion of US intervention to overthrow the Taliban before they were accused of harboring Al Qaeda after the latter's 9/11 attacks. Defensive or punitive response to terrorism was clearly the factual cause of US entry into the war. The possible humanitarian benefits of overthrowing the Taliban were viewed as mostly a beneficial side-effect (Whitlock 2021, Chapter 1; Malkasian 2021, Chapter 4).

There are ways that incurred obligations can contribute to the justification of war consistent with my thesis. First, a new justifying cause of sufficient magnitude could arise in the course of a war. In Iraq, as well as Afghanistan, preventing human rights abuses was not the initial cause for intervention but became the primary justification later.[13] Second, if there is a just cause for continued fighting, the good of discharging obligations, including reparation and gratitude, could contribute to the *proportionality* of fighting for that cause, helping tip the balance to making it worthwhile when it would not be otherwise. Third, the satisfaction of the *ad bellum* criteria is typically only thought to make a war permissible, but incurred duties could make what is acceptable obligatory. Nonetheless, to be obligatory, the war must first be permissible according to *jus ad bellum*, per my thesis.

I would specifically reject one possible psychological cause of continued fighting as lacking moral weight. Having already lost lives and spent resources in a battle, a party tends to be reluctant to give up the fight short of victory, lest past losses be in vain. The idea that one must continue a dubious and costly venture because one has already spent so much on it, leading one to "throw good money after bad," is known as the "sunk cost fallacy." Notably, Jeff McMahan has argued that losses suffered can actually contribute to the justifiability of continued war, since "the unjust combatant must be liable to suffer some additional harm as a means of bringing about the good of partially redeeming the loss he has caused" (McMahan 2015, 714). Thus, punishing those who unjustly killed one's compatriots would add to the war cause and its proportionate benefits. Against this, the view assumes McMahan's moral inequality of combatants, so his principle is to be applied only by the just side. There remains reason to think, with Walzer, that even those lacking just cause are excused, if not justified, in fighting for their society's causes, such that they can be justly resisted but not punished. In any event, both sides to a conflict consider their own war just, so any additional fighting rights that are accorded to the just would be taken advantage of by all, making redemption of past losses a particularly dangerous cause to endorse. Finally, if the war would not be otherwise justified, with a sufficient cause, proportionate, and likely to succeed, it isn't clear that it constitutes positive respect for the dead to keep fighting such a struggle, repeating the misfortune of their loss. Punitive vengeance is dubious as a just cause, and if taken as a rationale for war could lead both parties to be trapped in an endless cycle of violence. Any value in redeeming deaths by continuing their struggle would seem to be small in comparison to the effect on the living.

5 The Pragmatic, Utilitarian Case for *Jus Ex Bello*

The above arguments give reason to think that the same principled conditions for initiating war also apply to extending it. However, there is another, pragmatic case for not applying the same strict standards. Arguably, the standard just cause threshold, requiring atrocity-level crimes for intervention, reflects a sort of rule-utilitarian calculation (Rocheleau 2022). Intervention to stop small-scale rights violations would generally be disproportionate, while intervening to stop genocides and other atrocities has a good chance of saving lives on balance. Similarly, the last resort principle seems at least partly based on the relative costs of violent as opposed to non-violent means. However, such generalizations about wars' effects are contingent on circumstances. Some types of war to stop smaller scale injustices or wars despite alternative diplomatic resorts might be proportionate, with desirable consequences on balance.

In particular, the expected utility of war *continuation* might be thought generally better than that of war *initiation*, such that the former should be accepted more readily on rule utilitarian grounds. A party already engaged in a conflict might be able to more accurately forecast the costs and potential benefits of its fight, such that proportionality and likely success judgments get more reliable and carry more justificatory weight as the war goes on. Also, in war continuation, one will have already paid many of the war's costs, not only materially in sending forces to the battlefield but also politically by rallying public support and infringing sovereignty, so there is reason to think that the marginal expense of continuation tends to be lower than that for initiation. To withdraw forces, only to have to redeploy later when just cause and last resort are clearly satisfied, could be costly. For example, after President Obama withdrew troops from Iraq in 2011, ISIS was able to seize large amounts of territory, wreaking havoc on the civilian population. Only a return of US-led airpower starting in 2014 was eventually able to dislodge ISIS. This fueled the criticism that the 2011 withdrawal had been premature (Brennan 2014).[14] There are also distinct costs associated with withdrawing from a war, including the failures of obligations discussed in the previous section. Military defeat may also have political costs, such as loss of respect and of the ability to deter potential aggressive or rights-violating behavior in the future.[15]

In terms of the utility of fighting without *last resort*, there may be a flawed diplomatic option which nevertheless substantially achieves a just cause, making war no longer the only feasible alternative. Yet, refusing such a deal and fighting longer might allow one a chance at achieving the cause more completely or with greater long-term stability. Continued deployment and fighting might allow one to bargain for a better peace agreement, if not retain the leverage needed to get a deal at all.[16] In Afghanistan, one might think that the promise of ongoing diplomacy with the Taliban, plus possible US redeployment if needed in the future, were feasible resorts short of continued war, but still think that it made sense to fight further for a more just peace while intervening forces were deployed.[17] Arguably, eagerness to end a long and costly war, both in a hastily negotiated, undemanding agreement with the Taliban under Trump, and final unilateral withdrawal under Biden, lost an opportunity to use the threat of continued force to bargain for a deal preventing Taliban control of the whole country (Bergen and Tillman 2023; Malkasian 2021). My requirement of strict continual observance of *jus ad bellum* conditions is thus in tension with optimal strategy.

These utility considerations provide an argument for reducing the cause threshold and loosening last resort for war continuation. It is in line with Moellendorf's idea that in war exit, "due haste" should be balanced with "costs minimization" even absent a just cause; and that in wars with just cause, last resort should be balanced with "injustice mitigation."

6 Rejection of Pragmatic War Continuation without *Jus Ad Bellum*

Against this suggestion, I argue that in addition to principled limits to utilitarian justifications of violence, continued war tends to be less proportionate and successful than forecast. The fog of war, including evolving strategies and circumstances, makes consequences uncertain and ends elusive. This is particularly true in state-building operations, the success of which depends on popular support and local leadership, institutions, and culture. There is a psychological tendency to excessive optimism, exacerbated by groupthink, causing military decision-makers to overestimate likely benefits and underestimate challenges and costs (Rocheleau 2020, Chap. 5).

Although some costs have already been incurred in war continuation calculations, reducing uncertainty and costs going forward, it is still impossible to know long-term outcomes. Experience of a prolonged war increases miscalculation based on sunk-cost thinking. This leads to an overestimation of the importance and likely success of war continuation.

Although the withdrawal from Afghanistan has been criticized as overhasty, the 20-year mission, which left a corrupt government even less able to stand against the Taliban than the Northern Alliance rebels in 2001, might instead be taken as a cautionary lesson about the limits of state-building through military force and the difficulty of extracting oneself from a failing war. In the *Afghanistan Papers*, Craig Whitlock (2021) reports that despite years of rosy public reports, military officials knew that nation-building was going poorly and the Taliban insurgency was strengthening, in an eerie echo of Vietnam's Pentagon Papers. Carter Malkasian's (2021) history of the US intervention argues that the Taliban's deep reflection of Afghan identification with the Islamic faith and resistance to foreign intervention, combined with the corrupt and flawed governance of the US-backed regime, made the battle for hearts and minds, and thus the counterinsurgency, unwinnable. Some additionally argue that the mission failed because of insufficiently large force commitment to the counterinsurgency campaign, or due to excessive restraint in targeting the Taliban. Others counter that the problem was a too-ambitious plan with unattainable state-building goals (Stewart 2021), including dubious attempts to meddle in internal Afghan politics and the local drug trade (Whitlock 2021, chaps. 10–15).[18] Economic assistance varied from stingy during the Bush years, with the overarching commitment to Iraq, to so free-flowing during Obama that it undermined local markets and exacerbated corruption. The lessons learned are contradictory, with much more clarity about decided mistakes than about any path that was likely to yield victory or justice (Malkasian 2021; Whitlock 2021). I would suggest that the biggest lesson is that state-building intervention is so problematic that it is unlikely to lead to humanitarian improvement unless it is used narrowly for atrocity prevention.

Interestingly, some proponents of continued intervention acknowledge the war against the Taliban was unwinnable but argue that it was worthwhile to continue to fight to stave off defeat (Patterson 2022). Malkasian supports the view of his former commanding officer, General Dunford, that an ongoing small deployment, aided by air support, served as a "term life insurance – good only as long you pay" (2021, 357) that could keep the Taliban from overthrowing the government, with a hope that a longer commitment in tandem with negotiations might have eventually secured a sustainable agreement with the Taliban permitting a more successful US exit (481–482). It is also argued that the 2,500 troops still deployed in

Afghanistan in 2021 was a fairly small US commitment, such that it could have been worthwhile to continue to prevent the Taliban takeover that rapidly followed the withdrawal. However, it is doubtful whether that level of force would have continued to keep the Taliban at bay. They had been gathering strength and making advances, saving their major push for after the US withdrawal. Moreover, to keep the Taliban from overwhelming government forces, the United States relied increasingly on heavy airstrikes, exacerbating civilian casualties and further alienating Afghans (Whitlock 2021; Malkasian 2021). Thus, the temporarily reduced cost for the United States did not necessarily result in overall proportionality.

While there may be political costs to accepting less than total victory, these are likely lower than the costs of being embroiled in an ongoing war with questionable cause and benefits. Admittedly, military withdrawal may leave instability and conflict behind. Yet, the ongoing intervention has been found to escalate and prolong conflict and instability (Rocheleau 2022, Chap. 5). Among its costs are the delegitimization of the dependent local government and increased support for insurgents, both of which plagued Afghanistan. Malkasian's citation of Odd Arne Westad is apropos: "Superpower interventions … helped put a number of Third World countries in a state of semipermanent civil war," and as a result "caused untold harm to their peoples in pursuit of marginal interests" (484). As I discuss in the next section, there are also ways of avoiding the feared harms of withdrawal without continued war.

In regards to last resort, one is inherently on dubious grounds in killing and infringing sovereignty unnecessarily. Moreover, the anticipated benefits of continued fighting are apt to be illusory, based again on overoptimism and sunk-cost thinking. In Afghanistan, it was not likely that additional war would significantly weaken the Taliban, who had been gaining strength for years during the US intervention, even weathering troop surges. Nor was it likely that the Taliban would be convinced to share power with a government that they refused to recognize and were beating in the war. They correctly recognized that time was on their side, and to convince them otherwise would probably have required a massive US commitment, with ongoing costs, including further delegitimizing the Afghan government.

While some proposed peace deals would fail to achieve a just cause sufficiently to require (or even justify) ending the war – other deals which are not maximally just should be accepted if they adequately achieve the just cause. The last resort principle that one should stop fighting if a reasonable alternative exists should not be waived on the chance that there might someday be a better solution, much less because one fears being held accountable for withdrawal but not continuation of the status quo. The requirement to fight until injustice is minimized implies a bias toward continued fighting in poor situations, like Afghanistan, and thus further embroilment in a war that may actually make things worse.[19] Indeed, bias toward the status quo of ongoing war is exactly what one sees in practice, and it is why a more rigorous test of the justification of war continuation is needed.

Admittedly, a single case does not prove a universal law. There may be *other* wars in which fighting without just cause or as a last resort *would* be worthwhile. However, I have argued that there are general tendencies to underestimate costs and overestimate the likelihood of success. The United States' two-decade intervention in Afghanistan provides a powerfully illustrative case study. Given the dubiousness of anticipated benefits and the probability of underestimated harm, it is not good humanitarian policy to fight wars on the basis of calculations of marginal utility without definite just cause and last resort. Continuing war only when the *ad bellum* criteria are all met makes practical as well as principled sense.

7 Ending War vs. Ending Humanitarian Measures

One might still think that it is a mistake to require the cessation of war *as soon as* any of the *ad bellum* criteria are lacking. Fighting a little longer in some cases, possibly including Afghanistan, might prevent harm and fulfill relational duties at a proportionate cost. My call for an immediate end to wars without definitive just cause or with any other feasible resort might seem rigidly legalistic and irresponsible. Without blanket permission to continue such wars, one still might think, with Moellendorf, that they should be ended "in due haste," but according to a timetable with the most humane results.[20] In Afghanistan, the fight could have continued longer, holding the Taliban at bay while evacuating larger numbers of Afghanis along with allied forces.

To counter this, I would point out that ending a war does not mean doing nothing at all to avoid harm and to fulfill obligations. Most obviously, even after forced withdrawal, it is possible to use diplomacy, including persuasion, incentives, and pressures, along with humanitarian aid to secure just goals. Ongoing attempts to do this in Afghanistan and elsewhere could be given more resources. Military intervention is relatively expensive, and more lives could be saved by redirecting these resources to humanitarian assistance (Valentino 2011). New or ongoing threats to human rights can be countered by targeted strikes and rescue operations without commitment to a full-scale war. And, should rights violations escalate to the level of atrocity crimes, redeployment could be undertaken as a last resort.

Second, stopping the prosecution of a war does not necessarily mean immediate troop withdrawal or the cessation of all force. To use a typical definition, war is a large-scale conflict between groups over governance

(Orend 2013, 3). Armed force not aimed at defeating a group or vying for political control but only at protecting individuals is a measure short of war and, thus, does not need to meet the atrocity threshold or be a last resort. I take it that in Afghanistan, US forces were seeking to help the government defeat the Taliban and retain control of the country, and thus they were involved in a war, at least up until the final weeks after President Biden's announced withdrawal. In the end, US forces switched from a war against the Taliban to providing immediate security as they prepared to withdraw and evacuate some Afghans. Arguably, a more widespread and longer-lasting attempt to provide security short of war could have been undertaken, as well as a more prompt evacuation.[21,22] These measures short of war would have had to focus on the immediate protection of human rights, including self-defense, with narrower targeting rules than the permissiveness in war of killing anyone affiliated with enemy forces and acceptance of collateral damage.

Admittedly, at some point, an effort to provide security against advancing forces amounts to a war. A prolonged US fight to hold Kabul against the Taliban would constitute continuing or renewed military intervention and thus require *jus ad bellum*. If attacks by advancing counterinsurgents on retreating forces or civilians become widespread, this would amount to a defensive or humanitarian just cause that could give a right to attempt to defeat the attacking party. In any event, continued immediate self-defense and defense of individual human rights would be allowed while preparing to withdraw in due haste. There is a tension between sovereignty and human rights here, where sovereignty rights point toward immediate withdrawal of forces as soon as possible, and human rights claims toward protecting individuals in the area to be surrendered, paralleling on a smaller scale the dilemma of whether to intervene militarily at all in contravention to sovereignty. It is difficult to specify how exactly to adjudicate between these claims. One cannot take up the goal of guaranteeing human rights throughout society without denying sovereignty rights and giving blanket rights to use cross-border force; that is, in effect, going to war. So long as the atrocity just cause threshold, or last resort, is not met, efforts to defeat a party to a civil war, including general efforts to weaken its forces through targeted strikes, should be stopped. On the other hand, still-present forces can seek to protect the basic rights of those in their immediate purview.

The truce reached between the Taliban and withdrawing US forces in August 2021, permitting the latter's evacuation from the Kabul airport and the former's occupation of the rest of the city, was in large part a strategic *modus vivendi* between the two parties. However, it arguably reflected what justice required of one party which could no longer justify its intervention, and of another that, although the new legitimate governing authority, must allow the former's peaceful but reasonably hasty withdrawal. One might object that if the intervener lacked *jus ad bellum*, the advancing insurgents could justly attack them. However, if the "intervener" is no longer seeking to control territory, it is no longer fighting for its unjust cause (or without last resort), and the insurgents coming to power cannot justly attack. It would retain a right to self-defense and defense of the rights of other individuals in their vicinity. That continuous *jus ad bellum* does not require immediate troop withdrawal, or the cessation of all force, helps to allay pragmatic and humanitarian concerns about its implications.

8 Conclusion

I have argued that neither pragmatism nor acquired obligations provide special hurdles to ending a war that obviate the need to satisfy just recourse principles. Afghanistan does not provide a counterexample. The obligation to end a war when any of the *jus ad bellum* criteria, including just cause and last resort, are lacking helps to support the conclusion that the United States was obligated to withdraw from Afghanistan when it did, and probably many years before. If one thinks that just cause and last resort were satisfied, I have also given reasons to think that the war was disproportionate and unlikely to succeed.[23] A combination of these points, in tandem with narrower prudential and national interest considerations, seems to have reasonably persuaded the Biden Administration to end the intervention in Afghanistan.

It is difficult to pinpoint an exact date when the war should have been stopped. Arguably, after destroying the Al Qaeda camp at Tora Bora and helping to dislodge the harboring Taliban in 2001–2002, the cause was achieved, and the war could have properly ended. There is reason to think that willing Taliban and other marginalized groups could have been included in the government, preventing the future insurgency. The Bush Administration, confident with initial victory and riding the anti-Taliban wave after 9/11, refused to allow negotiation and reconciliation with the Taliban when it would have been favorable and would have permitted an early US exit. If there was an obligation to reconstruct, forces invited by the Afghan government could have assisted with this, unless or until it meant engaging in renewed civil war. When the Taliban resurged in 2005, it is doubtful that the United States had a just defensive or humanitarian cause for renewed warfare. After the Obama surge in 2009–2011 and the killing of bin Laden in Pakistan, Al Qaeda was further decimated, obviating the initial cause, so continuing the war became still more dubious. As the surge failed to eradicate the Taliban, who were clearly gaining the support of many Afghans, ongoing intervention to stop them lacked proportionality and likely success, as well as just cause. There were also various times at which greater willingness to negotiate with the Taliban might have achieved a political settlement that would have prevented their control of the whole country, such that last resort was no longer met even if there was a just cause to prevent a Taliban overthrow of the government (Malkasian 2021). It appears that there was a paradoxical unwillingness to negotiate, either when the war was going well (why be nice when we have them on the ropes?) or badly (we aren't in a strong place to bargain), that scuttled diplomacy and inclined to continued war. Failure to recognize loss of just cause, disproportionality, and the possibility of peace negotiations resulted in twenty years of war with devastating effects for Afghanistan and high costs for the United States.[24]

Notes

1 Despite his previous condemnation of nation building, US President George W. Bush's initial mission of disrupting Al Qaeda and toppling the Taliban evolved increasingly into exactly this (Whitlock 2021, chap. 3; Malkasian 2021, 83). President Barack Obama was also ambivalent but defended intervention in order to, among other things, guard against the Taliban's "denial of basic human rights to the Afghan people – especially women and girls." (quoted in Malkasian 2021, 223). The goals of Obama's troop surge included not just "deny[ing] Al Qaeda a safe haven" but also "revers[ing] Taliban momentum against the government, and strengthening the Afghan armed forces and government so they could secure Afghanistan on their own" (quoted in Malkasian, 237).

2 Dobbins et al. (2019) cautioned against a hasty exit in 2019 following a directive from then president Trump to prepare withdrawal. In response to Miller's (2011) call for immediate withdrawal from Afghanistan on just war grounds, Moellendorf (2011) cautions that it may be a case in which, though unjustifiable to continue, it is not yet justifiable to end the war.

3 Especially regarding proportionality but also potentially regarding just cause, one might realize that one's war never satisfied the criteria, so that it is isn't so much the war's status that changes as one's awareness of the status. In any event, such awareness would create an even clearer duty to stop fighting.

4 For such reasons, Moellendorf says that last resort does not apply to war continuation (2008, 127), but he proposes a "principle of the pursuit of diplomatic remedies" (2008, 134), which amounts to a requirement of last resort for war continuation. Ultimately, however, as I discuss in Section 3, Moellendorf allows remedies to be rejected if they fail to minimize harm or achieve other humanitarian goals, such that the principle is looser than a traditional last resort principle.

5 It is beyond the scope of this chapter to argue that the intervention definitely failed to meet the criteria and was unjust, as this would require detailed analysis of the facts on the ground and an interpretation and application of each *jus ad bellum* criterion. My thesis here – that the norms of *jus ad bellum* apply to war continuation – does not rest on a conclusion about whether Afghanistan met those criteria in 2021.

6 One of the few is John Lango (2014, 103–106), who calls for the "temporalization" of just war principles, with ongoing application of all the criteria to continuing acts of war.

7 Alternatively, David Rodin (2015) terms the ethics of war cessation "*jus terminatio bellum*." I focus on Moellendorf's view and use his terminology.
8 It is also clear that for Moellendorf, likely success can also be overridden, especially if success means the complete realization of one's just cause (2015, 670). I do not dispute this, largely because I do not consider likely success a *jus ad bellum* requirement separate from proportionality (Rocheleau 2022, 27–28).
9 Of course, as my argument here supports, the intervention may have become unjust over time. This means that continued war may have in turn created some duty of reparation. So one might object that my own argument paradoxically implies a duty to stay to repair wrongs. However, I would argue that the best way of repairing the harms of fighting too long is not doing more of the same but rather some other form of reparation, for example, financial remuneration and apologies, providing non-military services or security short of war, and so forth.
10 One might object that if harm to civilians were proportionate and unintended, it would be justified by double-effect. However, even if the act was justified, it isn't true to say that the evil side-effect was justified. It is also true that the wrongdoer who gave initial cause to the war should bear some, perhaps primary responsibility, for such innocents killed. Nonetheless, moral common sense is that this does not nullify all responsibility on the part of the immediate injurer.
11 The US intervention in Afghanistan, taking the form of assistance to the Northern Alliance in their fight against the Taliban, did not directly overthrow their government in the same way it did that of Hussein in Iraq. The initial US fight in Afghanistan had a more plausible defensive cause than the invasion of Iraq. Nonetheless, in the former case, the United States also took up a mission to provide security and help with state-building, along with defeating the Taliban resistance, in acknowledgment of some of the obligations discussed here.
12 At a presentation of a draft of this chapter at a meeting of the International Society for Military Ethics in 2023, Crystal Allen-Gunasekera raised this point about the implications of the adoption of individualism as opposed to the legalist conception of just recourse that I generally adopt.
13 As Rodin (2015) notes, this is a reason to have a high bar against initiating war, as one may be trapped in fighting for a more pressing cause. I would add that another way to avoid being trapped in a war is to require that the just cause and last resort thresholds truly be met throughout the conflict, rather than presuming continued justification.
14 Brennan (2014) explicitly extended the lesson of Iraq to caution about withdrawing from Afghanistan.
15 Rodin (2015) mentions these costs as part of the "war trap" that makes it rational to fight even when costs are greater than one initially would have been willing to pay. This cost assumes that the national military reputation of the group in question is a positive good and that it could outweigh the immediate harms of continued war.
16 Peace overtures with the Taliban were contemplated from early on and periodically attempted. At least since the end of the Obama surge in 2014, including throughout the Trump Administration, the overarching US exit strategy was to achieve an acceptable peace treaty with the Taliban (Malkasian 2021).
17 Note that just cause and last resort have to be satisfied for the same action. If it is no longer a last resort to make war for the just cause (e.g., national defense in Afghanistan), then the fact that war is a last resort for a non-justifying cause (humanitarian improvement of Afghanistan short of atrocity prevention) cannot justify the fight.

18 For another argument that defeat in Afghanistan was prefigured for years, see McKinley (2021).

19 Moellendorf might counter that if one accepted, with me, that fighting will likely have harmful results, then injustice would be minimized by ending the war immediately, so that I am in a sense adhering to his principle. Although I agree that this would frequently be the correct interpretation, the unfortunate tendency of a principle that requires optimal conditions to end a war is to recommend erring on the side of the status quo of war continuation.

20 Moellendorf's early (2008) article on *jus ex bello* distinguished between decisions of "when" versus "how" to exit a war, placing considerations of cost minimization under the "how." This seems to accord with the common view that the withdrawal ordered by Biden was too rapid even if the war as a whole was no longer justified. However, slowness in ending a war ultimately amounts to a delay in ending it, such that the how impacts the when. If my argument here is correct, any prolongation of warfare needs an ongoing *ad bellum* justification.

21 In 2014, Obama ordered a policy along these lines, directing that US forces cease targeting the Taliban except in emergencies (Malkasian), thus limiting the mission to targeting terrorists and defending against imminent threats to human rights instead of defeating the Taliban. Malkasian objects that the Taliban made significant advances during this time. However, ongoing intervention against the Taliban was not likely to defeat them, as Malkasian acknowledges, and was going to cause further harm to civilian bystanders and US forces and was going to further increase the perceived legitimacy of the Taliban as opposed to the Afghan government.

22 A US State Department review faulted the Trump and Biden Administrations for failure to plan for evacuation (Crowley 2023).

23 Biden's decision to withdraw forces was probably in large part based on proportionality and likely success grounds and, more basically, on prudential national interest considerations about ongoing US resource expenditure. Of course, some thought continued war was proportionate and could achieve valuable results, or at least prevent worse ones. While I have given reasons to think that ongoing war was disproportionate, my central argument has been against those who would waive questions of just cause and last resort for war continuation, justifying continued war only on grounds of utility or cost and injustice mitigation.

24 Earlier versions of this paper were presented at the American Philosophical Association Conference in Chicago, February 2022, and the International Society for Military Ethics Conference in Colorado Springs, July 2023. The paper benefited from comments by the audiences at both events.

References

Bergen, Peter, and Laura Tillman. 2023. "Opinion: How Trump Made One of 'the Worst Diplomatic Agreements' in US History and How Biden Carried It Out." *CNN*. August 9, 2023. https://www.cnn.com/2023/08/09/opinions/trump-biden-afghanistan-withdrawal-taliban-bergen-tillman/index.html

Brennan, Rick. 2014. "Withdrawal Symptoms: The Bungling of the Iraq Exit." *Foreign Affairs* 93 (6): 25–30.

Coppieters, Bruno, and Nick Fotion. 2008. *Moral Constraints on War: Principles and Cases*. Lanham, MD: Lexington Books.

Crowley, Michael. 2023. "State Department Report on Afghanistan Exit Urges 'Worst Case' Thinking." *New York Times*, July 1, 2023. https://www.nytimes.com/2023/06/30/us/politics/afghan-war-report.html
Dobbins, James, Jason H. Campbell, Sean Mann, and Laurel E. Miller. 2019. *Consequences of a Precipitous U.S. Withdrawal from Afghanistan*. Rand Corporation. JSTOR. http://www.jstor.org/stable/resrep19894
Griscelli, Nina. 2023. "Operation Nation Building: How International Humanitarian Law Left Afghanistan Open on the Operating Table." *University of Miami Law Review* 77 (3). https://repository.law.miami.edu/umlr/vol77/iss3/8
Griswold, Eliza. 2021. "The Afghans America Left Behind." *The New Yorker*, December 20, 2021. https://www.newyorker.com/magazine/2021/12/27/the-afghans-america-left-behind
Lango, John W. 2014. *The Ethics of Armed Conflict: A Cosmopolitan Just War Theory*. Edinburgh: Edinburgh University Press.
Malkasian, Carter. 2021. *The American War in Afghanistan*. New York: Oxford University Press.
McKinley, P. Michael. 2021. "We All Lost Afghanistan." *Foreign Affairs* (Online), August 16, 2021. https://www.foreignaffairs.com/articles/united-states/2021-08-16/we-all-lost-afghanistan-taliban
McMahan, Jeff. 2015. "Proportionality and Time." *Ethics* 125 (April): 696–719.
Miller, Richard W. 2011. "The Ethics of America's Afghan War." *Ethics & International Affairs* 25 (2): 103–131. https://doi.org/10.1017/S0892679411000098
Moellendorf, Darrel. 2008. "*Jus Ex Bello*." *Journal of Political Philosophy* 16 (2): 123–136. https://doi.org/10.1111/j.1467-9760.2008.00310.x
Moellendorf, Darrel. 2011. "*Jus Ex Bello* in Afghanistan." *Ethics & International Affairs* 25 (2): 155–164. https://doi.org/10.1017/S0892679411000128
Moellendorf, Darrel. 2015. "Two Doctrines of *Jus Ex Bello*." *Ethics* 125 (3): 653–673.
Orend, Brian. 2013. *The Morality of War*. 2nd ed. Peterborough, ON; Buffalo, NY: Broadview Press.
Patterson, Eric. 2022. "The Afghanistan War and *Jus Post Bellum*." *Washington University Review of Philosophy* 2: 62–77.
Plato. 1996. *The Collected Dialogues of Plato*. Edited by Edith Hamilton and Cairns Huntington. 16. print. Bollingen Series 71. Princeton: Princeton University Press.
Rocheleau, Jordy. 2010. "From Aggression to Just Occupation? The Temporal Application of *Jus Ad Bellum* Principles and the Case of Iraq." *Journal of Military Ethics* 9 (2): 123–138.
Rocheleau, Jordy. 2020. "Legitimate Authority as a *Jus Ad Bellum* Condition: Defense of a Procedural Requirement in Just War Theory." *Journal of Military Ethics* 19 (2): 99–117. https://doi.org/10.1080/15027570.2020.1799486
Rocheleau, Jordy. 2022. *New Interventionist Just War Theory: A Critique*. Routledge Studies in Intervention and Statebuilding. Abingdon, Oxon, New York:Routledge.
Rodin, David. 2015. "The War Trap: Dilemmas of *Jus Terminatio*." *Ethics* 125 (3): 674–695.
Stewart, Rory. 2021. "The Last Days of Intervention: Afghanistan and the Delusions of Maximalism." *Foreign Affairs* 100 (6): 60–73.
The Hague. 1907. Hague Convention (IV) Respecting the Laws and Customs of War on Land and Its Annex: Regulations Concerning the Laws and Customs of

War on Land. *International Conferences (The Hague)*, October 18. https://www.refworld.org/legal/agreements/hague/1907/en/31788 (accessed 1 May 2024).
Valentino, Benjamin. 2011. "The True Costs of Humanitarian Intervention: The Hard Truths about a Noble Notion." *Foreign Affairs* 90 (6): 60–73.
Walzer, Michael. 1977. *Just and Unjust Wars*. New York: Basic Books.
Whitlock, Craig. 2021. *The Afghanistan Papers: A Secret History of the War*. New York: Simon & Schuster.

8 The Afghanistan War and *Jus Post Bellum*: A Look at Three Milestones for Peace and Security*

Eric Patterson

When considering the long-enduring Afghanistan War, it may seem that Afghanistan has come full circle after a rapid and chaotic withdrawal of the United States and international peacekeeping forces. However, when analyzing the war, there remains a responsibility on the part of those involved to consider the cause, conduct, and sudden ending based upon just war criteria, including *jus post bellum*. Was it a just war in how it began and how it was conducted, and what is the status of the country and its people at the war's end (*jus post bellum*)?

Understanding the morality of the Afghanistan War is complicated for at least two reasons. The first reason involves the scale: the war involved four United States presidencies over twenty years, $2.3 trillion dollars, and hundreds of thousands of United States and allied troops with the involvement of dozens of NATO allies and UN partners. Part of the scale of this complex war's timeline involves al Qaeda's presence and activities in the region and throughout the world—emanating initially from Afghanistan. Osama bin Laden and his associates went to war with the United States in the first attack on the World Trade Center in 1993, then the bombing of the Khobar Towers housing complex in 1994 and the United States embassies in Kenya and Tanzania in 1998, then attacking the *USS Cole* in 1999, and the second attack on the World Trade Center's Twin Towers in 2001. In addition, the group murdered many innocent civilians in New York, Bali, London, Madrid, and Paris, among several other locations. Al Qaeda's actions and the way the global terrorist organization inspired other violent Islamists around the world led to the Global War on Terrorism. Afghanistan,

* Some framing for this chapter was first used in a series of lectures and conference papers, including the American Philosophical Association's Central Division Meeting in New Orleans (2024) as well as in the *Washington University Review of Philosophy* (2022). I thank the editors of the *Review* for permission to re-use some material. I thank Linda Waits-Kamau for her assistance with the manuscript.

DOI: 10.4324/9781003454144-11

therefore, was a major part of this much longer, larger-scale global war involving al Qaeda and other terrorist groups inspired by al Qaeda.

The second complexity involves how to think about the morality of a conflict on this scale. Just war thinking provides a framework for doing so by analyzing the three criteria for just war: (1) Under what conditions is it moral to employ force, and were these conditions met in the Afghanistan War? (2) After the decision to use force was made by proper authorities, how was force employed? (3) What were the conditions at the end of the war for *jus post bellum*? This paper concludes with a brief discussion of how to think about victory, that is, in terms of winning, losing, and the moral character of the victor's political program.

1 Analyzing Just War Criteria and *Jus Post Bellum* in Afghanistan

The just war framework states that *legitimate political authorities* may act on a *just cause* with the *right intention*. Authorities—meaning legitimate national leaders such as governors, prime ministers, or presidents—have a responsibility to protect the lives, livelihoods, and way of life of their citizens on a daily basis and especially to respond when they are attacked—whether on December 7, 1941, or September 11, 2001. Leaders also should take into account the secondary, prudential criteria: the *likelihood of success* of the decision to go to war and consideration of whether appropriate non-military options have been reasonably tried (*reasonable last resort* and strategic *proportionality*). Clearly, the decision to bring al Qaeda and its allies to justice and thwart future attacks met these criteria.

When it comes to the second set of just war criteria—the ethics of how the war was fought, or *jus in bello*—America and its allies were required to act *proportionately* and *discriminately*. For the first several years, its modest force of just 25,000 troops on the ground was not an "invasion" in a rugged country of over 30 million people. The United States did not carpet bomb cities or devastate the countryside. United States forces and its allies tried very hard to *discriminate* between combatants and noncombatants through the application of rigorous rules of engagement, often putting their own military personnel at increased risk.

That brings us to the primary focus of this paper—the ethics and responsibility after the war's ending (*jus post bellum*). Although low-intensity conflict seemed to never end in Afghanistan, there were efforts to lay the foundation for a just and enduring long-term peace. Perhaps most importantly, massive investments were made in education, training, and infrastructure for the Afghan people. There was no plan to pillage the Afghan people or rob the country of its natural resources. In fact, the United States actually left behind millions of dollars of military equipment to equip Afghanistan's

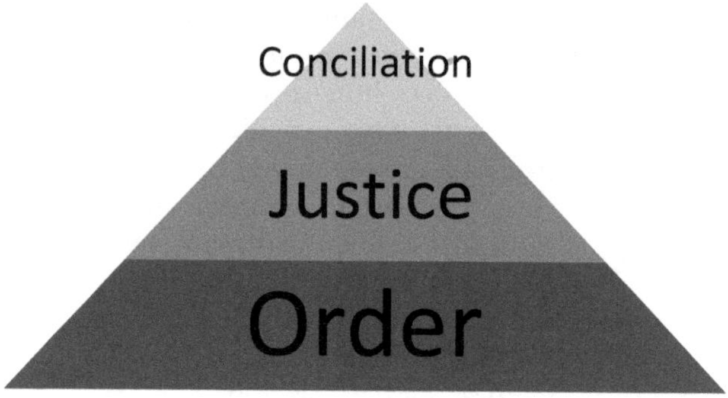

Figure 8.1 Jus Post Bellum: Order, Justice, and *Conciliation.*

military that had been trained by the United States and its allies. However, Afghanistan's military, such as it was, dissolved rapidly, even before the United States and other allies left the country in August 2021.

A morally satisfying peace begins with *order* (governance, rule of law) that develops into *justice* and takes steps toward long-term *conciliation. Conciliation* means coming to terms with the past and seeing former enemies as partners in a future peace. However, one cannot establish enduring *justice* and *conciliation* without basic *order*—the first step.

A word about nomenclature is necessary. For most of the last two millennia, discussions of just war statecraft focused attention on the decision to go to war and how war was fought. The issues of late- and post-conflict peace and security were largely seen as being obvious. Philosophers and theologians such as Augustine (1994), as well as Cicero and more recently B.L. Hart, usually said something along the lines of the following: "the end of war is a better state of peace." Aquinas famously argued for the pursuit of order, justice, and peace. Some have argued that *jus post bellum* was implicit in the war aims or in efforts at post-conflict juridical forms of justice (e.g., Nuremberg). Thus, it was mostly since the immediate aftermath of 9/11 that a group of scholars such as Eric Patterson, Brian Orend, and others have increasingly highlighted the late- and post-conflict dynamics, emphasizing the term *jus post bellum*. Strangely, and largely without citing the important *jus post bellum* literature of the early 2000s, a hazy new term has developed that sometimes seeks to distance itself from *jus post bellum*: "*jus ex bello*." The idea of *jus ex bello*, according to one author, is "the set of considerations that govern whether a war, once begun, should be brought to an end and if so how" (Mollendorf 2008, 123). The basic idea here is important, but it seems to have fallen into a simplistic view that this is somehow distinct from a wider *jus post bellum*.

Unfortunately, quite a bit of scholarship views war as linear and the three phases of just war statecraft as somehow distinct categories, with little interaction or overlap. This has been particularly true of Americans in the past, for whom the experience of war was often quite truncated and linear: Americans typically think about the beginning and successful termination of war: the Civil War (1861–1865) and the First World War (1917–1918) being cases in point. Perhaps the most obvious example is the Second World War, where nearly every American adult can quote the start date (December 7, 1941) and get close to the end dates (V-E and V-J days, summer of 1945). This type of reasoning is wrong because, for most people in most places, war has a way of ebbing and flowing, or, better, raging and subsiding, and cooling off and flaring up. This type of reasoning is also wrong because war has phases that include other forms of security competition, engagement, and deterrence.

Thus, the term *jus post bellum* captures two major trends in war. The first is the fact that many regions of conflict, such as Central Asia, the Great Lakes region of Africa, and Sudan, are zones of ongoing conflict. It is hard to know when they started, and it is hard to know if a peace deal, such as Rwanda's 1992 Arusha Accords, symbolizes a secure peace or merely an interregnum (Rwanda's genocide broke out in April 1994, after a massive arming of the Hutu population that began in December 1993). Tied to this is the fact that government authorities are responsible for diplomacy, economic statecraft, national defense and deterrence, and all the other elements of politics at all times. Thus, when one thinks of what the US Department of Defense now labels the five phases of the war, leaders are thinking about ethics and strategy at all times:

- Phase 0 ("Shape"): the period of diplomacy, intergovernmental relations, economic statecraft, etc. ("Shaping").
- Phase I ("Deter"): the preparation, training, and explicit activities designed to move beyond passive preparation to actively deter threats from rivals and aggressors.
- Phases II–III ("Seize the Initiative" and "Dominate"): what we call "hot war," that is, the activities to engage military power in ways to bring secure victory.
- Phase IV ("Stabilize"): the activities of military, legal, diplomatic, humanitarian, and other agencies to bring a secure and enduring order. In other words, phases 0 and IV, as well as phase V below, overlap and should deepen toward peace and away from armed conflict.
- Phase V ("Enable Civil Authority"): involves the end goal of establishing the first element of order following war (Otto 2017, Fig. 1, 79).[1]

The point being made here is that it is probably best to think in terms of *jus post bellum*, for even in the course of the hot war, as context changes for any of a number of reasons, proper government authorities should be assessing and re-assessing war aims and intentions. This is true at every phase of warfare and on every day of a hot war. In other words, *jus ad bellum* is inextricably linked at all times with *jus in bello* and with *jus post bellum*, because authorities are deciding as the campaigns go on about matters of just cause and right intention in the light of battlefield activities and political considerations, and, at all times, with a vision through this battlefield or campaign toward the objective of peace.

Therefore, this chapter looks at three *jus post bellum* milestones in Afghanistan. The first is the immediate aftermath of the smashing of al Qaeda and the fall of the Taliban—the early years of UN and US-NATO efforts to stabilize the country and foster representative law and order. The second milestone is at approximately the one-decade mark—from 2009 to 2012, when unsuccessful peacemaking efforts included indigenous councils (*loya jirga*) and the inclusion of Taliban representatives. The final milestone is the 20-year mark and includes the precipitous abandonment of Afghanistan by President Biden, accompanied by our allies. It is noteworthy how rarely the term "victory" is used when elites talk about Afghanistan at any stage of the war. We will also examine the relationship of types of victory to the morality of winning, as well as how to think about *jus post bellum* after September 11, 2021.

2 Starting with Order

The fundamental responsibility of political actors, in war or peace, is to work toward *order*. In post-conflict settings, *order* begins when the killing dramatically diminishes and the exercise of sovereignty by a single point of authority is established. *Order* extends its roots through the maturation of government capacity and services. There are military (traditional security), governance (domestic politics), and international security conditions to a basic post-conflict *order* that must be met and extended if there is to be lasting peace.

The *military* dimension regards the definitive termination of "hot" conflict, with the tools of warfare resting solely in the hands of legitimate authorities. This means that all belligerents have agreed to the cessation of conflict; there are no organized, armed spoilers or insurgents lurking in the countryside to destabilize the peace deal, and all parties support the new security arrangement by no longer challenging it via military force. Military considerations of *order* also begin to take into account the appropriate structuring of military strength and forces to sustain a robust defense without undermining the security of formal rivals.

All of these efforts to confirm military aspects of post-conflict *order* should work in tandem with domestic and international political objectives while being careful to buttress, rather than erode, the basic peace settlement. Hence, the *governance* dimension of *order* is the imposition and maintenance of the domestic rule of law. It implies a national political entity which exercises sovereignty over the legitimate use of force at home, as well as political sovereignty over its policies at home and in relations with its neighbors. However, in some cases, the resumption of sovereignty follows a period of political rehabilitation, whether in the aftermath of military defeat (post-Second World War Japan) or instituting political tutelage and reconstruction (East Timor). In either case, *order* means focusing on the fundamental tasks of governance, including governance over the economic sector.

The third dimension of *order* is the *international security* dimension, which means that the state no longer faces an imminent threat from an internal or external foe, nor is the country a threat to the peace and security of its neighbors (e.g., refugee flows). The international security dimension is intertwined with and reinforces both basic internal security and efforts at governance. In sum, the very first steps toward a longer-term, more robust domestic and national situation of security begin with the grueling task of implementing *order* with these three dimensions.

Just getting to the first stage of *jus post bellum—order*—can be a herculean ordeal. *Order* is most likely to occur when one side convincingly defeats its adversary on the battlefield, as the Union battered the Confederacy, as the Entente defeated the Triple Alliance in 1918, and as the Allies crushed the Nazis and Imperial Japan in 1945. More recently were the decisive victories by the RPF in Rwanda (1994) and by the Sri Lankan government (2009). Decisive victories allow a window for the uncontested elimination of threats to security and the establishment of the basics of *political order*. History attests to how costly and difficult such victories can be to win, as in each of these cases, but victory does provide an opportunity to found a secure post-conflict *order*. We will discuss victory at the end of the essay, but suffice it to say at this point there was no international consensus to achieve total victory against all of the violent extremist elements in Afghanistan.

3 A Richer *Jus Post Bellum*—Justice

Order is a necessary condition for *jus post bellum*. Nonetheless, at the end of some conflicts, particularly since the Second World War, a richer dimension of *jus post bellum* has been employed—provisions for *justice* in addition to creating a situation of security. Aggressors are held accountable in some way for their actions. Accountability is a moral principle based on the notion of responsibility—political and military leaders have a responsibility to their citizens and their neighbors to promote security. This is expected in domestic society, and when possible, we should employ the notion of *justice* at the end of inter- and intra-state wars. The same also applies to warriors and political leaders who, during the fighting, violate the war convention: these should be held responsible when possible.[2]

Most wars conclude with *order*, not *justice*. Indeed, *justice* is not available at the end of every war. The reality of warfare is that ending the carnage soon is often preferable to prolonging the conflict in hopes of "ending war with *justice*." Nevertheless, in those cases where *justice* is possible, it should be pursued. Although in practice *justice* is problematic, it may take the form of *restitution*—a payment of some sort to the aggrieved or the victim(s). A better mechanism for *justice* in international politics is punishment—a penalty for employing violence in the first place or for how violence was perpetrated. In any event, *justice* is desirable and may lead to a better peace that both sides can find acceptable (Mani 2002; Walzer 2004).

In theory, a holistic notion of *justice* takes into account the losses of victims as well as the responsibility of the aggressors. In other words, there is a need for *restitution* to the victims and punishment of the aggressors. Both sides of the coin are necessary for comprehensive *justice* to be achieved. The concept of *restitution* is that victims or their representatives are entitled to the *restoration* of something. Unfortunately, there are many flaws with employing reparations in international politics, not the least of which is that it is often impossible to return what was taken: personal property, a home filled with memories, or the life of a loved one.

4 Conciliation/Reconciliation

If *order* is the attainable and *justice* the possible, then *(re)conciliation* is the desirable. *Conciliation* is future-focused in that it sees former enemies as partners in a shared future. Sometimes, particularly in intra-state conflict, it is *reconciliation*—building bridges between parties that have some shared past. In international conflict, it is more likely that the goal is *conciliation*—the mutual effort of both sides to overcome past hostility and reframe the relationship as one of partnership to rebuild together. If the fundamental goals of just war thinking are to promote international security and to protect human life, then *conciliation* does this by ameliorating the conditions that can lead to new or renewed violence.

The Christian foundation for classic just war theory derives from a theological basis for *reconciliation*, which is based upon neighbor-love (*caritas*). *Caritas*, also translated as "charity," is the notion of concern for one's neighbor as for oneself. Love calls on individuals to protect their neighbors and may result in self-defensive war or intervention on behalf of allies or those who are defenseless. Love may also motivate just punishment, the righting of wrongs, and restitution for the victim. Love questions our motives, restrains our behavior, and foresees a better peace approximating the ideal as described in Augustine's *City of God* (Augustine 1994, see also Ramsey 1961).

Although I believe that *reconciliation* based on *caritas* is important in individual human relationships and can be called on in intra-state conflicts, it is a tricky notion for international affairs (Boraine et al. 1997, Frost 1991, Gibson and Gouws 1999, Kritz 1995, Markel 1999, Minow 1998, Rigby 2001, Stahn 2001, Walter 1997). The international system is based primarily on national interests, and unless common interests are engaged, *conciliation* is unlikely to occur at war's end. In other words, *states' common interests can provide the basis for conciliation.* In most conflicts, enemies have a history of tension and competition and have probably fought openly numerous times in the past. In these cases, a change in interests is the usual mechanism for *conciliation* to be possible.

Conciliation based on evolving interests is not a new idea. Rousseau and Kant both argued for a perpetual peace based, in part, on sovereigns realizing that war was not in the long-term interest of their nations (Kant 1983; Rousseau 1997). However, in the real world, such relational changes usually take a long period of time (e.g., the United States and Canada) and/or may require a shared threat to provide a context for shared interests (e.g., France and Germany facing a common threat during the Cold War). The Scandinavian countries provide a case in point. Formerly a region of competition and violence, today it is difficult to imagine a more pacific set of relationships than those among the Nordic countries. What inspired the *conciliation* of these governments? The answer is not culture, language, religion, trade, or some formal acts of forgiveness. Rather, the basis of *conciliation* was provided by balance-of-power struggles in the 19th century. First the Napoleonic wars, and later the Franco-Prussian wars, created a situation of shared interests for the Nordic countries. Moreover, this process of *conciliation* has weathered the tests of the two World Wars, the Cold War (including Finnish alignment with the Soviet Union and Swedish neutrality), and the rise of the "New Europe" (European Union).

Of course, in international life, *justice* might be a mechanism that helps change the socio-political context in such a way as to allow for a positive change in relationships. Certainly, one outcome of the Nuremberg Trials was the effect that the punishment of Third Reich leaders had on thawing relations between Germany and its neighbors. Acts of *justice* can bring vindication to the victims and provide conditions wherein a change in the quality of relationships is possible.

However, it is more likely that the looming Soviet threat played a larger role in Germany and its former adversaries coming to a shared set of strategic interests. The development of Western European institutions, including the regional Coal and Steel Community, atomic cooperation, NATO, and the European Economic Community (EEC), was rooted in mutual interests and shared threats, not forgiveness and *reconciliation*.

Idealists, however, argue that forgiveness and mercy form the fulcrum for *conciliation* in international affairs. I remain skeptical that this is the case. There are almost no examples in international life of heads of state asking for forgiveness from their neighbors or nations they have been at war with, resulting in acts of *conciliation* among states. The reasons for this are numerous, but the primary among them is the multi-causal nature of conflict and the recognition that states go to war because they feel that it is in their interest to do so. States are self-interested and it is folly to expect them, except under the most unique of circumstances, to plead, "We were wrong, won't you please forgive us?"[3] Consequently, the mercy/forgiveness path to *conciliation* among states is improbable at best; however, as indicated, *conciliation* could be possible based on the evolution or re-interpretation of national interests (Stassen 1997).[4]

When it comes to *reconciliation* in domestic politics, such as after the overthrow of a tyrannical regime or oligarchy or following a civil war, thoughtful policies of *justice* and political *conciliation* are important. There is a large amount of literature on the different mechanisms for this—South Africa's Truth and Reconciliation Commission, international tribunals such as those for the former Yugoslavia and Rwanda, as well as the informal community (*Gacaca*) courts in Rwanda, various truth commissions in Latin America and East Timor, transparency initiatives such as East Germany's lustration policies, as well as various forms of amnesty from the US Civil War until today.[5] As we look at the Afghanistan case, we will see a variety of policies designed to promote the reconstruction of the country while prosecuting security operations against terrorists and other agents of instability.

5 The First Phase of the Afghanistan War: The Early Years (2002–2005)

In December 2001, donors met in Bonn; then in subsequent months, the UN, United States, and others pledged billions of dollars (or the equivalent) to help construct a modern Afghanistan after decades of violence and intermittent civil war. These were good-faith efforts over a number of years to establish the rule of law, de-mobilize combatants, and develop a government of national unity. These approaches, however, were rooted in secularist cookie-cutter models employed with only limited success elsewhere, such as in Africa and Latin America. As I have argued elsewhere, such approaches tend to fail, in part, because they do not engage disenfranchised leaders (e.g., low-level Taliban) and because they lack culturally relevant mechanisms for peace (Patterson 2011a). The Bonn Agreement committed global resources to build Afghan institutions, invest in development and reconstruction, and ensure that Afghan citizens not only had livelihoods, human rights, and civil liberties but also that violent jihadists no longer had a base to work from in Afghanistan.

In 2003, the United Nations Development Program (UNDP) launched a disarmament, de-mobilization, and reintegration (DDR) campaign like those previously implemented in other post-conflict environments from the Balkans to Africa to Central America. The campaign was titled the "Afghan New Beginnings Program" (ANBP). The goal was to de-mobilize the many armed, competing power centers around the country, thus diluting the power of warlords and the potential for renewed conflict. The ANBP's budget was the equivalent of $140.9 million, and the program mandated the de-mobilization of 100,000 soldiers from the umbrella Afghan Militia Forces who had helped topple the Taliban. However, senior leaders were often co-opted by giving them high-ranking government positions. Combatants who were de-mobilized participated in a formal military ceremony, often with a military parade or review, handed in a weapon (often an antique model inferior to what they kept hidden), attended a seminar, and received compensation consisting primarily of food and clothing. The former militia members, after two decades of war, were to return to their families and become productive citizens. According to the International Center for Transitional Justice (ICTJ), more than 62,000 former combatants, 11,000 children, and nearly 25,000 women were recipients of assistance through ANBP at a cost of $100 million. Moreover, much of the heavy weaponry (e.g., tanks) were turned in at cantonment sites.[6]

A second phase of DDR began with Presidential Decree 50 in the summer of 2004. This Decree declared any extant militias to be "illegally armed groups" and essentially was a final chance for such individuals and their leaders to de-mobilize. With the advent of national assembly elections the next year and concerns about Afghan security, a second formal program called Disarmament of Illegally Armed Groups (DIAG) began. The "carrot" was that the leaders of illegally armed groups (regional and local militias) could participate in the elections if their groups disarmed; the "stick" was that those who had not/would not disband their fighting forces were barred from holding office. DIAG was largely unsuccessful except in a few cases.

Finally, it should be noted that during this period, the Government of Afghanistan's Afghan Independent Human Rights Commission (AIHRC) adopted an "Action Plan on Peace, Reconciliation, and Justice" in December 2005. Four years later, there were few results, particularly as the security situation deteriorated with the rebounding of the Taliban.

The AIHRC's Action Plan called for a) formal remembrance of past victims of abuse, b) human rights (and corruption) vetting of government officials, c) truth-seeking, d) reconciliation, and e) creation of a Task Force to recommend further measures.

It is also worth noting that these approaches were all good-faith efforts based on what was considered state-of-the-art Western approaches to post-conflict stabilization and reconstruction. There are numerous reasons why these approaches have not brought safety and security to Afghanistan, but one of them is simply that these efforts often did not take root because they lacked cultural and religious relevance to the local population. Secular human rights approaches, rather than those that appeal to the religious authority of Islam, seem unlikely to provide a firm foundation for respecting human rights in Afghanistan. Secular reconciliation efforts that disregard the cultural symbols of weapons and neglect the role of tribal and religious leaders in "waging peace" have proven their futility in engaging so-called "reconcilable" elements of the Taliban and other illegally armed groups. What was needed to complement other efforts was a religiously relevant approach to dialogue for *reconciliation*. Islamic concepts of arbitration and consultation (*takhim*, *sulh*) may have provided such an approach (Patterson 2011a).

During this time period, the Western military footprint in the country deliberately tried to be a *stabilizing*, rather than an *occupying*, force. The United States only placed about 25,000 troops in Afghanistan for the first several years, and NATO and other international forces played a large role. During these years, the equivalent of billions of dollars was spent by the UN and donor countries on Afghanistan, and the equivalent of hundreds of millions of dollars was provided in various forms of assistance to Pakistan as well. The international community had tried a variety of efforts to ensure a post-conflict future for Afghanistan that no longer threatens other nations and that provides security, opportunity, and human rights protections for its citizens. In short, the West wanted to get out and allow the locals to run their own affairs, assuming that Western citizens would remain safe from Islamist terrorism at home.

The fundamental problem with the Afghanistan War, however, was that the foundational aspect of *order* was never achieved after the initial defeat of the Taliban. The West and their allies, working with the government of Afghanistan, never achieved domestic security for individual Afghans during this time. There was no martial law, no imposition of *order*, and no part of the country that remained immune from terrorist attacks. This all became increasingly obvious when the first suicide bombers—a historical and religious anathema for Afghanistan's Muslims—arrived on the scene in 2007. Without securing *order* for domestic and governance dimensions rooted in appropriate cultural norms, Afghanistan did not have an adequate chance for peace and security—hence, the failure to provide the foundational requirement for *jus post bellum* during the first phase of the Afghanistan War within the larger scenario of the "Global War on Terror."

6 Second Phase of the Afghanistan War: 2009 to the End of the First Decade (2012)

As the Bush Administration (2001–2008) was preparing to leave office in January 2009, the administration had increased its efforts to stabilize Afghanistan through a modest buildup of US forces, changes in strategy (counter-terrorism vs. counter-insurgency), and simultaneously building Afghan institutions with allies. There was increasing donor and supporter fatigue, but few could imagine a way out of Afghanistan. In the late Bush Administration and into the early Obama Administration, there was a reluctant willingness to begin negotiations with Taliban leaders, many of whom were living in exile in nearby Pakistan. After a decade of low-intensity conflict, recognizing the reality of needing to include these actors was a significant departure from past policies but yielded no local ethno-religious and security realities.

Part of the reality was an uncertain political situation that never truly stabilized under President Hamid Karzai and cultural resistance to Western norms (e.g., empowerment of women and tolerance for religious minorities), in addition to increasing instability from suicide bombers, invigorated Taliban-led insurgency, and terrorism. Thus, the Afghan government and its Western allies were at the time stymied in their efforts to provide a basic level of security. Washington, along with the allies working for stabilization in Afghanistan, came to realize that some sort of orderly future would have to include some sort of *reconciliation* with individuals and families that in the past have been associated with the Taliban—perhaps even senior figures in the Taliban. Building schools, clearing minefields, and paving roads simply were not going to do the job.

The West faced a dilemma in trying to find a political arrangement that would be appealing enough to cause a reappraisal of common interests without also bringing the Taliban in "from the cold." That reappraisal could have been based on major military victories that left the Taliban and its tribal allies stricken and on the verge of collapse, allowing its members to switch sides. A reframing of the Taliban's and tribal interests might have included the opportunity for some members of the Taliban to participate in governance, such as by evolving into a political party. We have seen elsewhere how rebel groups can disband and become part of the political process, such as occurred with Colombia's M-19 in 1991.

Most importantly, however, such a "reframing" of interests could take place in the context of arbitration (*sulh*) and/or a formal Afghan *loya jirga*.

At the time, counterinsurgency expert David Kilcullen and others argued that it was possible to strip away "second- and third-tier Taliban" from the hardened, "irreconcilable" leadership of the Taliban (and al Qaeda) (Kilcullen 2007). This might be accomplished primarily by reaching out to tribal leaders as points of authority, rather than to the Taliban's leadership, and could follow the first model of reconciliation noted above. For such to have happened, there needed to have been a reappraisal of interests combined with religiously-informed appeals to dialogue, not unlike what happened in Iraq's Sunni Awakening in 2007. In the Iraqi case, not only did the West commit to increasing security (through the "surge"), but tribal and religious leaders concluded that al Qaeda in Iraq (AQI) was morally corrupt and that it was no longer in Sunni interests to avoid national reconciliation. A major summit of religious leaders—the Iraqi Interreligious Congress of July 2007, which included Muqtada al Sadr and dozens of other key religious figures—helped to establish a modest basis for national *reconciliation*, at least on security matters of mutual interest (Patterson 2011b).

Related efforts toward *reconciliation* in Afghanistan could include religiously relevant post-conflict efforts at *justice* and *reconciliation*, be it through a blanket amnesty rooted in "forgiveness" or one like the model employed in East Timor. The Government of East Timor had a two-tier transitional justice system. The first included a Special Crimes Investigation Unit and courts to try egregious crimes as defined in terms of the Rome Statute's war crimes, including murder and rape. However, the vast majority of East Timorese went before a separate juridical institution based in local communities that often included religious leaders. Perpetrators confessed their guilt publicly and were "sentenced" to modest community service. This quasi-amnesty allowed thousands to return to their homes while paying their debt to society and establishing the "truth" of what happened. Moreover, it is likely that Muslim leadership on this issue could have helped, perhaps in the way that Malaysia had been a peace agent between Mindanao and Manila, such as through the offices of the Organization of Islamic Countries.

Let me just sum up the argument just made: Security *(order)* was not achieved in the first decade of the Afghanistan war. Had a newly invigorated security force determinedly sought and crushed the Taliban in 2009–2010, then it would have ceased to be an effective military force, and lower levels of its supporters would have either been killed, incarcerated, or quietly slipped away. Surviving elements may have been integrated into national politics as they saw their interests shift. National and provincial councils (*loya jirgas*) may have been employed to bring them in from the cold.

However, what happened in 2010 was the opposite. When a senior Taliban figure—a revered fighter from the 1990s—was enroute to attend a peace conference, his motorcade was blown apart by a rival Taliban faction. There was little stomach among many Taliban to negotiate. Moreover, they rightly judged that the Obama Administration and its allies did not have the stomach for a massive military intervention that would turn the tide against the Taliban (the Obama Administration did increase drone strikes but not multi-year boots-on-the-ground commitments).

7 The Afghanistan War's Second Decade Since 2012 and Beyond 2022

Whither Afghanistan today? Whither US policy toward Afghanistan today? The principles of *order, justice*, and *conciliation* continue to inform the situation. First, the Taliban do want a level of *order* in Afghanistan. They need public services, such as trash collection, medical provision, and safe drinking water, to be available. These common goods raise their legitimacy, and the citizenry will increasingly demand such services. Afghanistan does not have a major international threat on its borders, though at present its porous borders make it notorious for trafficking of all kinds. Afghanistan's neighbors had previously looked the other way and even encouraged lawless borders in the past, but with the refugee crisis caused by America's pull-out in 2021, many have moved to increase the level of security on those borders. The real question for the Taliban, then, is how to provide domestic security and how to impose their normative commitments on the population (moral order).

The Taliban have multiple competitors within Afghanistan, the most lethal being pockets of al Qaeda and ISIS-K fighters. These militants provide at least two threats to the Taliban. The first is a sense of attack at home that destabilizes, or interrupts, domestic peace and the legitimacy of the Taliban as an effective government. They become seen as inadequate in providing basic internal security. The second is related: should external powers believe that ISIS-K and others are preparing to launch attacks on Western targets, they could strike preemptively. There seems to be no current desire in Washington, DC, Turtle Bay, or Brussels to take out the Taliban and re-invade the country. Nevertheless, the fact that senior defense officials testified to the US Congress that terrorists could strike North America within six months was seen as a concern for the Biden Administration. Thus, Western powers are no doubt preparing for contingencies.

Over time, no one knows for certain if the Taliban will be effective in governing and how strong its various political rivals will turn out to be. Of course, the Taliban has its own moral vision, a preferred moral *order* for Afghanistan. I have written elsewhere that one form of victory is moral victory: the vindication of the value structure of the winners and the imposition of that value structure on the losers (Patterson 2019). Just as the

Western allies imposed a liberal system and accompanying institutions on Western Germany in 1945 and the Soviet Union imposed a Communist system in Eastern Germany, so too the Taliban is imposing its version of Sharia law as the law of the land. Only time will tell how this will actually work in practice.

When it comes to *justice* and *conciliation*, the Taliban has been divided internally on how to deal with its formal rivals. Although there has been some amnesty for those associated with the previous regime, there have also been murders, executions, and reprisals. A big question is what to do with hundreds of thousands of low-level government officials, policemen, soldiers, and other civil servants who will likely not face persecution as long as they appear and act loyally. Indeed, the best way for the Taliban to cement its legitimacy at home and abroad is for it to be magnanimous in victory.

On the international stage, how are countries such as the United States to respond? The Biden administration irresponsibly left a security vacuum in Central Asia, one that plays into the interests of China and Russia. The Western alliance needs to take seriously the continuing threats of terrorism, narco-trafficking, population displacement, and the regional dynamics of Iran, Pakistan, and India, as well as China and Russia.

The West has long wanted *justice* for war crimes that included leaders of the Taliban and especially some of its allies, such as the Haqqani network, for the murder and mayhem caused over the past 20 years. It is very difficult to imagine this happening in the short term. It would require a popular revolt that led to a political transition that isolated senior Taliban leaders and their accomplices so they could be detained to face a domestic or international tribunal. The former happened to Saddam Hussein and his henchman after 2003, but it is hard to imagine this in Afghanistan in 2022. Similarly, is there enough civil society momentum in Afghanistan to force a "pacted" transition at some point in the future, such as what happened in many Latin American countries in the 1980s and 1990s? There may be the opportunity for a domestic accounting, such as occurred with South Africa's Truth and Reconciliation Commission, or just a reporting as happened with East Timor's local community-run courts. As of early 2022, all of these seem like impossible dreams for a peaceful, just Afghanistan.

8 Conclusion

In 2001, a fairly new US president first faced challenges from China and Russia. Little did he anticipate that after just eight months in office, the United States would face the largest attack on United States soil since Pearl Harbor. President Bush, standing at the head of a united country, called for *justice*. The first mission of what became known as the Global War on Terrorism—to smash al Qaeda and its allies—was temporarily accomplished, but what became the longer-term goal, of making Afghanistan a stable, modern contributor to the security of its own people and that region, remains unfulfilled at this juncture. A secure and just political *order* was never fully established. Victory was never declared or ceded. Victory, in this context, is winning or success in war. More specifically, *victory in war* can mean one or more of the following three definitional actions:

1 defeating an opponent;
2 not allowing an opponent to win; and/or
3 the vindication of values (Patterson 2019).

The first type of victory is outright beating one's opponent. The second is a Fabian strategy of avoiding defeat by outlasting an adversary (Patterson 2019). We have typically thought that the United States should mobilize its massive resources and only do the former, as happened in 1865, 1918, and 1945. The second type of victory is not unknown to the United States: this was George Washington's strategy, and it was successfully employed against us in Vietnam.

Many may wish that the United States had smashed the Taliban a decade ago, but that was not what happened. However, a middle ground was certainly possible and was possible for many years: a sort of strategic muddling along that kept terrorists from openly operating out of Afghanistan and kept the Taliban somewhat at bay, maintained a regional "cold peace," and continued the slow evolution of Afghan society and institutions. Such an approach would also have had a diplomatic component, but we are now seeing that China, Russia, and others are successfully outmaneuvering Western allies in the political realm. It was stunning to see Americans fleeing in August 2021 while the Russian ambassador in Kabul graciously entertained a Taliban delegation.

Part of what makes the Afghanistan debacle so heart-rending has to do with a third type of winning, *victory* that has a *moral* dimension. This is difficult in the case of Afghanistan because the opponents represent utterly different views on what the world should look like. Take a step back for a moment to the 1940s to fully comprehend moral victory. The United States and the Allies won, decimating long-term threats to world peace and imposing a set of moral principles into international relations, including the Universal Declaration of Human Rights and United Nations Charter, the Geneva Conventions of 1949, and similar standards such as the Genocide Convention and International Human Rights Law, as well as a set of related institutions including the Marshall Plan and Bretton Woods system (Patterson 2019).

Imagine, in contrast, how an Axis victory would have resulted in a different set of opportunities and institutionalized values. Had the Nazis won, it still would have been a form of moral victory, but in a catastrophic, wicked sense. The Nazi and Japanese value systems of racialism and superiority would have been vindicated; it would have been a victor's justice, so to speak. "Vindication" is not a moral judgment in retrospect about which values are superior—it is the recognition that at the end of some wars, "victory" means more than going home with some material losses for the loser. "Vindication" means that the values of the victor become the worldview framing a new status quo. We have seen this throughout history: Tours confirmed continental Europe as Christian, setting the foundations of the Carolingian Empire; Alexander's victories brought Hellenism to the Near East; Napoleon's victories and the "Continental System" changed the role of church-state relations, legal codes, and many other elements of life across Europe; and the US Civil War abolished slavery once and for all and dramatically altered the course of the country. So too, victors such as Lenin, Mao, and the Khmer Rouge imposed a value system on their populaces and foes after winning. In each case, victory had far-reaching moral, social, and political consequences (Patterson 2019).

Fast forward to today. The fact that global human rights norms, such as religious freedom for all and the equal citizenship of all adults—including women and religious minorities—never fully took root in Afghanistan is clearly a failure. However, it is one that could be predicted because from the earliest period, including US counsel on Afghanistan's Constitution, the Americans pulled their punches on these critical human rights issues. None would expect Afghanistan to look like Canada, but it should have more of a flavor of Pakistan and India, where large swathes of the country are pro-democratic, despite terrorism, violence, criminality, and inequality.

Even though the Afghan government surrendered as its Western allies left the country, the United States still has responsibilities, both to ensure that Afghanistan never becomes a focal point for threats to the United States and to protect Afghan friends who fought for their country.

There are a number of potential questions raised by the Afghanistan war and the "Global War on Terrorism" that are beyond this essay but worth mentioning. One is simply the relationship between the two: if al Qaeda had been eliminated or surrendered, how should we think about operations in Afghanistan against the indigenous Taliban? There is scholarship on the wide-ranging Authorization to Use Military Force, provided to the Bush and Obama Administrations to prosecute terrorism globally. It is interesting to think about narrower objectives (e.g., just crushing al Qaeda and departing Afghanistan) and narrower theatres rather than a global effort that considers any and all terrorist networks as targets. As of this writing, that Authorization is no longer valid, but the US military and intelligence services remain vigilant in watching potential terrorist centers, such as Yemen, ungoverned parts of Pakistan and Afghanistan, West Africa, and parts of the Middle East.

Another thing worth more scholarship is careful scrutiny of the permanence or impermanence of war aims, such as in the case of Afghanistan. I have written about this in the Vietnam case, how statements of war rationale by Eisenhower, Kennedy, Johnson, and Nixon all pointed to a specific context ("the domino theory"), strategy (containment), and moral purpose (safeguarding democracy and allies) (Patterson 2019). Perhaps we need to think about "campaigns" and "theatres" rather than a *global* war on terrorist organizations and individuals. Perhaps the Cold War is an analogue here: one could imagine a major victory in one area (e.g., holding West Berlin, frustrating French and Italian communists, and liberating Grenada) but not in others (e.g., Cuba and Vietnam). In other words, a global, multi-year "war" may be conceptually stretched beyond being useful for more focused analysis.

At this vantage point, the calamitous abandonment of Afghanistan by the Biden Administration and other allies in 2021 hurt US national security: one Administration official recently testified that a resurgent al Qaeda and ISIS would be able to hit the United States from Afghanistan within six months. This is not *order*, much less *justice* or *conciliation*.

However, that does not mean that the decisions to enter the fight and prosecute terrorists and criminals, along with the West's extraordinary generosity and resolve to help the Afghan people achieve stability and peace, were craven in intent or application. What was needed was most likely another generation of patient security assistance and national construction, similar to the way that there are still troops securing the peace in Europe and Asia long after the surrender of the Axis Powers in 1945. Let us hope that the millions of Afghans who benefitted from training, education, and the vision of a better future offered over the past 20 years, after their victory over the Soviet Union, may be able to help their country move toward a more secure, more free, and more peaceful future, which will secure *order* and call for *justice* and *conciliation*.

Notes

1 Gustav Otto's article describes the DoD's operational phases 0, I, II, III, IV, and V in Figure 1 showing how Phase 0 "Shaping/Diplomacy" and IV (Stabilizing) overlap at https://thesimonscenter.org/wp-content/uploads/2017/08/IAJ-8-3-2017-pg78-86.pdf.

2 The codification of the Geneva protocols as well as the American Uniform Code of Military Justice became the basis for numerous trials of American GIs during and after the Vietnam conflict.

3 Interestingly, we observe countries that experience significant regime change (e.g., in Latin America and Eastern Europe in the early 1990s) making public

statements breaking with the past, but we do not see these countries ask for forgiveness or offer restitution to neighbors they have threatened or harmed.

4 A relatively newer literature championed by Glen Stassen and others called "just peacemaking" takes most of its proponents from the pacifist tradition; nonetheless the efforts of Stassen and his colleagues are to address the real-world dilemmas in bedeviled areas of intractable conflict.

5 A place to start is Patterson 2011c. Georgetown University's Berkley Center for Religion, Peace, and World Affairs has a set of case studies on transitional justice, peacemaking, and related topics. See: https://berkleycenter.georgetown.edu/projects/case-studies-on-religion-and-conflict. Accessed June 1, 2024.

6 Technically speaking, the ANBP program was formalized at the Tokyo Donor Conference of February 2003. Japan was to take the lead on Security Sector Reform (as agreed in Bonn).

References

Augustine, St. 1994. *The City of God*. Cambridge: Cambridge University Press.

Boraine, Alex, Janet Levy, and Ronel Scheffer. 1997. *Dealing with the Past: Truth and Reconciliation in South Africa*. Cape Town: IDASA.

Frost, Brian. 1991. *The Politics of Peace*. London: Darton, Longman, and Todd, Ltd.

Gibson, James L., and Amanda Gouws. 1999. "Truth and Reconciliation in South Africa: Attributions of Blame and the Struggle over Apartheid." *The American Political Science Review* 93, no. 3 (September): 501–517. https://doi.org/10.2307/2585571

Kant, Immanuel. 1983. *Perpetual Peace and Other Essays*. Translated by T. Humphrey. Indianapolis, IN: Hackett.

Kilcullen, David. 2007. *The Accidental Guerrilla*. Oxford: Oxford University Press.

Kritz, Neil J. 1995. *Transitional Justice: How Emerging Democracies Reckon with Former Regimes*, vol. 2. Washington, DC: US Institute of Peace.

Mani, Rami. 2002. *Beyond Retribution: Seeking Justice in the Shadows of War*. Cambridge: Polity Press.

Markel, Dan. 1999. "The Justice of Amnesty? Towards a Theory of Retributivism in Recovering States." *The University of Toronto Law Journal* 49, no. 3 (Summer): 389–445. https://doi.org/10.2307/826004

Minow, Martha. 1998. *Between Vengeance and Forgiveness*. Boston, Beacon Press.

Mollendorf, Darrel. 2008. "Jus ex Bello." *The Journal of Political Philosophy* 16, no. 2: 123–136. https://www.fb03.uni-frankfurt.de/58976166/jus-ex-bello.pdf

Otto, Gustav A. 2017. "The End of Operational Phases at Last." *InterAgency Journal* 8, no. 3: 78–86. https://thesimonscenter.org/wp-content/uploads/2017/08/IAJ-8-3-2017-pg78-86.pdf

Patterson, Eric. 2011a. "Bury the Bloody Hatchet: Secularism, Islam, and Reconciliation in Afghanistan." *Interreligious Studies Forum* 5, no. 5 (February). https://acrobat.adobe.com/id/urn:aaid:sc:VA6C2:b40be510-f10d-4abd-9cdc-0ee2832aa005

Patterson, Eric. 2011b. *Politics in a Religious World: Toward a Religiously Literate U.S. Foreign Policy*. New York: Continuum.

Patterson, Eric, 2011c. *Ethics Beyond War's End*. Washington, DC: Georgetown University Press.

Patterson, Eric. 2019. *Just American Wars: Ethical Dilemmas in U.S. Military History*. New York: Routledge.
Ramsey, Paul. 1961. *War and the Christian Conscience: How Shall Modern War Be Conducted Justly?* Cambridge: Cambridge University Press.
Rigby, Andrew. 2001. *Justice and Reconciliation*. Boulder, CO: Lynne Rienner.
Rousseau, Jean Jacques. 1997. *The Social Contract and Other Later Political Writings*. Edited by Victor Gourevitch. Cambridge: Cambridge University Press.
Stahn, Carsten. 2001. "Accommodating Individual Criminal Responsibility and National Reconciliation: The UN Truth Commission for East Timor." *The American Journal of International Law* 95, no. 4 (October): 952–966. https://doi.org/10.2307/2674655
Stassen, Glen. 1997. "New Paradigm: Just Peacemaking Theory." *Council of the Societies for the Study of Religion Bulletin* (Spring). http://catalog.gcah.org/publicdata/files/5849/Just_Peacemaking.pdf
Walter, Barbara F. 1997. "The Critical Barrier to Civil War Settlement." *International Organization* 51, no. 3 (Summer): 335–364. http://www.jstor.org/stable/2703607
Walzer, Michael. 2004. "Just and Unjust Occupations." *Dissent* 51 (Winter): 61–63.

9 Meaningful Lives and Meaningful Deaths: Narrative Values and the Retreat from Afghanistan

Michael Blake

In 1971, John Kerry – who had recently joined the organization Vietnam Veterans Against the War – gave testimony to the Senate Foreign Relations Committee, which was considering how to end the war in Vietnam. As part of his testimony, Kerry asked a question for which he has become famous: How do you ask a man to be the last man to die for a mistake? (Kerry 2004 [1971]). The question has returned to prominence following the recent withdrawal of American service personnel from Afghanistan, after a 20-year military presence, and the return to power within Afghanistan of the Taliban. Kerry's question was intended, 50 years ago, as a distinctive sort of argument against a demand for further sacrifice on the part of American soldiers; even if the United States can sometimes rightly ask American soldiers to risk their lives, goes this argument, a *mistaken* war cannot justly ask so much of them.

This argument has obvious power; if it did not, Kerry would not be so closely associated with the question in which the argument was first raised. And yet that argument's contours are hardly obvious; what, exactly, would make a military action a *mistake* in the relevant sense? And why is it less morally troubling for a soldier's life to be lost in the service of a non-mistaken war, as opposed to a mistaken one? The soldier in question, after all, loses as much in either case, or so it seems; if there is something more troubling about the continued deaths of American service personnel in Vietnam than, say, the deaths of such personnel during World War II, in what can that moral distinction be found?

In this paper, I want to provide some partial and tentative answers to these questions. I will begin by arguing that the best construal of *mistake* in the argumentative pattern given here refers not to the overall justice of the war but to the success of that war in achieving its ends. I want to make the case, put more simply, that it is easier to ask people to die in the service of wars that succeed in their goals – whether or not those goals were sufficient to have justified such military action in the first place. The reason

DOI: 10.4324/9781003454144-12

for this, however, requires us to make an excursion into what it is that makes meaning in life possible – and how such meaning might ascribe value within a given life to what happens after that life's end. I want to make the case that the success of war makes a difference to the success of a life given in pursuit of that war – and that this fact persists regardless of whether the individual lives long enough to discover the relevant empirical facts about that war's success. I will conclude this paper by relating these thoughts more explicitly to the retreat from Afghanistan and to the ways in which the withdrawal from Afghanistan might be understood as a sort of moral tragedy in which the United States would bear some moral costs regardless of what choice they made.

In these thoughts, I follow some ideas of David Rodin about the ways in which time matters for the morality of war-making. Rodin has discussed the ways in which the moral costs of a war may shift, such that it might become morally obligatory to continue to fight a war that is, all-things-considered, "foolish, self-destructive, and immoral" (Rodin 2015, at 695). Such pathologies of warfare – which Rodin terms the "war trap" – can give us additional reasons to take great care before undertaking any particular military endeavor. My present task is to demonstrate that these ideas have some purchase, not only for the decisions of those charged with the giving of orders but also with reference to the lives of those who must follow such orders on the battlefield. A soldier who sheds blood in the pursuit of a goal that is achieved, I will argue, is provided with the tools needed to tell a story markedly unlike that available to a soldier similarly harmed in the pursuit of a war whose goals are not so achieved. As is the case for Rodin's war trap, these moral facts become more difficult as the war continues; after 20 years of warfare, there may be no way to exit a war without incurring significant moral costs. The account of meaning I provide here might give us some way in which these moral costs might be understood.

Or so I hope to show. I would start, though, by focusing on an obvious interpretation of the notion of a *mistake* in Kerry's question. This thought is that only a just war, justly pursued, could count as anything other than a mistake in the relevant sense. On this account, the death of a soldier in a just war is sometimes taken to be a legitimately borne cost, by that soldier and by his nation; anything other than this, however, is unjust and therefore could not be justified to the soldier in question. This narrow reading has appeal – it allows us to read Kerry's moral question through the traditional lens of just war theory, which has some advantages for theoretical parsimony – but I do not think it is quite adequate to explain the moral phenomenon to which Kerry is appealing. To see this, we might make two distinctions. The first is between wars which are unjust because they aim at an insufficient good and wars which are unjust because they aim at no genuine good at all, and the second is between a death which has some causal role in bringing about the good putatively thought to justify that war and a death which fails to bring that good into the world. We can deal with these in turn.

Thus, we can start by dividing the two ways in which an unjust war might be condemned as unjust. The first, and more profoundly unjust war, involves a form of warfare which proposes to bring about a state of affairs which is no better than the world prior to that warfare – or, indeed, one which proposes to make the world actively worse, from the standpoint of justice. The invasion of Poland in 1939 might be taken as an example of this sort of unjust war – as might the more recent invasion of Ukraine by Russia. In both cases, the invasion was (and, in the latter case, continues to be) enormously bloody, and the best explanation for why that blood is being shed has more to do with the balance of power within Europe and Eurasia than any defensible moral ideal such as human rights or liberal democracy. Russia's plutocracy is less demonic than Hitler's Nazism, but what emerges from a Russia that absorbs the nation of Ukraine is – putting things mildly – unlikely to be better, from the standpoint of democratic legitimacy, than the present state of affairs (Anderson 2024). The war, understood from the standpoint of a morally permissible vision of what makes a political state of affairs a good one, is unjust in that its success would make the world no better – and, often, significantly worse – than the world without that war.

The second sort of unjust war, I think, is perhaps less common than this, but also philosophically more interesting. It involves warfare in pursuit of an ideal which is rightly described as good – but one which is morally insufficient, taken as a ground for military action of the sort entailed. The war is unjust here, not because it aims at the bad, but because it aims at a good that isn't quite good enough – quite urgent enough, that is, or quite significant enough – to ground the war in question. What falls under this sort of vision of injustice, I think, might be subject to an enormous amount of disagreement – it depends, after all, on a vision of what could be defended, morally speaking, and that notion is unlikely to be something on which all disputants (military or philosophical) will find agreement. However, I think there are some examples that might be plausible; the invasion of Iraq, on Michael Ignatieff's construal of it, could have been regarded *ex ante* as likely to improve the respect given to Iraqi human rights, given the demonic nature of the Baath party's human rights record throughout the 1990s (Ignatieff 2004). It should be noted, on this account, that Ignatieff did *not* have to say that the invasion of Iraq was justified, as a just war is justified; it was unclear, even before the war, that the intention of the Bush administration was adequately oriented toward human rights, and it was equally unclear that the imagined benefits for human rights were sufficient to justify the invasion's potentially enormous cost in human lives; it rapidly became clear, moreover, that the Bush administration had made empirical errors about both the progress of the war on the ground and the likely effects of that war on the Arab world more generally. If we do not regard these empirical errors as sufficiently obvious as to render judgments made on their basis to be morally culpable, then the war in Iraq could be taken – on a view like Ignatieff's – to be an unjust war which had some potential to rebuild some part of the world in a manner we could rightly regard as an improvement of that world.

This would not, again, make the war in Iraq a just war, but it might have some effect upon how it is that those who participated in that war might understand their lives and the meanings they assigned to their lives. To see this, we can look at the second of the two distinctions I want to make – between lives that are lost in the service of building some good in the world and lives that are lost without any putatively justifying good being created out of the process in which that loss occurs. The most simple vision of this distinction would likely track victory or defeat within the war itself; a war that is won is, at least most of the time, one in which the victor has a greater role in remaking the world in accordance with its own interests and values. (For a demonic vision of this, we can see Hitler's plans to annihilate the city of Leningrad during Operation Barbarossa; the goal of Hitler's military operations was, quite simply, the annihilation of the native population of that city, in the service of *lebensraum* for his own citizens (Reid 2011).) Those who win a war set the terms of what those who lose will find available for themselves; those who participate in the winning of that war can take themselves to have a share, to a greater or smaller degree, in the remaking of the world that victory makes possible.

I should pause, at this juncture, to be more precise about the notion of *participation*. It seems, to my eyes at least, that one can gain meaning from a project that one does not sign up for freely; parents may derive meaning from the lives of children they did not freely choose to create, and those who are drafted may similarly obtain meaning from their role in remaking the world. We tend to think that intention matters for the assigning of moral responsibility; the soldiers who did not murder civilians at My Lai, for instance, bear no part in the blame rightly assigned to those soldiers who did. There is a difference, however, between the process of understanding the meaning of one's life and the process of assigning praise and blame for the acts done within that life. To blame is, in some sense, to open the door for punishment, and we cannot be blamed for what we did not choose to do. The meaning we assign to our lives, however, might have a wider ambit and could include aspects of the self for which we bear no particular responsibility – including those roles and acts which are assigned to us without our consent. If I am forced to feed the hungry, I deserve no praise for such an action; I might nonetheless take my having done that action as one of the actions which, in looking back on my life, renders that life retrospectively meaningful.[1]

If humans are, as theorists like Susan Wolf suppose, inclined to seek meaning as one aspect of a good human life, then such meaning can be grounded in how the world is remade by those projects in which our labor is mixed. This meaning can be found, for Wolf, in how we devote our energies to projects that are worthy of those energies; a meaningful life is one that is devoted to bringing about some value outside of the individual whose life is in question. As Wolf has it: a meaningful life is one "in which a person contributes to something larger than himself" (Wolf 2010, 20). Wolf insists that there are conditions on what can be regarded as meaningful lives – two of which might concern us here. The first is that the value pursued must be capable of being regarded as valuable – that it does not represent such empty values as counting blades of grass or such demonic goods as Hitler's vision of *lebensraum*. The second is that the value in question is, in fact, brought into the world by the agency of the person in question. It may be impossible for us to be precise about the actual effects of that individual agency on that overall value; I might think I am doing my part in keeping the tradition of philosophy alive by teaching and writing about philosophy while being utterly ignorant about how much what I do is causally responsible for that tradition's survival. It is, indeed, always possible my contribution is zero, or indeed negative. What matters is that my life involves the sort of agency without which the successful joint pursuit of that good is impossible. If this participation is what offers meaning to a particular life, then we must hope that the good in question is actually obtained in the world for my efforts to effectively ground meaning in that particular life. Imagine a life in which a person's agency is directed – whether as an individual, or in concert with others – toward a particular good; Wolf insists that we cannot, from the standpoint of meaning, be neutral between a version of that life that succeeds in bringing that good into the world and one that does not:

> Think first about… the scientist whose life's work has come to naught, or been superseded by another colleague's results; the farmer whose farm, which he had hoped to hand down to his children, goes into foreclosure; the woman who, after years of sacrifice and devotion, discovers that the man around whom she has built her life has been lying to her and using her all along. If these people were to think of their lives as wasted, a total loss, it would not be unnatural or surprising, and such a thought is at least somewhat akin to the thought that one's life (or this period of it) has been meaningless. To deny that the success or failure of such projects is relevant to the meaningfulness of one's life would fly in the face of such reasonable reaction.
>
> (Wolf 2010, 105)

If this is right, however, then there might be a link between meaning in the life of a soldier and the success of that war in which the soldier participates. Imagine, for instance, a soldier whose health and youth are sacrificed in pursuit of a particular good – say, a vision of human rights or liberal democratic self-government, which that soldier takes to be of sufficient value to bear the weight of his concerned efforts. He joins up to defend these values, perhaps, or comforts himself after conscription by considering his commitment to them. Imagine, further, that in one world, the military action to which his energies are devoted succeeds in making the world more just, by his lights, than the world prior to his work – not solely because of his work, to be sure, but in virtue of the collective labor with which he participated. Imagine, finally, that in another world, the soldier lives to see his work as a soldier come to ruin; the collective work of the military ended up not increasing respect for human rights but, if anything, impugning it, bringing it into disrepute, or, at any rate, failing to increase its prevalence within the human world. The latter soldier has reason, on Wolf's account, to regard his life as a less meaningful one than the former soldier's. He may not actually think in this way, of course; in many lives, such questions may not arise, and it is far from clear that those lives are worse for being unexamined (Schlick 1979 [1927]). What matters, instead, is whether – were such a question of meaning to arise – the soldier would be able to respond to such questions with reference to his participation in such a war. This conclusion, moreover, does not depend upon the war in question as being rightly described as justified, all things considered. The soldier might be wrong about his ideals: these might be inadequate, poorly described, or otherwise flawed. However, a life that succeeds in building these flawed values into the fabric of the social world is a better one – a more meaningful one – than a life in which the entirety of the agent's time and labor does nothing, or less than nothing, to bring these flawed values into being.

These ideas, I think, or something like them, might be enough to ground the conviction that empirical success in warfare might be a part of the best story of what Kerry must mean by the notion of a *mistake*. A war might, of course, be a mistake for any number of reasons; it might be a mistake because there is no plausible moral value capable of providing it with justification. Alternatively, it might be a mistake, and I think Kerry means this sense of mistake, when it is no longer capable of doing what it wants to do in the world. By 1971, it was clear – to John Kerry, if not to Richard Nixon – that the war in Vietnam could not serve the cause of liberal democracy; continuing the war would, instead, simply act to push more people – and more peoples – away from American political ideals and practices. If it is hard to ask a man to be the last one to die for a mistake, it might be because it is hard to ask a man to die without a reasonable prospect of that death's making the world better for those left behind, and this, for Kerry at least, seems to have been the situation in 1971.

I think, however, that we can go further than this and inquire even about the meaning of those lives that have already been lost in the service of a military operation. How a war ends – whether or not it accomplishes its goals – might affect the meaning of those lives devoted to that collective enterprise, even if those who have died are themselves unaware of this fact. This much is implicit in Wolf's thought that the scientist whose life is devoted to the pursuit of a false theory has wasted his life, even if she dies before this fact becomes available to her. At first glance, this seems to have the air of paradox; how can that which happens after a life's end affect the meaning of that life, for the one living it? This paradox, however, is potentially an illusion; many of us find our energies bound up with the success of enterprises we will not live to see come to completion. The medical researcher working on the cure for cancer might be aware that her work will not, during her lifetime, provide the key to that cure, but she might see her energies here as justifiable as part of a collective enterprise, which will extend past her own lifetime into an indefinite future. If her energies are part of a successful collective enterprise, then her life can be regarded as having meaning, in virtue of the ways in which that enterprise has remade the world for the better. The collective enterprise here is intertemporal, rather than a collective venture amongst fellow citizens; the logic, however, is much the same. We take our lives to have meaning, based not simply upon how we try to improve the world but upon whether we – together with others – succeed at doing so. Whether this success occurs before or after our deaths seems not, in principle, to affect our judgment that facts in the world matter, and matter crucially, to the question of whether or not our lives have proven meaningful.

These ideas, of course, are expressed in the work of Samuel Scheffler, who coined the idea of the *collective afterlife* as a method of explaining them (Scheffler 2013). Very few of us, argues Scheffler, are indifferent to what happens in the world after we die; if we were to discover that the world would end shortly after our own individual deaths, we would not regard that fact with equanimity. Indeed, in such a world we would likely find it difficult to find any reason to value much of anything; the fact that there would be no people to come into being would make it difficult for us to build lives of value in the here and now, despite the fact that those people are – by definition – those we are not capable of meeting or encountering during our own lifetimes:

> People cheerfully engage in cancer research and similar activities despite their recognition that the primary payoff of these activities is not likely to be achieved before their own deaths. Yet, if my argument is correct,

> their motivation to engage in these same activities would be weakened or even completely undermined by the prospect that, in consequence of the earth's destruction, there would be no payoff after their deaths. In other words, there are many projects and activities whose importance to us is not diminished by the prospect of our own deaths but would be diminished by the prospect that everyone else will soon die. So if by the afterlife we mean the continuation of human life on earth after our own deaths, then it seems difficult to avoid the conclusion that, in some significant respects, the existence of the afterlife matters more to us than our own continued existence.
>
> (Scheffler 2013, 25–26)

These ideas, however, are applied with equal ease to the lives of soldiers as to the lives of medical researchers. The sacrifice of a given life is made meaningful by the existence of people for whom that sacrifice has made a genuine and positive difference. If the soldier were to discover the fact that there would be no people around, shortly after her death, to experience the benefits of her sacrifice, that fact would seem to make her sacrifice less capable of being regarded as meaningful – as part of, and as a fitting end to, a meaningful life. However, it seems equally true that the meaning of her sacrifice would be undermined by the absence of people for whom her sacrifice made a difference, in the more conventional case in which that sacrifice simply failed to make the world a better place. The one case renders her sacrifice meaningless because no one is there to live in the better world she built; the other renders her sacrifice meaningless because she did not build a better world, and there is no one around whose world is better because of her efforts. In each case, it seems possible for us to read back meaning – or its absence – into her life in virtue of the facts that would obtain after that life's permanent and irreversible ending.

I would go further than this, however, and suggest that we want our descendants to not only live in the world that we have built but also to value that world in ways similar to how we valued it. We might ground this vision of meaning in what Todd May calls "narrative values" – the values that ground the stories we tell, to ourselves and to others, about the choices we make about what we pursue in our individual and limited lives (May 2015). The stories we tell involve choices about what values we will pursue – and these stories, in a meaningful life, are intended to ground both interpersonal and intertemporal communities. A life devoted to defending the importance of human rights, on this account, could be frustrated by a sudden catastrophe, which would annihilate all humans, and therefore any relevance to the rights held by such humans. Furthermore, it would also be frustrated by the absence of any persons for whom the values we sacrificed are comprehensible or attractive. If I take human rights to be worth the risk of premature death, on this account, then I hope not only for there to be people in the future whose lives are respected; I hope, as well, for the existence of people who will continue – after my death – the project of explaining, defending, and interpreting those rights. I hope, in short, that the stories I tell about *my* sacrifice are told by others, after my death; not stories about me, of course, but stories that are comprehensible to me and stories that render my life – and its loss – comprehensible, were it to be examined by those who come after me.

It is now likely time to return to the idea that we might find it difficult to ask a man to die for a mistake. An individual death might be rendered meaningful, on this account, when the sacrifice is made in the course of a collective effort that succeeds in remaking the world; Nathan Hale's declaration that he regrets that he has only one life to give for his country is taken as heroic, in large part, because of those who continued the project of nation-building in which he participated (My neighborhood high school, I would note, is Nathan Hale High; it would not have been so named had the American Revolution failed.). The stories we tell about Nathan Hale are those that mesh, in important ways, with his own story about why his sacrifice was worth making.[2] Other deaths, however, seem incapable of bearing this normative weight. Death in service to a plausible ideal, where that death does not form part of a collective project that benefits the world, seems less meaningful; the death does not issue in a world remade in the image of that benefit, and so the death itself might be in service of a mistake. The mistake, however, is not best understood as a simple matter of moral error. John Kerry, in saying that those sent to die in 1971 would be dying for a mistake, did not commit himself to the superiority of the Vietcong over liberal democracy. His words are best taken to signify, instead, that the war was lost, and these deaths could not be made meaningful by their contribution to a world in which liberal democracy was globally dominant over revolutionary Communism. That world, if it were to be made real, would have to be made so by means other than continued military force in Vietnam.

I want to conclude this paper with the exploration of two amplifications of these ideas, both of which seem – to me – relevant to the American retreat from Afghanistan.

The first is that we might supplement the above considerations with an examination not just of the empirical success of a military action, but also with the reasons for that success – or failure. We might, in particular, think that the moral sting from a life lost in a losing cause is made worse when that loss is the result not of inevitability or the decisions of the winning side but of the decisions of the defeated side. Imagine a war that might be won, but for the decision of a new administration to deprive a previous one of a perceived success; or, perhaps, imagine decisions made with culpable lack of planning or good sense – such as, in Kerry's view, the decision to continue military action in 1971, long after it became clear that the war in Vietnam could not be won. On an expanded view of the argument that Kerry was making, it is not simply that the soldiers sent to Vietnam would be dying in the service of a lost – and, hence, a mistaken – cause; it is that those charged with the execution of that cause were mistaken, and culpably so, in their belief that the war could still be won.

This leads me to the second amplification of the view presented here – one which focuses on time and the ways in which past losses may prove relevant to the decision to continue the fight.

If what I have said here is correct, then any given war might involve a normative trap – one which has a tendency to get worse as the war goes on. On one side is something like a normative momentum: the more lives that are lost in the pursuit of a given cause, the worse it is for that cause to be lost. David Rodin, again, has outlined how this might be true in virtue of the considerations of justice in warfare, as understood with reference to the decisions made by the powerful, but I think it might be true with reference to the meanings of the lives – and the deaths – of those who have no particular share in the decision-making about war but must instead pursue that war on the ground. Those lives now ended would be, in the ways I discuss, rendered less meaningful in the case that the war does not succeed in remaking the world. Each individual death thus provides some additional reason to continue the process of intervention, so long as any hope remains of success. There might be, if this side of the dilemma were all that needed to be considered, a sort of moral event horizon, past which the loss of meaning to the world would become so significant – would entail so many deaths now made meaningless – that the war could not be rightly ended. This moral event horizon would have to weigh the certainty of deaths to come against the difference made in the meaning of the sacrifices already made, but there might come a point at which those future deaths might be outweighed by that which has come before, so that we cannot rightly cease to continue sacrificing, so long as any hope remains that such sacrifice might eventually render those deaths meaningful.

There is, however, another side to this dilemma, and it is something like normative corruption – the moral difficulty encountered in accurately determining how likely or possible eventual success in a given military mission is. John Kerry, in 1971, felt that the war was lost; the leaders of the Nixon Administration did not agree. The conflict between such parties, I believe, reflects not simply a difference in how to understand future probabilities but also a response to the felt moral weight of what has gone before. The Nixon Administration did not *want* to make the deaths in Vietnam meaningless by failing in the overall mission of that war; John Kerry, in response, was concerned to avoid adding to the number of meaningless deaths. As time passed, the moral costs of both remaining and leaving that war increased – which had a tendency to amplify the moral differences undergirding the two positions and make any neutral evaluation of possibility less likely. As the war continued, moral clarity is lost – not simply because of the fog of war, but because of the greater moral costs entailed both by leaving that war and by failing to do so.

These two amplifications, I suggest, are reasons to think that those who authorized the retreat from Afghanistan are rightly ascribed with bringing some loss into the world because of their decision to cease intervening under circumstances in which some continued striving for success was possible. To leave Afghanistan would be to render the deaths experienced in Afghanistan by American service personnel less meaningful; those deaths did not remake Afghanistan but simply forestalled the return to power of the same agents dislodged 20 years ago by American military action. I do not, of course, say that this renders the decision to remain in Afghanistan superior. To remain in Afghanistan would be to make it inevitably the case that more deaths would follow those that have already taken place. Both options would involve, I think, a loss to the world that cannot be simply or obviously compensated for – in part because the losses are not easily evaluated on the same scale; causing a person's death is not easily weighed against causing death to become meaningless. It might be – and I think it is – plausible that there is, here, a genuine moral tragedy at work, in which neither decision – to stay or to go – is one without reason for moral self-reproach and shame.

My point in highlighting these losses, instead, is one directed toward the future. I propose that we view these factors as predictable moral implications for any future military undertaking – and, therefore, as reasons to be exceptionally cautious prior to undertaking such military intervention in the future. If we fail to exercise such caution, we not only act unjustly – but may also find ourselves in circumstances in which even ceasing our unjust actions might prove morally difficult. Understanding the ways in which failing to succeed at war can affect the meaning of life – and the meaning of its end – should make us hesitant to begin the process of war, given how morally dangerous the end of that process must be understood to be.

Notes

1 I am grateful to David Chan for urging me to be precise on these points.

2 David Chan has pointed out to me that some memorial practices begin in other places than in success – as in, for instance, the Lost Cause narrative in the American South and the explicit memorialization of martyrs to the Confederate efforts to perpetuate chattel slavery. Examining these practices fully would require answers to at least two questions: can meaning be derived from projects in the world that are fundamentally unjust? And – on a broader note – is it

possible for there to be meaning gained in a human life from participation in a failed collective endeavor? I cannot, in the present context, offer worked-out answers to either question, but I suspect that the notion of meaning is distinct from other normative values to such a degree that meaning can be ascribed to lives from participation in malignant projects – and that there might be some subsidiary form of meaning which emerges from participation in failed projects. I suspect such meaning might work rather differently than what I have considered here; it might emerge in virtue of participation with the longer task of, eventually, returning to the failed task to rectify those failures – as, indeed, those who began the task of memorializing the Confederacy generally hoped to reinstate white supremacy in the American polity (or, on a less malignant note, the memorialization of members of the International Brigades in the Spanish Civil War). My contention in the present context is more narrow – namely, that where meaning in life is assigned in virtue of participation in a shared effort that might make the world more just, we are more easily able to ascribe such meaning for shared efforts that succeed than for those which fail. I am grateful to David Chan for his conversation about these issues.

References

Anderson, Stuart. 2024. "Human Rights in Russia Plummet to Post-Soviet Low." *Forbes Magazine*, January 25, 2024.

Ignatieff, Michael. 2004. "The Year of Living Dangerously." *The New York Times Magazine*, March 14, 2004.

Kerry, John. 1971. "Testimony to Senate Foreign Relations Committee." Reprinted in *The Washington Post*, February 20, 2004.

May, Todd. 2015. *A Significant Life*. Chicago: University of Chicago Press.

Reid, Anna. 2011. *Leningrad: Tragedy of a City Under Siege, 1941–44*. London: Bloomsbury.

Rodin, David. 2015. "The War Trap: Dilemmas of *jus terminatio*." *Ethics* 125(3): 674–695.

Scheffler, Samuel. 2013. *Death and the Afterlife*. Oxford: Oxford University Press.

Schlick, Moritz. 1979. (1927). "On the Meaning of Life." In *Philosophical Papers, Vol. 2*, edited by E. D. Klemke, and S. M. Cahn. Dordrecht: D. Reidel.

Wolf, Susan. 2010. *Meaning in Life and Why it Matters*. New York: Princeton University Press.

Index

Pages followed by "n" refer to notes

FSC
www.fsc.org
MIX
Papier | Fördert
gute Waldnutzung
FSC® C083411

Kolibri 360 GmbH
Ferdinand-Jühlke-Straße 7
99095 Erfurt, Deutschland
produktsicherheit@kolibri360.de